THE METROPOLITAN AIRPORT

AMERICAN BUSINESS, POLITICS, AND SOCIETY

Series editors: Andrew Wender Cohen, Pamela Walker Laird,
Mark H. Rose, and Elizabeth Tandy Shermer

Books in the series American Business, Politics, and Society
explore the relationships over time between governmental
institutions and the creation and performance of markets, firms,
and industries large and small. The central theme of this series
is that politics, law, and public policy—understood broadly to
embrace not only lawmaking but also the structuring presence
of governmental institutions—has been fundamental to the
evolution of American business from the colonial era to the
present. The series aims to explore, in particular, developments
that have enduring consequences.

A complete list of books in the series is available from the
publisher.

THE
METROPOLITAN
AIRPORT

JFK INTERNATIONAL
AND MODERN NEW YORK

NICHOLAS DAGEN BLOOM

PENN

UNIVERSITY OF PENNSYLVANIA PRESS

PHILADELPHIA

Published by
University of Pennsylvania Press
Philadelphia, Pennsylvania 19104-4112
www.upenn.edu/pennpress

Printed in the United States of America
on acid-free paper

10 9 8 7 6 5 4 3 2 1

A catalogue record for this book is available from the
Library of Congress
ISBN 978-0-8122-4741-1

To Roxie Bloom, who loves to travel . . .

CONTENTS

Seven years' residence in Kew Gardens, New York, inspired my interest in airport history. This quaint neighborhood, situated in the borough of Queens roughly equidistant between JFK International and LaGuardia Airports, is one of many points of contact between the aviation industry and ordinary urban life. Jets flew loud and low over the neighborhood on many cloudy, rainy nights, disturbing the peace in otherwise quiet streets. Kew Gardens also sheltered airline pilots and flight attendants in crowded "crash pad" apartments where they caught some sleep, partied, and collected their dry cleaning. Refreshed and rested, they waited in their pressed uniforms on Lefferts Boulevard for airport coaches to whisk them off to their next destinations.

The areas surrounding Kew Gardens progressively revealed additional airport influences. Our family trips to the Atlantic Ocean at nearby Long Beach were accompanied by an overhead parade of descending international flights on their way into JFK. On the way back from the beach, we spent a lot of time strategizing routes to avoid the chronic traffic jams on the Van Wyck Expressway—the primary highway link from JFK to Manhattan, Westchester County, and more distant points. Like many before us, we discovered that complicated alternative routes on local streets were even worse than the crawl of taxis, trucks, and shuttle buses on the Van Wyck.

A more satisfying experience, as a Long Island Rail Road commuter in those years, was watching firsthand the growing popularity of the new Air-Train system (2003) linking JFK to subways and commuter rail. Transit advocates were proved right that airline travelers would use a train to go from the city and surrounding suburbs to their terminals. Finally, as a frequent air traveler bound for both conferences and leisure, I was impressed by JFK's new terminals, such as Terminal 4, but also concerned by the jerry-rigged system employees had created to funnel leaking ceiling water away from passengers at the decaying Pan Am (then Delta) terminal. Like most regular travelers at JFK, my family and I also endured our share of flight delays and inconveniences there.

The front seat that Kew Gardens and the surrounding region provided on JFK International—one of the world's oldest and busiest international airports—provoked a number of reflections that coalesced into the single, broader question this book addresses: what has been, and what is today, the relationship and cumulative impact of such a large airport to a modern American metropolis? JFK International, as it turned out, provided a particularly good subject because this airport has been open and in the public eye for so long, is surrounded by dense urban and suburban neighborhoods, and has been the subject of so many previous studies and conflicts concerning airport impact in the fields of economics, the environment, traffic, and labor relations, to name a few. Those looking for an architectural history of the airport, a catalogue of airlines and operations, or a plan for future growth should look to other sources described in the notes. *The Metropolitan Airport* is a book for those who seek to understand the revolutionary impact that airports have had on the modern American metropolis.

The name John F. Kennedy International Airport, or JFK, is primarily used throughout the text to minimize confusion for readers, even though the airport was only renamed in memory of President John F. Kennedy in 1963. Idlewild Airport is, however, sometimes used in the text for the period from 1941 to 1963 (Chapters 1 and 2) in order to align with the public and media use of that name for the airport at the time. The official name of the airport from 1947 to 1963, according to the Port Authority, was New York International Airport, a name rarely used by anyone but Port Authority administrators. The term Port Authority is primarily used for brevity to refer to the Port Authority of New York and New Jersey (PANYNJ). The bi-state agency (cooperatively run by New York and New Jersey) was established in 1921 as the Port Authority of New York and renamed in 1972 as the Port Authority of New York and New Jersey.

Introduction

John F. Kennedy International Airport (JFK) was and remains one of the most successful and influential of all of New York City's many modern redevelopment projects. Despite decades of bad press accruing from jammed and confusing roads, epic flight delays, persistent crime, decaying terminals, smelly bathrooms, noise pollution, and abrasive employees, JFK has had far-reaching influence on the shape not just of New York City but also of the metropolitan area's international prestige, economic vitality, and quality of life.

New Yorkers bound for adventure and business have enjoyed the privilege and advantage of boarding planes headed to the distant corners of the globe. Billions of tourists have flowed back into the city and region through the airport's enormous, if imperfect, terminals. The air-cargo facilities have enlarged the market and options for the region's industries, consumers, and service sector. At the same time, the New York metropolitan area—crowded, competitive, wealthy, and outspoken—has influenced distinctive aspects of JFK for both better and worse, defining the airport's scale, market, and ambience. Postwar New York, both the city and surrounding suburbs, makes little sense without JFK in the frame.[1]

JFK opened in 1948 in a city and nation still shaped by railroads, trucks, automobiles, ports, and steamships. Beginning in the 1950s, affluent passengers and high-value cargo shifted from boats to planes for transatlantic travel, lured by the swiftness, comfort, and prestige of air travel. For most of the 1960s, JFK handled approximately 80 percent of all American-bound traffic for Europe, a significant share of national domestic travelers, and a majority of the nation's air cargo. By the 1960s, and as a result of its importance to so many companies, the airport also served as the hub of globalized airline companies such as Pan Am Airlines.[2] The airport had achieved the goal of city leaders who, in the 1940s, viewed it as a key to preserving the city's preeminence in the nation's trade and travel patterns.

The hectic air and ground activity at JFK dramatically affected the surrounding skies, waters, and neighborhoods on both sides of the city-suburban divide. By the 1960s, JFK International (along with the Port Authority's other two airports, LaGuardia and Newark International, and the Port Authority Bus Terminal) had helped divert long-distance transportation in New York away from train tracks and waterfronts. Magnificent rail hubs, such as Pennsylvania Station (built in 1910), and the companies behind them lost their central functions in urban life and vanished from the landscape. So too did the steamship docks, thousands of dockworkers, and small manufacturing plants that once filled New York's industrial districts.

By the 1950s and 1960s, millions of cars, taxis, and heavily loaded trucks every year poured out of the airport into surrounding highways and parkways. Immigrants and tourists from distant lands made their way from the airport to the region's neighborhoods and attractions. JFK International was a massive construction project that generated billions of dollars in investments. Tens of thousands of New Yorkers found work there and in its related industries, making the airport (with LaGuardia Airport) a leading source of employment in Queens and suburban Nassau County. By dint of its dominant role in international routes at the time, the airport created a competitive advantage for managerial services and air cargo in a deindustrializing city. Today, JFK still generates billions of dollars in regional trade, supports hundreds of thousands of jobs (thirty-six thousand jobs on site), and is a key element in New York's modern economic and touristic success.

The growing scale of JFK in the 1950s and 1960s helped redefine metropolitan patterns of labor, transportation, and residence, encouraging dispersion of the population to the outer boroughs and suburbs. Living and working miles from railroad stations and ports was no disadvantage for businessmen in the new office parks of Nassau or Westchester County, who could easily drive or take cabs directly to the airport for business trips. Prosperous suburban families, bound for exotic lands, did not have to travel to aging rail or port terminals in a crowded, increasingly minority-dominated city center. High-value freight, such as electronic equipment and pharmaceuticals, did not have to journey to and from the center of the city either, enabling suburban warehouses and factories to send their goods

AIR TRAVEL DEMAND AT NEW YORK AIRPORTS: 1948 TO 2009
Source: Port Authority and Regional Plan Association

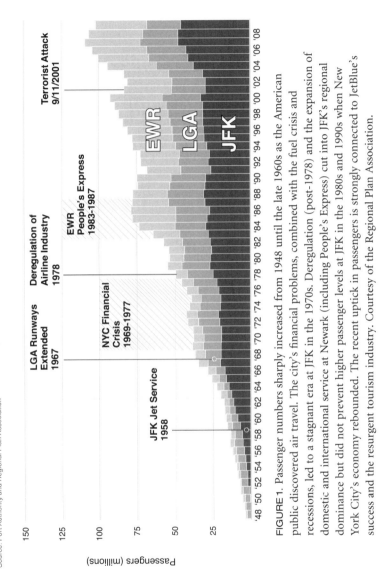

FIGURE 1. Passenger numbers sharply increased from 1948 until the late 1960s as the American public discovered air travel. The city's financial problems, combined with the fuel crisis and recessions, led to a stagnant era at JFK in the 1970s. Deregulation (post-1978) and the expansion of domestic and international service at Newark (including People's Express) cut into JFK's regional dominance but did not prevent higher passenger levels at JFK in the 1980s and 1990s when New York City's economy rebounded. The recent uptick in passengers is strongly connected to JetBlue's success and the resurgent tourism industry. Courtesy of the Regional Plan Association.

through the airport cargo terminal to the most distant lands overnight. Mayor Fiorello La Guardia (in office from 1933 to 1945) may have conceived the airport in 1941 as a guarantor of the city's leading role in transportation—and as a vast renewal project—but it also encouraged suburbanization by equalizing transportation benefits across the metropolitan area.

If the airport was, in fact, one of the premier projects in New York's postwar redevelopment program, why has it never been recognized as such? First, many observers have treated JFK as a failure because of the airport's shabby treatment of the public. New Yorkers did not agree about much for the past half century, but most of them shared a low opinion of this airport based upon their visits. During the 1940s and much of the 1950s, for instance, passengers might have expected a futuristic experience, but they actually trundled through a grubby, crowded "temporary" terminal complex. In the decades that followed, passengers in modern terminals continued to encounter a bewildering number of reconstructions, temporary walkways, crowded roadways, miserable food service, and aggressive hustlers. By the 1980s and 1990s, formerly modern terminals remained for too long as faltering airlines, such as Pan Am and Delta, refused to invest in their reconstruction. When terminal reconstruction finally started, passengers had to endure year after year of reconstruction at one terminal after another.

This constant throwing up and tearing down, the restructuring of the entire airline business starting in the 1970s, and the distracted management style of the overextended Port Authority cumulatively rendered the airport's Terminal City (the central hub of terminals since the 1950s) a mixture of confusing and unpleasant. JFK, for instance, is consistently rated by travelers today as one of the worst airports in the country. While most of the terminals have been modernized since the 1990s or are in a process of renovation, decades of inferior passenger experiences, uneven daily management, and persistent flight and ground delays have blinded most of us to the enduring value of the airport to the region.

The most important reason for the failure to recognize JFK as a major factor in urban affairs is that airports, even those within traditional urban boundaries like JFK, are artifacts of a metropolitan-scale redevelopment program. Metropolitan renewal, rather than a spatially defined, limited urban-renewal program, is harder for both the public and scholars to conceptualize.[3] Mayor La Guardia and other civic leaders may have envisioned the airport as part of New York City's renewal, but the scale of the airport that developed aided not just the city but areas far beyond the city's boundaries. Publications and statements by both the Port Authority and the Regional Plan Association have over the years tried with little success to explain the metropolitan scale and profound importance of JFK and other airports to New Yorkers. Metropolitan impact, flowing to and from such a vast and complicated institution, is difficult to conceptualize.[4]

Airports have traditionally been treated in urban history as isolated institutions because it is difficult to account for and describe economic, social, or political influence flowing from airport to urban region, and vice versa, over such a large area. While some airports gather office and hotel infrastructure around them, becoming what some now call an aerotropolis, the fact that airplanes fly in and out at great heights from sprawling, seemingly self-contained airport complexes has made it difficult to document their relationship to traditional urban historical patterns, such as urban redevelopment, deindustrialization, suburbanization, neighborhood change, immigration, citizen activism, globalization, and even the most obvious connection, the rise of the tourist city.[5] That it is difficult to make airport-metropolitan connections, however, does not mean that they do not exist. Airports are in every respect as influential in shaping modern cities as freeways, public housing, redlining, urban renewal, suburban development, and any other of the more familiar and much more studied topics in urban history.[6]

The Master Builders

Airports are often viewed as isolated dimensions of urban life, part of a standardized global system, but just below the surface are distinct characteristics that result from choices made by local leaders. The influence of New York's outsized urban personalities and the competing institutions they guided have left enduring marks on JFK International that are explored in detail throughout *Metropolitan Airport*. Three key figures in particular—Mayor Fiorello La Guardia, Robert Moses, and Austin Tobin—have helped define the airport that is so famous today.

Mayor La Guardia set the initial scale and ambition for what is today's JFK. La Guardia's interest in aviation is permanently linked to the comparatively small and particularly unpleasant airport that bears his name, but JFK International better reflects the global ambition he had for New York

City in the coming aviation era. Decades later, Robert Moses, the powerful city administrator who aggressively rebuilt much of New York's infrastructure from the 1920s to the 1960s, praised the mayor for understanding the future importance of aviation when few others did: "Mayor La Guardia was way ahead of his time and so were his aides. The future of air travel was not dimly apprehended at this time and we were ridiculed for the size of this airport."[7] The mayor's determination that New York lead the region and nation in air travel made it possible to grab such an enormous parcel of land for the airport before an era of environmental regulation. It was well known at the time that JFK was his "pet project" to which he committed substantial city resources, including the talents of Robert Moses, to bring to fruition.

La Guardia's attempts to reform and rebuild so many areas of urban life (housing, schools, hospitals, parks, and so on), and his aim of creating two major airports within just a few miles of each other, made it unlikely that the city he loved would end up managing both airports in the long term. The state-imposed limits on New York City's debt meant there was not enough capital for the investments needed for vast airfields and terminals. To build a second airport on over four thousand acres at the cost of potentially hundreds of millions of dollars (many billions of dollars in today's money) led to a crisis of confidence on the part of city officials in the mid-1940s. La Guardia's successor, Mayor William O'Dwyer (in office from 1946 to 1950), transferred governance of both city airports to the Port Authority of New York in 1947.[8]

Robert Moses is still infamous for his controversial slum clearance program that made space for modern housing projects, cultural centers, parkways and highways, bridges, and new parks. His name is not, however, often associated with aviation as he failed to keep the airports out of the hands of the Port Authority. It could have turned out differently. In 1946, he convinced the newly elected mayor to spin off the airport into a City Airport Authority so that its development costs could be privately financed and thus left off the books of the city government. The authority would also, not coincidentally, give Moses another source of funds and power. In this instance, however, the notion of Robert Moses as an unstoppable power broker fails to explain his loss of airport control. Moses made a number of strategic errors in the 1940s that allowed the City Airport Authority to slip from his grasp. First, he was far too publicly honest about the enormous costs the airport would entail. Second, he demanded that the airlines renegotiate leases they had signed earlier, thus turning powerful executives against him. Moses's biggest error, it turned out, was in underestimating the Port Authority. Moses viewed the organization as a barely functional regional entity. In truth, however, executive director Austin Tobin and his staff outfoxed Moses by shaping the opinion of newspaper editors, the mayor, financiers, and the airlines.

It would be a mistake, however, to believe that Moses's lack of direct control of the airport equates with lack of influence. Moses was pushed aside at the airport, but he still played a critical role in the creation of the metropolitan infrastructure that made possible the use of Jamaica Bay as an airport site. His determination to build out the regional road system, for instance, brought Jamaica Bay and the Idlewild site into the orbit of Manhattan and the region's growing suburbs. His decision to build and maintain so many of the metropolitan highways as landscaped parkways for cars, however, in the long term limited the efficiency of the region's road network in relationship to the airport.

Moses's vision of Jamaica Bay as a metropolitan-scale park also had significant effects on the shape of the airport we know today. From the 1930s to the 1960s, Moses and park officials proved successful in restoring the natural beauty and even some of the ecological integrity of Jamaica Bay. On the basis of the conservation achievement, activists successfully resisted the Port Authority's plans for expansion into Jamaica Bay. Moses's postwar promotion of high-density housing around the bay and in the Rockaways also put tens of thousands of additional people near the airport's noisy flight paths. Protection of these residents from noise pollution would become a major factor in the creation of limits for JFK operations. Moses, in sum, may not have run the airport, but he powerfully influenced its operations.

The most important figure to shape the airport is also the one least familiar to New Yorkers and scholars. Austin Tobin, executive director of the Port Authority for thirty years (from 1942 to 1972), is New York's forgotten power broker.[9] Moses is usually given most of the credit and blame for the shape of modern New York, as his flamboyant personality, nasty sense of humor, and high-profile projects make for dramatic storytelling. Tobin, however, the low-key grandson of an Irish immigrant, was an equally aggressive empire builder who rivaled Moses in his talent for using a public authority as a tool for radical urban reconstruction. Tobin, as executive director, was given a relatively free hand by Port Authority chairmen,

such as Howard Cullman and Donald Love, wealthy civic leaders who were
too busy with many other business and charitable activities to meddle
deeply in everyday operations run by an obviously competent executive
director. Tobin diligently expanded the Port Authority from just three hundred to over eight thousand employees during his long tenure and ended up
controlling billions of dollars in assets, including the World Trade Center,
tunnels, container ports, bridges, heliports, and the very profitable metropolitan airport system (including JFK International, LaGuardia, and Newark International).

Tobin showed a particular talent for choosing infrastructure projects,
including airports, that had the potential to turn a profit. That profitability,
in turn, attracted billions in private funding for the Port Authority's bonds.
As with Moses, this business orientation gave the Port Authority a great
deal of independence. The Port Authority's takeover of the region's airports
in the 1940s, including JFK International in 1947, shaped the airport in
profound ways. The Port Authority's ability to negotiate hard with the airlines to secure better rates (even though the authority had initially promised
it would honor the original leases), and its ability to borrow vast sums
through bond sales, enabled the rapid completion of airports on a grand
scale in the New York region. The rapid opening of JFK in 1948 helped
secure the city's early aviation leadership in the United States for global
travel.

Tobin's sponsorship of the Terminal City design for JFK in the 1950s
and 1960s, with operations distilled into enormous freestanding unit terminals frequently operated by just one airline, distinguished JFK from many
of its peers—and not always for the better. JFK International was not the
only airport of its day to employ the terminal unit system (Los Angeles
International Airport—LAX—was roughly similar), but JFK was the largest
and most ambitious terminal unit airport of its day. This new city, with its
distantly separated terminals and sole reliance on highway links to the city
center, was a creature of Tobin's ambitions and values. Like Moses, Tobin
largely turned his back on traditional rail and subway lines in order to
maximize investments in infrastructure that would deliver future profits.
His main emphasis, therefore, was on tunnels, bridges, airports, and other
lucrative facilities related to modern transport, including cars, trucks, buses,
airplanes, and containerized cargo.[10] The Port Authority thus unfolded a
futuristic transportation vision at JFK—making Terminal City entirely
dependent on planes, cars, trucks, and buses—as a clear contrast to sweaty

and crowded subways, crumbling and corrupt docks, and grimy rail stations of a receding industrial age.

Tobin's empire building, despite its contribution to modernization of urban infrastructure, undermined JFK's reputation in a number of key areas. For most of JFK's history, the Port Authority resisted calls, and even legislation that accompanied those calls, for a mass-transit link to JFK because of the institution's bias to cars and trucks and because such a system would be a sure money loser. A mass-transit link could have reduced the hassle of terminal transfers within the airport and airport-city connections for many passengers. Yet it was not until 2003 that JFK had an effective mass-transit link or terminal connector. Tobin's growing focus on real-estate development in the 1960s, including the World Trade Center project, by many accounts also distracted Port Authority figures from the efficient management of its many mass transportation facilities. Modernization was expensive, but it is also true that Tobin and his successors, such as Peter Goldmark (executive director from 1977 to 1985), diverted airport profits into the Port Authority's real estate and other activities rather than reinvesting the money in the airports. The great power wielded by Tobin and subsequent Port Authority leaders meant that changing managers or forcing upgrades in service proved very difficult for unhappy metropolitan political leaders.

This short list of leading personalities necessarily excludes many other important actors and institutions, including airline executives, governors, mayors, Congressmen, local environmentalists, Port Authority civil servants, and Federal Aviation Administration (FAA) administrators who also contributed to the development and management of JFK—and who make appearances in the story that follows. Yet even this brief description of three major personalities provides a glimpse into the complexity of the environment in which New York airports, and JFK in particular, developed. The cumulative impact of strong personalities and the powerful political forces and organizations they represented contributed to a lack of metropolitan cooperation in the long term. Indeed, with so many authorities, departments, jurisdictions, and egos, it is remarkable that the airport works as well as it does. Most American cities suffer from a similar lack of central coordination, but there is no denying that New York, where the scale of any enterprise demands considerable funds and planning, boasts an excess of powerful institutions and agendas that has made metropolitan cooperation and planning difficult.[11] A complex web of patronage shaped JFK as a place in specific ways that make it different from other airports, even those in the New York region.

Metropolitan Relationships

The personalities and choices of leaders such as La Guardia, Moses, and Tobin matter a great deal, but the surrounding urban context is just as important to understanding the history of JFK. The story thus returns at different points to a number of themes that situate JFK within the broader history of the New York region in the twentieth century. These themes, taken together and over time, illustrate that there exist powerful and enduring reciprocal relationships between an airport and its surrounding metropolitan area.[12]

In particular, the wealthy and globalized New York metropolitan population played a key role in establishing JFK's early aviation leadership and dominant postwar firms such as Pan Am and Eastern Airlines. Without the lucrative New York market, and brave souls in a hurry, both American aviation and New York's air industry would have had a hard time taking off in the 1930s and 1940s. The Port Authority, which took over the airport in 1947, was able to negotiate higher fees with airlines in the late 1940s because the airlines could not abandon a comparatively well-developed and profitable market. These higher rates collected steady revenue that allowed for a massive expansion of airport facilities and a high-quality system not only in New York but also across the country from the 1950s to the present.

This influence of New York as a population center continued to be critical to JFK's success in the decades that followed. The steady uptick in the airport's ridership, notwithstanding the airport's poor reputation for service, cleanliness, and personal safety since the 1960s, reflects the fact that the region's population continued to grow in size and wealth despite New York City's well-publicized problems in the postwar period. Widespread housing abandonment, municipal financial troubles, and population loss in the 1970s overshadowed the continuing growth of the metropolitan area as a whole. The success of the massive Boeing 747s in the 1970s and 1980s, and Airbus 380s today, results from the existence of concentrated urban populations like those found only in New York and other massive world cities such as Tokyo, Paris, and London.

New York's current (2014) metropolitan population of eighteen million people includes such lush suburban counties as Westchester, Nassau, and

Fairfield (with their own edge cities such as Stamford and White Plains) that provide a solid base for the airport's continuing growth even in the face of national competition. The high incomes of this vast suburban belt surrounding New York, filled with affluent and globally oriented residents, generates a steady market for global air travel at JFK; leisure travel, in fact, accounts for three-quarters of JFK's passenger business. The establishment and rapid success of JetBlue starting in 1999 was and remains as much dependent on the particular travel needs of New Yorkers who journey often to Florida, California, and the Caribbean as it does on the demonstrated business leadership of JetBlue's founder, David Neeleman. The enormous number of tourists (now topping fifty million visitors per year), many of whom arrive by air, has created an additional transient urban population that sustains international air travel year round and helps keep ticket prices reasonable. The rebirth of New York as an immigrant city has added further to JFK's market power. The close connections between immigrants and their families in the Caribbean, South America, Africa, and Asia make possible a range of daily flights to these regions that surpasses in frequency all but a few other airports in the United States.

The growing density of New York's metropolitan population surrounding the airport has also affected airport operations. JFK, located in a corner of the city with limited transit connections, has contributed to overloaded highways such as the Van Wyck Expressway. Master builder Robert Moses envisioned that expressway as a double-duty road that would speed both airport traffic (including trucks) and suburban commuters to midtown; at the same time, he made the congestion that much worse by banning truck and bus traffic from his landscaped parkways. As a result of these early decisions, sustained by later politicians, the Van Wyck has never been large enough to handle airport traffic effectively and has a deserved reputation for near-permanent congestion. Above all, the growing density of population surrounding the airport placed limits on the ability of the Port Authority and airlines to operate as they saw fit. Neighborhoods bothered by aircraft operations produced both unlikely metropolitan alliances and unusually affluent activists.

In addition to demographics, neighborhood activism is a key theme influencing JFK's development. The widespread notion that airports are disconnected from neighborhoods is the result of the lack of historical perspective on community activism related to noise and the environment. That airplanes zoom over houses at hundreds of miles an hour does not mean that aviation does not profoundly affect neighborhood life. Aircraft noise became one of many new sources of pollution in the postwar era—and its impact was not restricted to one side of a city line.

The growing density of housing surrounding JFK in both Queens and Nassau County, and the affluence of many of these residents, had a major impact on the airport's operations. By failing to limit growth around the airport, as some experts at the time suggested, political leaders created an inevitable conflict between the airport and surrounding neighbors that began in the 1950s and continues today. Center-city neighborhood activists of the 1960s successfully pushed back on the bulldozer technique of urban renewal, and suburban activists discovered their own local environmental causes related to water quality and habitat loss. Airport activists, for their part, found common cause across city-suburban boundaries in opposing a bigger and noisier airport and in preserving Jamaica Bay. The activist spirit of the 1960s dramatically affected airport operations and expansion programs for decades to come.[13]

If Austin Tobin had gotten his way in the 1960s, JFK International today would have doubled in size, filling up much of Jamaica Bay in order to meet the demands of growing traffic and sending many more planes over the surrounding neighborhoods. During the 1940s, for instance, the site that became JFK was expanded to include almost 5,000 acres, which was considered large at the time of the airport's founding. But other cities have subsequently found even more land for their airports. Chicago's O'Hare International, for instance, was expanded in the 1950s to include 7,200 acres, allowing for additional facilities, taxiways, and runways. Port Authority leaders failed to expand much at all in New York, however, because an aggrieved citizenry rose up in protest in the 1960s.

Metropolitan activists, on the basis of limiting noise and environmental damage, restricted the growth of runways and additional hours of operation in the 1960s and 1970s that would have allowed for even more planes. Other activists stopped the expansion of the rail and road network at critical moments in the history of the airport. These restrictions improved the quality of life for those living adjacent to roads or rail lines but also damaged the efficiency of travel to and from the airport both in the air and on the ground. Preservationists and leading architects even forced the Port Authority and JetBlue to preserve the largest and most impressive nonfunctional historical building within an airport in the country, the former Trans World Airlines (TWA) terminal, which occupies valuable acres of Terminal

City land. That this gorgeous terminal is still standing in 2014, preserved if unused, is a result of metropolitan preservationist sentiment mindful of the heedless destruction of the original Penn Station.

Citizen impact on aviation is also visible by looking at New York's powerful legislative team, which, spurred on by activists in the region, pressured the Port Authority and worked tirelessly with other legislators from similarly unhappy communities in other states to get national noise-control standards in place. That continuous pressure, in turn, has ushered in an era of quieter, and in some cases larger, aircraft such as 747s and 757s as well as changes in operations to reduce noise during landing and takeoff. Conflict and context have ultimately been limiting factors in New York's aviation business, making the notion of restoring JFK as the world's leading global airport no more than a pipe dream. At the same time, activists' concerns have generated some creative fixes for the airport and airlines, such as quieter aircraft and carefully selected flight paths over parks and highways.

The history of crime at JFK speaks as well to the metropolitan context. The guardians of JFK International have been unable to isolate the airport from the region's criminal masterminds and desperate underclass. Criminals from surrounding neighborhoods, in fact, quickly found their way to the airport in the 1950s on the convenient and speedy highways. JFK has thus been subject to various forms of criminal behavior, including opportunistic cabbies, aggressive panhandling, theft, and extensive mob hijacking. Isolating the airport has proven to be a difficult task for the Port Authority; only the security crackdown after the terrorist attacks of September 11, 2001 in the United States (known as 9/11), and the closing of terminals to all but ticketed passengers have finally cut back on much of this irregularity. Yet JFK may still have the worst reputation in the country for passenger safety on the ground.

JFK International has taken its knocks as a result of its context, but it has also benefited from the shifting but comparatively resilient commercial fortunes of the New York metropolitan area. The willingness of business travelers to risk personal safety for speed made LaGuardia Airport and JFK successful in the 1940s and 1950s when air travel was far more dangerous. The airport received another boost in the postwar era from the New York region's high-value manufacturing sector that used air cargo to send goods to Europe for postwar reconstruction. JFK also profited from the early, tightly regulated government control of aviation. Rules governing routes and prices, promoted by traditional port cities like New York, limited airport and airline competition until the 1970s. These restrictions, on international routes, for instance, also gave global corporations such as Pan Am and their unionized workers enormous advantages at the expense, from our contemporary perspective in a deregulated system, of consumer value and choice. Airline corporations paid their workers well and established major maintenance and executive functions in the New York region because they were reliably profitable.

Federal deregulation of airline routes and prices, decentralization (both to suburbs and the Sunbelt), and deindustrialization appeared set to destroy JFK's commercial importance. Indeed, after 1978 these factors initially undercut JFK's national leadership as so-called legacy lines such as Pan Am either collapsed or restructured to limit their exposure to New York's high labor costs. Many workers lost their well-paid positions to lower-cost contract, nonunionized workers; many executive and maintenance functions simply disappeared or shifted to lower-cost areas of the country.[14]

The resilience of New York as a global financial and tourist center, however, has proven to be a key aspect of JFK's continuing health. While many predicted that business would abandon older cities like New York—and many corporations did seek greener suburban pastures—the confluence of capital, luxury neighborhoods, social connections, and specific skills made New York City's business districts, and its regional belt of edge cities and suburban office parks, key players in increasingly complex financial dealings of the finance, insurance, and real-estate sector. Rapid travel to any point on the globe, even with a delay getting to the airport, was still a great advantage for New York over cities such as Cleveland or Detroit that offered limited or no direct daily service to Shanghai or São Paulo. While the majority of travel at JFK shifted to nonbusiness travelers over the decades, a quarter of travelers (of a growing total number at JFK) are still in business sectors that pay a premium to be able to jump onto a plane going anywhere in the world.

The history of JFK International reveals that airports are more than just generic sets of buildings and runways cut off from their surrounding urban contexts. The choices Mayor La Guardia made about scale, Robert Moses about parkways, and Austin Tobin about terminal planning still influence the contemporary airport. The character of the metropolitan area has also defined key elements of the place that travelers still encountered in 2014. Some of the influences on an airport such as JFK are subtle, such as the metropolitan economy and noise regulation, while others are more obvious, such as crime and traffic. Knowledge of the actual history of JFK in its context—as opposed to one's subjective airport experience or the Port Authority's sanitized public relations—is more than just a matter of historical curiosity. The story of the real place and its context reveals many of the genuine limits and opportunities that must be taken into account when it comes to future planning for aviation in the New York metropolitan area. It was, in fact, a refusal to acknowledge the character of New York City and its environs, in areas such as mass transit, that led to many planning errors at JFK in the 1940s and 1950s—fateful decisions that New York still wrestles with today.

CHAPTER 1

From Idlewild to New York International

Our commercial position has been the foundation of New York's leadership in many fields. . . . There have been those elsewhere in the land, and a few here at home, who have been all too ready to believe that New York City had no future. This is a part—only a part—of the answer to the timid, the unimaginative and the doubting Thomases. . . . We are determined that in the field of aviation, as in other fields of commerce, New York City shall lead the way.

—Joseph McGoldrick, Comptroller of the City of New York, 1945

New York City's leaders envisioned an immense airport in the marshland of Jamaica Bay to enhance and retain the commercial advantages the city had accrued over hundreds of years. Mayor Fiorello La Guardia and his team, including Robert Moses, made major progress in achieving that dream in the 1940s. They secured over four thousand acres of land within the city limits, arranged initial financing in the tens of millions, began building major runways and drainage systems, and linked high-speed roadways to the new airport. By the late 1940s, however, it had become clear to most of the city's financial and political elite that the scale of the airport demanded a broader metropolitan view and the deeper pockets of an institution like the Port Authority. As the decades passed, the metropolitan character of JFK would become even more pronounced.

The fact that New York City's political and business leaders attempted to dominate the aviation age should not come as much of a surprise. After all, the city's merchants had been aggressive leaders in trade and technology for centuries. In the 19th century, New York's global reach resulted not only from its natural advantages as the country's greatest natural port but as a result of human enterprise. The establishment of the Black Ball packet shipping lines in the early 1800s attracted goods from up and down the Eastern seaboard for shipment across the Atlantic. The building of the Erie Canal from 1817 to 1825 pioneered a waterborne route where no natural one had existed, solidifying New York's position as the nation's dominant coastal port. Later in the century, Cornelius Vanderbilt's ruthless consolidation of lines into the New York Central system, the steady multiplication of rail lines and terminals around New Jersey and Manhattan, and ever faster and more advanced steamships for coastal and oceangoing cargo and passengers advanced New York's formidable lead in America's global trade.

New York's long history as an ocean port thus multiplied its advantages in the dawning aviation age. The international travel industry, including sophisticated customs, package brokering, and immigration facilities, had for decades clustered in New York to address the needs of transatlantic cargo and passenger travel. Before World War II, New York still handled approximately 70 percent of overseas passengers and 50 percent of America's foreign trade (mostly on steamships), even though America's population center had been moving westward for decades. The *New York Times* in 1944 predicted only greater success: "The heaviest concentrations of the future, as of the past, may be expected along those routes and at that those terminals where the greatest concentration of business logically arises."[1]

New Yorkers' interest in aviation was built on a lengthy history. Even before 1920, the New York region housed an impressive share of leading-edge aviation firms. Entrepreneurs and aviators across Long Island in the early twentieth century helped pioneer the future of global aviation systems on makeshift fields and in massive factories standing in the shadow of the world's largest and richest industrial metropolis.[2] Queens in 1918 featured no less than fourteen aviation manufacturers at work on a variety of warplanes and associated technology. By the late 1920s, so congenial was Long Island's confluence of capital and technology that roughly 80 percent of all aviation activity in the United States could be found clustered on Long Island (including Queens and Brooklyn). Queens, for instance, as the "automobile center of the East," had the skilled workers and infrastructure needed for building airplanes.[3]

Defense spending for World War I and capital generated by the 1920s bull market expanded the aviation business both in New York and nationally. Glenn Curtis, for instance, established a manufacturing firm in 1917 to build navy seaplanes; Lindbergh's dramatic transatlantic flight in 1927 originated at Long Island's Roosevelt Field; and during the 1920s, Leroy Grumman opened an aircraft manufacturing business in Nassau County that would one day become a major player in defense production. Long Island was just one of many places where planes were designed, tested, built, and flown in the interwar period (Boeing and Douglas in the West were early leaders in designing and building new planes), but New York supported a dynamic cluster of creative, high-technology firms that borrowed from one another and innovated in close proximity.[4]

Much like their more modern counterparts in Silicon Valley who depended upon government funds for basic research leading to the Internet and silicon chips, aviation innovators in the New York region and elsewhere benefited from and lobbied for generous long-term government subsidies. The federal government during World War I paid for research into and the design of aircraft and airfields that led directly to postwar commercial aviation, not the least because decommissioned aircraft found their way into civilian hands after the war. But without the first airmail flight, lifting off from the infield at Belmont Park in 1918 and bound for Washington, D.C., there would have been a much more difficult growth curve for the commercial aviation industry in New York and the nation. The government footed the bill for a privately contracted airmail service (formalized in the Kelly Act of 1925) of dubious national necessity—train delivery was very fast at the time—in order to provide an entirely essential subsidy to private aviation companies. This airmail system eventually stretched across the nation and generated new planes, pilots, airlines, air-control facilities, and even airports. Federal subsidies time and again created a steady and healthy underpinning for a high-risk industry, providing everything from the planes to the roadways linking the new airports.[5]

An abundance of adventurous, wealthy residents traveling for business and pleasure, along with many profitable industrial corporations—such as General Electric, U.S. Steel, Union Carbide, and Standard Oil—residing in the city and its hinterlands piled up New York's golden advantages in commercial aviation's early years. New York in the 1930s led the way in the number of citizens applying for passports, and New Yorkers (taken as a region) dominated first-class and cabin steamship international travel. Approximately two-thirds of American citizens traveling overseas lived in the northeastern United States, with about 40 percent of those in the states of New York and New Jersey alone. The Northeast, as the most globally oriented region of the country, supported both steamship lines and the pioneering and risky international airplane flights out of New York in the 1930s.[6]

New York entrepreneurs helped create the modern, globally oriented aviation industry. Early investors in American Airways included leading New York financiers Robert Lehman and Averell Harriman. Juan Trippe, the talented and ambitious scion of a rich New York family, gathered a group of New York investors to create Long Island Airways to shuttle the wealthy to the Hamptons in the 1920s. While this effort failed financially, Trippe turned right around and invested in 1927 in Pan American Airways (Pan Am). Applying his obvious organizational and promotional skills and personal connections, he not only secured valuable airmail routes but built up profitable seaplane lines (then based in Miami) to the Caribbean and South America. Trippe forced his way into the New York market by merging with a New York-based competitor (NYRBA, or New York, Rio and Buenos Aires Airline) and seizing control. The ever-expansive Pan Am under Trippe ultimately set a global standard for airborne luxury in the 1930s, monopolized international travel, and became the basis for Pan Am's dominance of postwar global travel at JFK. Trippe was just one of many entrepreneurs who leveraged New York's wealthy travelers and lucrative postal contracts to create modern airlines. The dashing World War I pilot, Eddie Rickenbacker, for instance, also used New York as a hub for Eastern Airlines, which eventually dominated air travel on the East Coast.

New York's power brokers leveraged these advantages to stifle competition in the dawning air age. They demanded that federal officials, for instance, limit the operation of foreign airlines to established centers of trade such as New York. The Port Authority made the dubious claim that "the rapidity of air flight will make it necessary to establish much more rigid inspection of passengers and cargo, and planes themselves, to provide protection against disease. . . . It would be impossible practically to allow unlimited use by foreign operators of every airport certified for general civil domestic use." The threat of foreign contamination was partly used to justify the concentration of international service in large seaboard cities and remained in place for decades under the highly regulated air travel of the postwar period.[7] Regulated air travel, not coincidentally, limited competition for such large airlines as Pan Am and Eastern, with their high capital and labor costs.

These early advantages did not mean that New York would automatically retain its status as a leading city of the air age. A crowded urban center had the market, capital, and commercial tradition, but those legacies would have to be leveraged with technology. The long-term investment in docks, and the lack of convenient open space for airfields, posed substantial obstacles for those seeking to maintain New York City's lead. Mayor La Guardia made the first major effort to overcome these barriers by abandoning Floyd Bennett Field, the city's small municipal airport that opened in 1931 on a site in Jamaica Bay not too far from the future site of JFK. Floyd Bennett Field was considered to be too isolated (Robert Moses's parkways were not yet in place) and too small to function as a major airport for New York.

To overcome the lack of buildable land close in to built-up areas of the city, what became LaGuardia Airport (which opened in 1939) rose majestically on fill dumped into the Long Island Sound to give Manhattanites, and potentially those in affluent suburbs nearby, a convenient aerial gateway to the nation and the globe. LaGuardia Airport's regional success was, in part, the result of generous New Deal work programs, coordinated by Robert Moses, that made possible the creation of the Grand Central Parkway and Triborough Bridge (opened in 1936), both of which provided high-speed links from LaGuardia Airport to both center city and the suburbs.[8]

LaGuardia Airport's streamlined terminal structure, vast parking fields, and, for its day, runways of great length reflected the vision that Mayor La Guardia brought to so many of his urban redevelopment projects. While the airport's architecture echoed the leading modernist airports of the era, such as Tempelhof in Berlin and that in Copenhagen, it set a new international standard according to architectural historian Alastair Gordon: "Seen from the air, the 558 acre complex made a single, sweeping gesture, linking up disparate parts—appearing to grow as much from the curves of the Grand Central Parkway as out of the bend of the shoreline—a natural offspring of the city and its infrastructure." Or was it? The airport lacked a direct connection to the city's subway system, just as it does today; instead, it was linked to modern auto infrastructure. The federal government, through millions of dollars in Works Progress Administration (WPA) labor, again provided the necessary subsidy to make it all possible. By 1940 the airport's 250 daily landings and 3,000 daily passengers made it the busiest airport in the world. New Yorkers even paid for access to an observation deck overlooking this futuristic drama.[9]

In spite of the lavish praise for LaGuardia Airport, its limited scale for future air travel was obvious even to the mayor.[10] By 1941 the airport may have been handling one million passengers a year, but the limitations on its physical growth promised long-term challenges. Adding land in the deeper waters of Long Island Sound, for instance, would have been very expensive and technically complicated (even though the airport's runways were eventually extended over the water after World War II). Seaplanes, also accommodated in the open water astride LaGuardia, were on their way out for commercial aviation. Making matters worse, as the fill it was built on settled, the airport began to sink in the years after it opened, and the runways had to be reconstructed. Finally, houses, businesses, and the Grand Central Parkway hemmed in the airport on the land side. LaGuardia was simply too small to hold New York at the center of a global air network.[11]

The Regional Plan Association, the city's powerful planning think tank, had been of the opinion in 1929 that "in the New York region it is practically impossible to obtain any large airport site so central that it would be in immediate touch with the main business activities and the largest groups of populations."[12] A practical, if unorthodox, solution was found to this problem.

Redefining Jamaica Bay

In retrospect, Jamaica Bay was a likely place to build a grand airport. Long neglected as a natural environment, civic leaders had for decades shifted around for a suitable use of such a large and seemingly vestigial territory. Sewage had flowed from loosely regulated suburban development for much of the twentieth century; the city dumped trash directly into the bay's waters and lined its edges with unsightly landfills; and improvised fishing camps emptied human excrement directly into the once pure waters. Many considered the filling of marshlands for an airport in the 1940s to be the best possible outcome for this polluted marshland. Robert Moses's transformation of the Flushing Meadows from ash dump and swamp into park, lakes, and a grand setting for the World's Fair of 1939 provided a clear precedent for environmental transformation on this scale. As Hugh Quinn, a city councilman from Astoria, remarked on an exploratory visit to the field in 1941, an airport at the site would "eliminate a large area of mosquito-breeding marshlands."[13]

It could have turned out quite differently if the bay's environment had been protected earlier. Yachting had once been popular in the 1890s at the Jamaica Bay Yacht Club, a summer spot for Brooklyn's fashionable set. Families would spend weeks at the clubhouse or come for a weekend by train to enjoy regattas and the salty marsh air. Those rosy days had long passed by the 1930s, however. The poor water quality and industrial development of the bay's edges spoiled the natural beauty that could still be found in new elite clubs on Long Island's less developed south and north shores.[14] The Idlewild Park Hotel for decades had also been a fashionable destination for "swank society" in the nineteenth and early twentieth centuries, but it had long ago fallen out of fashion and was demolished in 1939. The only relic of the fashionable era, and a modest one at that, was the Idlewild Golf Course (from which the colloquial name of the airport derived) and a small, recreational airfield known as Jamaica Sea Airport.[15]

Jamaica Bay's glory days as a productive estuary had also passed. In the early twentieth century, the bay still supported a $5 million-a-year industry that rivaled the Chesapeake Bay and Long Island's Great South Bay in the quality of oysters and clams drawn from its waters. The shallow waters made harvesting shellfish easy, and the delicate bivalves enjoyed protection from many storms and predators. Approximately 1,500 hearty souls still harvested 750,000 to 1,000,000 bushels of oysters per year from Jamaica Bay in about 1917.[16] Shellfish harvesting ended abruptly, however, in 1921 when the city's health officials firmly linked a typhoid epidemic to bay shellfish. Alas, diseases of great variety had already traveled from the fetid bay to the urban masses; untreated sewage had been flowing for years from surrounding industries and improvised suburban housing. Illegal harvesting continued in the 1920s even with bans on the shellfish.[17]

The salty air and open space in the shadow of a crowded city continued to attract urban adventurers seeking diversion. A few fishermen, precariously lodged in stilt houses, still fished the waters in the 1930s but not on a commercial basis. Small suburban housing developments in the early twentieth century clustered on the edge of the future airport site, including both cottages and "substantial" homes.[18] Failure of other infrastructure projects in the marsh contributed to the desolation. A grandiose plan to turn Jamaica Bay into a great port in the early twentieth century seemed to prove the inaccessibility of the site.[19] New Jersey, plugged directly into

FIGURE 2. The Broad Channel neighborhood of Jamaica Bay showing hotels, stores, and other development in 1915. Jamaica Bay was once an important source of seafood and a leisure destination for New Yorkers in search of fresh air and warm saltwater for recreation. Queens officials hoped that a port or airport would create a use for the bay as the quality of the water and environment declined in the 1920s and 1930s. Library of Congress Prints and Photographs Division.

continental rail and road routes, stood better positioned than Jamaica Bay for port modernization. New Jersey interests also proved far more aggressive; they successfully convinced the Port Authority to improve Newark Bay for deep-water shipping, a decision that doomed not only the Jamaica Bay port plan but also almost all of New York City's direct participation in waterborne commerce.[20] Robert Moses loved to make fun of the failed plans to make a port in Jamaica Bay because its promoters had believed that such a facility could be "greater than the combined ports of Liverpool, Rotterdam, and Hamburg."[21]

The political and business leaders in Queens, still desperate to bring their borough into the mainstream of the city's economic life, pivoted in the late 1920s to promoting a transatlantic air terminal in their seemingly forgotten marsh. The Jamaica Chamber of Commerce in 1928 recommended that Mayor Jimmy Walker and the Board of Estimate create an airport at Idlewild. Remoteness and vast open spaces had once been a disadvantage, but in the aviation era, isolation was a distinct advantage for aircraft operations that demanded open air and ground space otherwise in short supply. The new airport could be deliberately tucked away into a huge, still underutilized corner of New York City primarily inhabited by ducks, horseshoe crabs, clams, and "sagging sea-bleached homes."[22] This early airport plan, like the port plan before it, was shelved after Queens business leaders shifted alliances and focused on the more convenient North Beach site for the new airport (what became LaGuardia Airport).[23]

The Jamaica Bay site came back into focus as LaGuardia Airport's physical limitations blurred its future as a massive global airport. Jamaica Bay offered comparatively endless space for growth because the shallow coastal plain could be filled and patched, and its many streams and inlets diverted into culverts, as the airport expanded. Few thought there would ever be much resistance to filling large sections of the bay; in fact, for decades there was not any organized opposition to reshaping the shoreline to suit urbanization of many types. The history of New York City, in fact, can be traced through the construction of artificial shorelines and docks in order to maximize economic returns.[24]

The regional network of highways and bridges Robert Moses had developed in the 1930s and 1940s also contributed to a reappraisal of the bay's function. Moses's Southern State and Belt Parkways eventually intersected near Idlewild and provided high-speed links to Brooklyn, Manhattan, and Long Island. The addition of a highway linking Idlewild Airport to Queens Boulevard (and later Grand Central Parkway) would theoretically whisk air passengers even faster from airport to Midtown Manhattan (twenty-six minutes) by linking the Southern State and Belt Parkways to the Grand Central Parkway that cut in a relatively straight line to Manhattan. The new Triborough and Whitestone Bridges also provided fast links from the Grand Central or Whitestone Parkways to the Bronx and Westchester.[25] The New York State Department of Public Works, helped by federal highway funds, created a connector to the Grand Central, what became the Van Wyck Expressway. Moses in 1945 took credit not only for conceiving such a practical link but also for arranging generous state and federal financing: "The City will have to contribute only 50% of the cost of land and nothing for construction." Again, subsidies proved crucial to the airport. The 26-minute prediction alas proved optimistic for most hours of the day.[26]

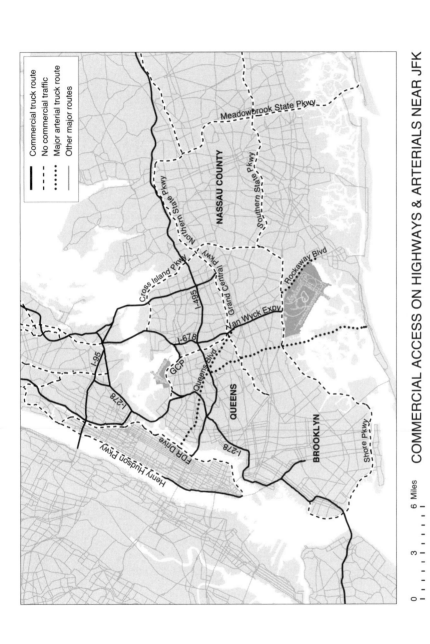

0 3 6 Miles

COMMERCIAL ACCESS ON HIGHWAYS & ARTERIALS NEAR JFK

FIGURE 3. JFK's location astride Moses's system of parkways. Moses, however, restricted his parkways, such as the Southern State, Shore Belt, and Grand Central Parkways, to passenger vehicles, and these limitations have been preserved today (2015). There remains only one high-speed bus and truck route to JFK (Interstate 678/Van Wyck Expressway). Courtesy of the Regional Plan Association.

FIGURE 4. This aerial view of the Van Wyck Expressway under construction in 1950 illustrates not only the density of residential neighborhoods near JFK but also the short distance between the airport and express subway and Long Island Rail Road routes (shown at the base of the image). The Port Authority did not establish a rail connection to mass transit from the airport until 2003 for a variety of reasons. Courtesy of the Queens Borough Public Library, Long Island Division, *New York Herald-Tribune* Photograph Morgue Collection.

Robert Moses, despite his work to open the marsh to development, maintained a broader ecological vision for Jamaica Bay. Moses began the long and steady process of converting the marsh into a desirable park and wildlife space. During the 1930s, he and the city administration began the hard and thankless task of cleaning up the bay. The city added chlorinating plants for sewage in 1937 to protect swimmers frequently sickened by the polluted waters. Moses also prevented the Department of Sanitation from siting an incinerator and associated ash dump in Jamaica Bay.[27] Moses blocked the dump by reminding Mayor La Guardia what Flushing Meadow Park had been before the ash dumps there had been shuttered and the space redesigned as a grand urban park and exposition grounds. Moses's interventions ringing Jamaica Bay included Jacob Riis Park's lovely beach, the new Marine Parkway Bridge, Rockaway Beach rehabilitation, and the Shore Parkway (now known as the Belt Parkway). He had big dreams for the combined effect of his action. His ultimate dream was to turn Jamaica Bay into an urban version of the beautiful Great South Bay that he had preserved as a result of the creation of Jones Beach in suburban Nassau County.[28]

Yet the war deferred and nearly wiped out Moses's vision of Jamaica Bay as a great urban wetland. Navy bombers, for instance, turned the bay's marshes into practice bombing fields in 1942. Construction of Idlewild Airport also led to the loss of thousands of acres of productive marshland and a massive trough in the bay where engineers pumped sand to raise the airport site above sea level.[29]

When Moses surveyed Jamaica Bay after the war, he still, however, saw something quite valuable for the city's urban masses. Moses affirmed his faith: "There is no other city in the country with an opportunity such as that presently available to the City of New York, to set aside within its corporate limits a large area in its native state as a natural preserve for wild life and for informal recreation, fishing, boating and the like." He believed that a park adjacent to the airport would aid operation of the airport rather than hinder it because there would be no tall industrial buildings in the way of the flight paths. Moses, an avid and strong swimmer, envisioned fellow city residents swimming and frolicking safely in the waters. He also envisioned birds reestablishing themselves as the dominant residents of the bay. On this prediction he proved entirely correct, much to the chagrin of pilots today.[30]

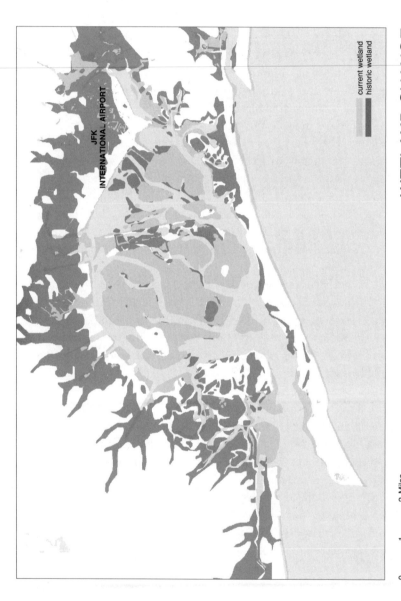

JFK
INTERNATIONAL AIRPORT

0   1   2 Miles

current wetland
historic wetland

WETLAND CHANGE

FIGURE 5. The transformation of Jamaica Bay through development, including
residential expansion, landfills, commercial expansion, and the creation of JFK
International. Minna Ninova.

Paying for the Treasure

Mayor La Guardia and other city officials in the 1940s fully realized the significance of a world-class airport to New York City's economic supremacy in the future. "We are building a great airport at Idlewild in New York City—the finest airport in the world, at a cost of $71 million—not in the hope that someday there will be need for it but because commercial aviation will need it as soon as it is completed."[31] Like much of the La Guardia legacy, it is all too easy to dismiss the degree to which his vision cleanly broke with everything that came before.

A sharp-eyed journalist directly linked the projected Idlewild Airport with Moses and La Guardia's spectacularly successful 1939–40 World's Fair in Flushing Meadow Park. At the fair, the public was captivated by General Motors' Futurama exhibition that included gleaming cities of the future tied together by high-speed expressways and vast air terminals: "The scene at Idlewild will resemble the famous Futurama come to life. Big land and sea planes will come and go" while visitors would marvel at helicopters that would "jump from one to another of New York's circling ring of airports." Air travel would become just another daily luxury for the affluent across the region, who would use "small private landing fields on their home estates" to fly their helicopters to Idlewild's projected helicopter parking lots.[32]

New Yorkers dreamed in aviation Technicolor, but the preeminence of New York in aviation remained less certain. The initial era of flight, when planes made frequent stops for refueling, offered New York advantages in transatlantic air commerce (the city was closer than all but a few American cities to Europe), but it was conceivable that as a result of wartime innovation airlines would dictate where and when they would land. That a remarkable 85 percent of national transatlantic traffic crowded through New York in 1946, mostly on stately ocean liners, did not necessarily guarantee anything. Experts working for the city estimated that by 1955, as a result of airport growth in other cities, New York would retain just 67 percent of transatlantic passengers. The Commerce and Industry Association of New York identified Idlewild as postwar project number-one "insofar as New York's prestige and commercial supremacy are concerned."[33]

The war proved essential to the new airport's development. Speedy condemnation of land for Idlewild, for instance, was justified on the basis of the national war emergency. The judge who enabled the condemnation remarked that "great new airfields with long ribbons of runways" would be needed for the war.[34] The biggest subsidy of the time came directly from the federal millions that flowed in from the sale of Floyd Bennett Field to the navy. This purchase helped pay for additional land sought for the new airport. A 1941 estimate of the total cost of Idlewild properties was $8.25 million that could conceivably be paid out of the navy's purchase of Floyd Bennett Field for $9.75 million.[35] Federal government officials also provided an initial grant of about $860,000 toward landfill and runway development in the Idlewild area. The federal government even subsidized hangar development and an administration building.[36]

The commercial aviation business got its biggest boost from federally funded aviation research. The U.S. Postal Service's airmail service continued to quietly subsidize airlines, but without the war, large-scale postwar commercial aviation would have grown more gradually. The massive bombers pioneered during the war proved easily remodeled for civilian conversion. With the addition of seats and other creature comforts such as bathrooms, they offered dependable commercial air travel. Planes that could safely fly thousands of miles under attack could pretty easily and safely ferry people from one city to another in peacetime. Government construction of extensive airfields in Europe also proved crucial. Seaplanes had been very popular before the war (in spite of high operating costs due to the fact that seawater was terrible for planes) for international travel because many crowded cities abroad lacked sufficient land or capital for runways, "but the exigencies of war made nations forget about expense. Big runways were laid down to support 4 engine bombers and big new land-based transports built for the military."[37] Radar systems developed for expertly detecting airborne enemies also simplified operations in dense urban airspace. By the late 1950s, a radar tower at Idlewild had the capacity to monitor planes at up to thirty thousand feet in the air and up to two hundred miles away.[38]

Airport construction at Idlewild gained speed as the war wound down. By 1945, 1,100 existing structures had been demolished and the site as a whole included 4,495 acres. Mayor La Guardia had condemned the first Idlewild area on December 30, 1941, and paid $723,000 in condemnation awards.[39] These were, in retrospect, modest down payments on a vast enterprise. The other properties condemned from 1941 to 1944 included 3,533 vacant lots and 1,867 improved sites. An estimated 500 acres of the site came directly from Jamaica Bay itself as the city undertook a massive pumping program to raise low marshlands to functional levels, an act of environmental destruction that would be unthinkable today.[40] Despite the fact that most of the land acquired was unimproved, by 1945 the city had spent about $9 million acquiring property (with a few parcels still desired at a cost of about $3 million more). Even marshland that one day might be filled was valuable in New York City; in fact, city officials rejoiced that they got their thousands of acres "at so modest a cost." In condemnation letters, the city frequently relied on a "defense" justification despite the remote chance that the airport would actually be brought into service during the war itself.[41]

In 1945, Mayor La Guardia boldly predicted that his new airport "will be one of the best investments the city ever made. It will pay for itself." Yet the dawning realization of just how much infrastructure a modern airport required made the promise of self-financing a more complicated proposition.[42] The visionary terminal plans favored by La Guardia and designed by architects Delano and Aldrich included "a monumental circular administration building, a three-mile long, two-story arcade, 2 hangars and miscellaneous utility structures." The price of constructing such a grand edifice, in an era when air travel was not yet profitable, raised serious questions about feasibility. Railroad companies, for instance, had built their own stations on a grand scale (at great cost to themselves), so why should the airlines not shoulder expenses for their airports?[43]

By 1945 city officials predicted that the total city investment in the field would eventually balloon to $90 million, most of which would have been funded out of long-term city bond sales. The city planned to ask for a federal grant of $25 million; to charge high rents for warehouse facilities, airline buildings, and retail facilities; and to provide concessions (food, shops, and so on) for visitors. But the rapidly escalating upfront costs were a reason for concern. The generous leases granted to the airlines (based on aircraft operations), only agreed to under threat that the airlines would move to Newark if they did not get their way, in no way covered future expenses.

For many onlookers, the airport program thus appeared to be another of La Guardia's many extravagant public programs. Mayor William O'Dwyer, who succeeded La Guardia in 1946, endorsed Robert Moses's plan for a City Airport Authority in 1946 out of financial desperation and his obvious admiration for Moses. O'Dwyer had inherited a budget deficit from La Guardia and was eager to both restore financial stability and rebuild the city's housing and other social infrastructure. The state legislature passed a provision to give the city the power to create its airport authority.

An airport authority promised to solve a number of problems inherent in large and complex public programs from both a managerial and financial perspective. New York was just one of many cities that sought to shift municipal airport management from the city to public authorities. Authorities theoretically circumvented messy political battles and patronage while adding much-needed managerial talent to complex urban functions. Authorities simultaneously created the possibility, as Robert Moses had demonstrated with the Triborough Bridge Authority, for additional long-term financing. Moving airport financing to an authority removed a major liability from the city's books and meant that the city did not surpass its state limit on borrowing. *New York Times* editorialists, in thrall of Moses at this time, came out for this airport authority plan in the short term to get the place built. The authors, however, hedged their bets by suggesting that the Port Authority might be the best organization to manage New York's airports because of its experience in transportation and its regional vision.[44]

Moses's plans, however, ran into a number of snags. The first was that many people were simply skeptical of giving Moses another set of responsibilities. O'Dwyer had already made him construction coordinator, giving him control over every major postwar project in the New York area, in addition to his continuing roles as parks commissioner, chairman of the Triborough Authority, and many other appointed positions. Even Mayor La Guardia, in a radio address after he left office, came out against Moses's plan because it was going to give Moses even more power. The second and more pressing issue was that the new City Airport Authority possessed limited borrowing capability because of banker skepticism. While the city signed over millions in airport improvements (estimated at $90 million) at no cost to the new authority, which some objected to as a giveaway, the unknown returns of airport investment meant that Airport Authority bonds were still a risky bet. More risk meant that financiers would demand higher interest. To some, this looked like another gift to the wealthy who would, by buying bonds, consume most of the future airport's profits.[45]

Moses, in a desperate attempt to bring airport costs in line with the debt capabilities, did make a number of changes in the plans that he thought would mollify critics and maintain the mayor's support. La Guardia's elaborate plan for the airport terminal, created by architects Delano and Aldrich, was scrapped with the encouragement of Mayor O'Dwyer. Unfortunately for Moses, the replacement plan was also elaborate: there was simply no inexpensive way to build a major terminal for a world-class airport.[46]

A leading landscape architect, Gilmour Clarke, and architect Wallace K. Harrison designed this new plan, which debuted in late 1946. Clarke was a favorite of Robert Moses and had been responsible for, among other projects, parkway design in the New York region. Harrison was the force behind the iconic Perisphere and Trylon at the 1939 World's Fair, Rockefeller Center, and would eventually coordinate the design of two of New York's iconic modernist ensembles: the United Nations and Lincoln Center. The revised airport plan included a streamlined administration (main terminal) building running north to south that connected to the Van Wyck Boulevard access road with escalators to the roadway. The architect's generous provisions for restaurants, which would benefit from panoramic views of the airport and make money, reflected harder financial realities: concessions were serious business.[47]

The revised plan as a whole for the airport (including terminal, hangars, runways, and so forth), when revealed in late 1946, still failed to reflect the economies necessary to bring the airport in line with the limited borrowing capacity of the City Airport Authority. Not only was the plan still expensive, but now the more modest plans for the airport (and plans for later expansion as revenues improved) as a whole failed to inspire additional support from those, such as airline executives, who still demanded that New York immediately build the best airport in the nation, even though they did not want to pay full freight for those costs.[48]

Moses's other strategy for funding the airport—raising the landing and other fees to the airlines and making them build their own hangars—also backfired. The airlines, and the oil companies who would fuel planes at the airport, resisted renegotiating their leases even if it was clear to them and everyone else that the revenues under those arrangements were insufficient to support the scale of airport they needed. They threatened to move their operations to Newark and to sue the city, but what they actually did was throw their support behind the Port Authority, which promised to honor their leases by generating the most revenue from other activities on site (for example, a hotel and concessions).

Moses, in the meantime, made trouble by exerting his outsized influence in the internal affairs of the airport authority. The famous aviator, Lieutenant General James Doolittle, had already resigned from the City Airport Authority board as a result of his connection to the fuel companies now up in arms over higher fees. When Harry F. Guggenheim, a prominent member of the airport authority, also resigned out of frustration, Mayor

O'Dwyer in 1946 asked the Port Authority to consider taking over the city's airports.[49] O'Dwyer still worried about the loss of the city's investment and "an abject surrender of the city's planning powers" to an agency whose important actions were subject to the vetoes of the governors of New York and New Jersey, but the scale, cost, and management requirements of the two airports were simply too daunting at the time.[50] O'Dwyer remained primarily concerned that the capital cost of the airport would drain money from other municipal services, but Moses's maladroit handling of the negotiations had also spiraled out of control and was undercutting the mayor's agenda and standing.

Part of the reason for Moses's loss of control was his failure to view the Port Authority as a serious rival. The Port Authority had been quietly plotting for some years to expand "by invitation" into the potentially profitable aviation business both in Newark and New York City. Created in 1921 as a self-supporting independent agency of New York and New Jersey, and able to develop terminal or transportation facilities within twenty-five miles of the Statue of Liberty, the Port Authority grew over the course of the twentieth century into one of the largest and wealthiest organizations in the region. By the 1940s, the Port Authority was growing rich from tolls it collected at the George Washington Bridge, Lincoln Tunnel, and other toll-producing crossings in the region. Executive director Austin Tobin argued that because the Port Authority operated using a self-supporting business model, and had a large professional staff, they would always perform better than the city government on complex, profit-oriented development projects in the public interest.[51]

In the 1940s, the Port Authority already controlled Newark's docks along with a number of bridges and tunnels. The authority's leaders realized full well that airports, despite the fact that they were money losers in this period, represented not only the future of passenger travel but also of high-value cargo as well. Even before the authority controlled a single airport, it had made its ambitions public. In 1944, the *New York Times* had reported that "not long ago the Port of New York authority declared its conviction that New York would remain, by reason of its traffic and of its commercial and financial importance, a major port of entry in the coming air age."[52]

Port Authority leaders starting with Tobin were convinced, according to historian and Port Authority expert Jameson Doig, that the city government was not up to the task of airport management: "Could these municipal governments be expected to replace patronage with merit in hiring workers, and could they attract and hold the kind of managerial talent needed to make these air and marine terminals vigorous competitors in the world market?"[53] Tobin also disliked the "artificial compartments of county and municipal boundary lines" that prevented metropolitan cooperation.[54]

Port Authority leaders quietly wooed opinion makers, politicians, and businessmen in part by successfully redefining airports as a regional issue that only they could handle. Chairman Howard Cullman and Tobin also offered the most ambitious plan for long-term development without specifying the creation of a very expensive terminal building (as Moses had done) or demanding more from the airlines. When necessary, they openly criticized Moses's proposals as unworkable from a financial point of view without revealing their own specific plans. Cullman liked to stress the urgency of the situation: "If the port district is to preserve its overseas air traffic against the competition of Boston, Philadelphia, Washington, Baltimore and Chicago, Idlewild airport must be put in service for overseas carriers as soon as possible."[55] *Colliers* reported that nationally "city fathers know that airports are to aviation what harbors are to shipping, and that only cities with the most ultramodern of airports can hope to become major terminals."[56]

After a period of study, the Port Authority announced in late 1946 that it desired a ninety-nine-year lease on both LaGuardia and Idlewild Airports. In a major embarrassment for Moses and O'Dwyer, Harry Guggenheim, the former chairman of the City Airport Authority, endorsed the Port Authority plan because the city's people "are offered airports and service removed from politics and without further debt obligations by the city." Members of the city's Board of Estimate, who in this era had the final say on the municipal expenditures, were nevertheless at first "cool" to the proposal and raised questions about honoring the old leases to the airlines. Many wondered, with some justification looking back from the present, about the future profits promised to the city: would they ever be delivered?[57]

The Port Authority, however, benefited from support for the transfer from the airlines, which hoped to retain their sweetheart lease deals at the new airport. Airline administrators, saddled with modest postwar air travel, high operating costs, and uncertainty about the future profitability of air travel, were rightly concerned that an independent airport authority would raise fees, as Moses promised to do, to cover high airport operating costs. The Port Authority leadership promised that the original lease arrangements would endure because they claimed that the additional revenue needed for operations would come from concessions and other commerce at the airport rather than from the airlines directly. The Port Authority could also pay for construction using long-term bonds that would be repaid out of airport revenues or failing that, from its profitable tolls on tunnels and bridges in the region.

In still another blow to Moses and his plan, the *New York Times* editorial writers expressed unequivocal support for the Port Authority takeover in early 1947. The newspaper was willing to abandon the City Airport Authority because of the Port Authority's demonstrated skills and vision: "The Port Authority is an experienced agency, ably staffed, with a background of twenty-five years testing in the handling of large enterprises. It is regional in its outlook, and this is a regional job." They called the City Airport Authority, on the other hand, "untried" and underfinanced.[58] The Regional Plan Association and Citizens Union, two of the most powerful nonpartisan public-policy organizations in the city, also endorsed the Port Authority's plan. The Regional Plan Association, assessing a decade of industrial trends in 1942, had long ago come to the conclusion that "the New York region faces a post-war world with momentum from the past but with no security for the future."[59] A massive, well-run airport was essential to a stable future.

Tobin cleverly lined up leading bankers willing to shoot holes in the financial plans presented by the City Airport Authority. He also criticized the construction costs as too low and the lack of nonaviation revenue sources. Not even a late push by Moses to build support for a revised City Airport Authority plan could stop the Board of Estimate (which included the mayor) from making the transfer. On June 1, 1947, the Port Authority assumed control and quickly set to work completing the runways and other airport infrastructure. Port Authority leaders fully understood that any delay might give New York's competition an edge.[60]

In the final transfer agreement in 1947, the Port Authority agreed to pay the city $72 million over a fifty-year term. The Port Authority estimated that it would have to spend about $191 million on capital expenditures at the two airports, mostly at Idlewild. This figure was roughly double the figure proposed by the City Airport Authority.[61] Even former Mayor La Guardia felt that the O'Dwyer administration's botching of the process ("criminal negligence and timidity") justified turning over the airports to the Port Authority. He also thought that if he had been mayor, he would have been able to develop the airports effectively. This lease agreement has been modestly revised in the decades since, but Port Authority control has been maintained nevertheless since 1947. It is hard to figure out how much profit has ever been turned over to the city by the Port Authority; such was the benefit of being an authority.[62]

Administrators at the Port Authority began the long march away from a central terminal structure serving all airlines. It was inconceivable to designers at the time that one building, especially an affordable one, could accommodate all the gates needed for the new airport and larger airplanes of the postwar period. A new plan by the Port Authority included forty-two plane positions in two large terminal structures (one for domestic and one for international traffic); they were considered to be "the largest and most modern air terminals in the world," with 1.35 million square feet, ten times the size of LaGuardia Airport. The terminals, positioned at each end of a 160-acre oval central area, were designed to handle the massive traffic of the future. An internal bus system to connect terminals and regional mass transit would also generate revenue.

This ambitious plan, like those before, was never built since the Port Authority, having won control, now appeared to be in no rush to spend the hundreds of millions (today's billions) necessary to create the world-class airport it had promised. The internal discussions are no longer available, but one imagines that administrators were understandably reluctant to commit to an expensive plan during such a dynamic era of air travel. Whatever the reasons might have been, and however logical, the passengers suffered: a temporary cinder-block building, expanded a number of times to meet growing capacity, served as New York's primary gateway until the International Arrivals Building opened in 1957.[63]

The Port Authority's leaders began to think big about the various functions the airport would fill, in part to envision a way to pay for such enormous facilities without raising rates for the airlines. Cullman predicted that consumer concessions would cover 70 percent of revenue in contrast to 30 percent from landing fees and fuel.[64] Idlewild "would be modeled after Grand Central terminal, where, he said, 'you can't spend 20 min. without buying something.'" The Port Authority, however, offered a description of the airport that sounded suburban in spite of the fact that the airport was located within the city limits.[65] At the airport, visitors and neighbors would find "a big air-conditioned, soundproofed hotel, huge service garage where your car can be fixed while you're flying, sports arena, auditorium, department store along with dozens of concession shops, restaurants and bars, as well as an outdoor swimming pool, outdoor movie theater, miniature golf course, tennis and badminton courts. . . . Bowling alleys, dart throwing, archery facilities and tremendous outdoor dance for playing host of big-name bands."[66] Not only would wealthier New Yorkers pay a premium to fly, but also they presumably would have leisure time to play sports such as tennis before and after. The emphasis on automobiles and open-air leisure demanded large areas of open space as one would find in the suburbs or perhaps the outer boroughs like Queens or Staten Island rather than in a crowded, aging city where most New Yorkers still lived. These ambitious and somewhat quirky recreational plans were never realized once the scale of airport operations came into focus in the 1950s, but the suburban flavor remained in the Terminal City that was finally built in the 1950s.[67]

The Port Authority updated and tinkered with plans but also changed the name of the airport. The official name changed from Major General Alexander E. Anderson Airport (so named by the City Council in 1943 after a Queens aviation hero), and known informally as Idlewild, to New York International Airport to "give the city added prestige as a center of airborne traffic."[68] The renaming reflected the Port Authority's vision of the field as part of a regional system of air travel, "a net of airports with each field having a special purpose." LaGuardia Airport would focus on domestic air service while New York International, with its long runways and planned grand terminal (and projected federal immigration, public health, and customs inspections), took the lead in international air travel. Newark was also slated for major upgrades and already had a strong air-cargo role.[69] Citizens did not, however, take to the name New York International and continued to refer to the airport as Idlewild until 1963 when the airport was successfully renamed after President John F. Kennedy.

To a visitor arriving soon after the opening in 1948, New York International might have looked rough and unimproved, but the space they had entered was one that had been dramatically reshaped in just a few short years. There had already been at least fifteen design changes to the airport, including shifting runways and various central structures, but in the meantime the city had cleared two thousand structures and a golf course, and had raised the marshy sections an average of eight-and-a-half feet by dredging sand from the depths of Jamaica Bay. Grasses from Montauk Point anchored this new desert to secure the blowing sands now exposed to the

FIGURE 6. Engineers quickly realized that the sand pumped up from Jamaica Bay created sandstorms that would hamper operations. Their solution was to use an adapted tobacco-planting machine to plant beach grass, August 20, 1945. Courtesy of the Queens Borough Public Library, Long Island Division, *New York Herald-Tribune* Photograph Morgue Collection.

blustery Atlantic winds. Over four thousand acres of the airport would eventually be carpeted with beach grass efficiently replanted using a converted tobacco-planting machine. The airport was already nine times larger than LaGuardia, and its central terminal area alone could comfortably fit twenty-five Yankee Stadiums. There was no urban renewal project in New York City that rivaled Idlewild in sheer scale at the time, and it was arguably, as La Guardia had hoped, the finest airfield in the country.[70]

To further transform marsh to airport, workers created a heroic and mostly hidden infrastructure to urbanize this wild space. Under the guidance of Jay Downer, one of Moses's favorite engineers, almost $60 million was spent on a complex system of sewers, drainage canals, and electrical conduits. Initial work had started on six reinforced concrete runways (varying

FIGURE 7. Runways on the sand: construction of runway "A" at Idlewild Airport, October 25, 1944. Courtesy of the Queens Borough Public Library, Long Island Division, *New York Herald-Tribune* Photograph Morgue Collection.

from 6,000 to 9,500 feet in length, with two held in reserve) that planners believed to be adequate for future operations. A complex tangential plan for twelve runways, providing a variety of directions for takeoff in changing wind conditions, had already been replaced with a simplified series of parallel runways, preferred by pilots, surrounding the planned but as yet undefined central terminal area. The new runways were designed to handle 300,000-pound airplanes, double the weight of a Stratocruiser, the largest plane in service at the time. They had been carefully designed for drainage and safe operations in even the most harrowing of conditions. New York International even included a grade-separated roadway that dove under a massive airplane taxi lane, a distant nod to Central Park's once-revolutionary separation of horse and pedestrian traffic. The new airport also included an instrument landing

FIGURE 8. New York International Airport, where the most advanced transportation systems of the era, planes and automobiles, coexisted in harmony, 1949. Gottscho-Schleisner, Inc. Library of Congress Prints and Photographs Division.

system on Runway C that enabled safe landings in poor weather. A radio beam guided pilots to ground-level rows of synchronized flashing lights, including powerful Krypton bulbs, bolted to a pier in Jamaica Bay. These lights at full power generated 115 billion candlepower.[71]

A temporary terminal and administration building was in place by spring 1947, as were three runways. The temporary terminal, a rough amalgam of concrete block and linoleum tile with just a bit of World's Fair flair, was already larger than the once cutting-edge terminal at LaGuardia; the runways were also longer than those at LaGuardia. In spite of the rough condition, the airport's scale impressed its main audience: aviation experts. Airlines were unanimous that "Idlewild is far superior . . . to facilities available at London, Paris, Berlin, Amsterdam or other big foreign centers."[72] Such remarkable facilities were expensive to build and maintain. With Tobin's Port Authority now fully in charge of the most valuable air market in the world, the airlines had no choice but to pay the bill.

The Port Authority's leaders had initially promised it would honor the original and very generous leases to airlines negotiated by Mayor La Guardia by generating most of its operating revenue from other sources, but there was no chance the new owner would honor these deals. The

FIGURE 9. Temporary terminal and parking lot, July 30, 1948. Courtesy of the Queens Borough Public Library, Long Island Division, *New York Herald-Tribune* Photograph Morgue Collection.

leases appeared to many at the time as an awful arrangement, and permitted anticompetitive practices such as volume rebates for the biggest operators that would limit competition. Mayor La Guardia had only signed these rates as a result of the airlines' threat that airline operations would decamp to Newark if the city's terms were unfavorable. The terms would have been equally bad for the Port Authority. Authority leaders claimed they were not fully aware of the financial implications of the leases when they made the case for assumption of the airports; Austin Tobin even claimed to feel deceived after the fact. Yet the unfavorable rates had been a matter of public record and had to have been known to Port Authority officials as well. Clearly, Tobin was determined to renegotiate rates after grabbing the airports.[73]

Austin Tobin now had the upper hand with the airlines. In fall 1948 the Port Authority dug in its heels, claiming that the leases signed with the airlines by the La Guardia administration would destroy aviation in the region and even the nation. It was the authority's contention, and that of other airport operators who joined it in a new national association to defend their interests (the Airport Operators Council), that the airlines unfairly burdened airports with capital and operating costs that were unsustainable in the long term. The airlines in New York threatened to move elsewhere unless they could pay very low fees. But they were bluffing. The Port Authority had the upper hand as a result of its control of the three regional airports. New York was the number-one air market in the country, and the authority's airport monopoly now established there could not be ignored. There was little time to waste, however, either for the airlines or the Port Authority. The new and more comfortable Stratocruisers, adapted from the B-29s of the war years, that the airlines wanted to use exceeded the weight limits for LaGuardia Airport. The Port Authority, on the other side, labored under the accumulated construction costs of $110 million at a barely utilized airfield.[74]

While the standoff included the Port Authority's tricky gambit of allowing airlines to land aircraft but not let passengers use the terminal, Governor Thomas E. Dewey of New York (and future presidential candidate) quickly settled the lease issue with the major airlines (including Pan Am, American, Northwest, and British Overseas Airways Corporation, or BOAC, forerunner of British Airways), and the Port Authority. The settlement included a major increase in fees that figured in weight of planes and the costs of hangar construction. The new fee structure from the airlines in 1950 already generated 15 percent of the cost of aviation operations at Idlewild for the Port Authority and set a national standard for airport fees—a bitter pill for the airlines but one they had to accept. By 1951 the Port Authority reported that Idlewild, not including the millions required annually for construction or the related debt service, generated over $900,000 in excess revenues from operations.[75]

New York City and its uniquely powerful authorities and market power thus influenced the shape of aviation by raising costs for all airlines. The Port Authority had set a national precedent by balancing public and private capital in airport operation. The deal actually proved valuable in the long term for airlines and the aviation industry by encouraging long-term investments in much larger and more modern airports throughout the nation because of the lucrative fees municipalities could expect from air-lines in exchange for their major financial commitments. By 1957 the Port Authority, for instance, had invested $167,100,000 in Idlewild alone; such largesse was only possible owing to the proceeds of a blend of higher fees and lucrative concessions.[76]

Crowded Skies and Highways

LaGuardia Airport seemed far from Idlewild by land, at least measured in crowded highway and street miles. For pilots at the controls of a Douglas DC3, a popular commercial craft at the time that traveled up to two hundred miles per hour, the descent into New York looked quite different. The airports actually crowded uncomfortably close together because the limited air-traffic guidance technology of the era demanded that such fast-moving planes remain tens of miles apart in the air in order to avoid any chance of midair collision. The new instrument runway added by the Port Authority in its 1946 plan eliminated a dangerous intersection of planes en route to Idlewild and LaGuardia, but three airports (including Newark) in such close proximity generated complexity.[77]

The total number of aircraft movements in the 1950s at Idlewild was still low compared with the crowded future, but the limited technological capacity then available meant that many precautions had to be taken over New York's airspace. Pilots had to constantly radio their altitude speed and heading to ground installations, which then relayed the positions to traffic control centers. Directions to pilots from the control centers had to be sent through the same ground installations. What this meant in practice was overloaded radio frequencies that limited accurate position information. For this reason, controllers had to keep at least ten minutes (or about sixty miles) between arriving planes in New York until the mid-1950s to maintain safety. Competition between commercial and military sponsors of new air-traffic control systems delayed the implementation of a new and better system. Further complicating the situation was the unregulated air force of small general aviation aircraft in the New York region that had a free run (at low cost) at the city's major airports. New York was quickly suffering as a result of the inadequate technology and lax regulation. In 1954, for instance, there was so much instrument traffic in the New York area that flights backed up, and during that year, 45,000 passengers experienced major delays.[78]

Federal officials installed new radar systems in 1955 to reduce backups and permit a reduced five-mile separation. Air control for the Northeast and much of the mid-Atlantic area shifted from LaGuardia to Idlewild in 1956, taking up residence in a cutting-edge air-control facility boasting the latest radar. Continuing congestion in the skies over Idlewild and other busy airports, and a head-on plane collision in the West in 1956, galvanized federal officials in the late 1950s to adopt an expensive program of flight-control modernization, including extensive long-range radar systems. The Civil Aeronautics Authority (CAA, the forerunner of today's FAA that regulated air control and safety) also established instrument-controlled trans-continental routes (essentially high-altitude, high-speed highways of the skies) in order to regulate what had been informal, often chaotic use of airspace by commercial, private, and military pilots using their eyes as guides. Airlines benefited from this process by, among other things, making transcontinental routes faster, safer, and more dependable—and ready for the jet age.[79]

As pilots closed in on Idlewild, there was still danger when landing over the marshes and through Atlantic fogs. In 1955 the Port Authority installed a flasher system on runway 4 on a dock that extended into Jamaica Bay. Pilots would be able to see the runway approach sooner, improving the chances of making a safe landing.[80] By the late 1950s the Port Authority was busily extending runways, enhancing lighting, and laying out high-speed taxiway exits. The capacity crisis sparked and encouraged technological innovation. Idlewild was one of the first commercial airports in the country, for instance, to feature advanced instrumentation for landing. Instrumentation boosted capacity because it minimized the amount of circling airplanes had to do under visual navigation in poor weather conditions.

The Port Authority benefited from continuing federal subsidy as it made these upgrades. President Harry Truman authorized $500 million in 1946 for national airport construction and development that would lead to 3,000 new airports and improvement of 1,600 more. New York City was not the only city that benefited, but federal aid was essential to the development of the airport program nationally. Already by 1949 the federal government had spent approximately $200 million on airport development,[81] and by 1965 that figure had reached $900 million. While New York's airports received a relatively small share of this money (of $500 million spent on New York City area airports by 1965, only about 5 percent could be directly linked to federal aid), the creation of a truly national system would have been impossible without federal subsidy.[82]

Idlewild's record growth positioned it during the 1950s as the second busiest airport in the country for all operations after Chicago's O'Hare International and the leading American airport for international travel. The growth in operations was driven by the growing popularity of faster and more comfortable air travel.[83] The level of service offered by the major airline companies aimed to turn flying into a predictable, comfortable, and luxurious service that would justify high fares. Most airlines suffered from an overcapacity problem in the postwar era because the growing size and speed of aircraft outpaced the market for seats on many routes. The big companies thus used government regulations to push out the smaller airlines that threatened to make overcapacity an even bigger problem. The government endorsed the objectively anticompetitive protection of the biggest firms, not only because of formidable lobbying by the most powerful airlines but because the government viewed an advanced, large, stable aviation industry (a Civil Air Reserve fleet) as a potential partner in military operations during times of crisis. Government officials wanted the best aircraft, and lots of them, for their troops in the future and were not necessarily worried about supporting what was most profitable.[84]

Under the regulated system, airfares remained comparatively high for most American travelers throughout the 1950s. TWA, for instance, in the immediate postwar era still prepared entire planes for sleeper service across the Atlantic. Men and women dressed formally and dined on expertly prepared meals. The Lockheed Super Constellations also offered deluxe sleeper-plane service on domestic routes between Idlewild and Los Angeles. A twelve-hour luxurious New York-Paris direct flight added profits in the luxury trade for Air France in 1953. In the early era of flight, wealthy passengers even rode on their own planes with amenities such as separate lounges. Fatality rates from flying dropped so dramatically in the postwar era that plane travel became an acceptable risk even for families.[85]

At the same time, fares became more reasonable over the course of the 1950s because federal regulators held prices steady (while wages improved), and airlines realized that they could expand the market for international travel beyond the elite.[86] Tourist service thus outpaced luxury service by the late 1950s. Tourist-class flights (made possible by cheap fuel, faster planes, and greater capacity) introduced by Pan Am in 1952 between New York and London catalyzed the expansion of lower-fare transatlantic service to the most popular foreign travel destinations.[87] Tourist service proved so popular that it accounted for three-quarters of air travelers by 1957. Once airlines realized that planes with mixed levels of seating and higher seat density did not discourage travelers and actually encouraged business, economy (or coach) class was introduced in 1958 in order to crowd even more passengers on planes. A New York-London round trip in first class was very expensive in 1950: $385 ($3,607 in 2012 dollars). By 1960, however, that same trip in a more comfortable and faster jet was more reasonable at $350 ($2,710 in 2012 dollars) and a far better value in terms of time, comfort, and safety. Most jets, in fact, included both first-class and coach seating in order to achieve more efficient operations; by 1960, airlines actually designated half of their seats as coach.[88]

Flying was not yet for everyman, but by 1960 it was becoming a settled upper-middle-class phenomenon and a necessity for many business managers. In 1960 Idlewild alone handled 248,686 plane movements that shuttled 8.8 million passengers through the airport. Approximately 85 percent of the nation's transatlantic passengers came through Idlewild that year, a reduced percentage from the immediate postwar years but still impressive for one airport. Perhaps even more impressive was that Idlewild handled approximately half of all of the nation's international airline traffic that year. Airports, and Idlewild in particular, had been built optimistically, but rapid democratization of air travel quickly tested even those generous boundaries. The fact that Pan Am led the world's international travel market, for instance, meant that Idlewild was already crowded.[89]

From Water Ports to Air Ports

The booming consumer society of the postwar years also swelled air-cargo operations at Idlewild. Air cargo boosted Idlewild's competitive advantages by subsidizing many otherwise unprofitable or under-capacity international routes (air cargo could be stowed in the holds of passenger planes), helping Idlewild remain at the center of global air travel. Air cargo seemed financially promising because, as promoters noted in 1945, the New York metro region was already "one of the great centers of high-class package freight, which is the type most likely to use airplanes in overseas transport."[90] The region's wealth and extensive trade were key to creating Idlewild's early lead in the air-cargo industry.

The Port Authority leadership closely calculated the future of trade in the region and the nation. After the war, the Port Authority adopted additional new technologies for the maintenance of the port's supremacy. These investments, planned by the authority's able team of economists and engineers, proved crucial to the region's future health. At the docks, this would mean in the 1950s the creation of a modern, containerized shipping facility in Newark-Elizabeth. These new facilities, made possible in part by generous deals to protect current longshoremen, in the long term eliminated the raison d'être for much of the aging port infrastructure and unionized staff on New York's waterfront. Air cargo was also a new frontier. The service may have been expensive compared with traditional means of shipping (almost one-third more expensive), but the high value or time sensitivity of the cargo more than compensated for the additional costs. In addition, combining passenger flights and cargo flights kept many routes relatively profitable for airlines.

New York built on its leadership of oceangoing trade as it entered the modern air-cargo era. Freight forwarders of the maritime era, who handled paperwork for international shipping, made a successful transition from ocean vessels to airplanes because they realized that planes represented just another way to move goods faster and over greater distances. They understood that "forwarding is a complex, many faceted service," and they had to be "expert in paperwork that covers the spectrum of U.S. and foreign government regulations; and had to be capable of performing a full range of ground services between the shipper and the airline."[91] New York's history as a global center of commerce gave it a significant advantage and helped secure the city as an early leader in air cargo.

The defense industry also played a role in inspiring and subsidizing this service. The Berlin airlift is frequently cited as a key demonstration of the potential for airfreight in the postwar period because a city's basic needs were sustained by air cargo alone for months. Just as important were the surplus aircraft sold off at war's end. New Yorkers quickly jumped into this profitable game. New York was, after all, in its last years as the nation's leading industrial region and still produced many high-value industrial products, such as machine parts and business machines. Sperry's vast electronics plant in Lake Success on Long Island was just one of many Long Island enterprises that benefited from the transition of wartime contracts to both Cold War defense spending and the rise in commercial aviation.

Seaboard and Western Airlines, for instance, started with one air freighter in May 1947 and operated solely in the freight business between New York and European points. The founders of the company had been part of the Air Transport Command during the war, which distinguished itself by flying almost anything anywhere under almost any conditions, and they also had experience in aviation insurance before the war. About 40 percent of the company's tonnage was in wearing apparel, accessories, and textiles, not just high-value industrial items like machine parts. By 1948, the company had five planes in constant rotation and, in fact, got a profitable bump from the contract it secured during the Berlin airlift.[92]

It did not hurt the development of aviation in the region that Long Island was, by the end of World War II and during the height of the Cold War, one of the nation's aviation hubs, with massive plants and operations of Grumman, Republic, Fairchild, and Sperry driving industrial growth. So important was aviation on Long Island that in 1954, for instance, the industry accounted for 45.4 percent of Nassau-Suffolk's total manufacturing employment. The contracts generated by the Korean War mainlined federal cash to these booming suburbs. Even though this high level of aircraft employment was not maintained in the long term, the importing and exporting of advanced electronics, machine tools, and other materials needed for the aviation business boosted Idlewild's air-cargo industry for decades.[93]

The postwar defense industrial complex provided key subsidies for the emerging air-cargo business. Not only was the technology for air-cargo planes pioneered during the war and after (Hercules turboprop C-130s easily became cargo carriers), but also "propping up the airfreight business were fat contracts channeled to the carriers by the government and the Defense Department. In fiscal 1956, the Pentagon spent a whopping $67.5 million to ship goods and personnel by commercial carriers." The Flying Tiger line alone received almost $3 million in contracts from the military air transportation service.[94] The Eisenhower administration also promoted air cargo by encouraging federal agencies to use civil cargo airlift. Volume reduced costs and improved systems for everyone, not just the military.[95]

The air-cargo center at Idlewild, dedicated in 1956, was its own Terminal City for cargo. The four warehouses and five buildings provided space where the freight forwarders, customs inspection, and quarantine could all be conducted. Separate hangars of ever-increasing size and complexity sheltered planes that carried this complex and popular trade. New York's cargo companies were also able to leverage the growing number of passenger routes by including cargos in the holds of these frequently scheduled flights. By 1960, the Port Authority realized that even though the cargo facility was by their account the largest air-cargo center in the world, it was already far too small to preserve its leadership; administrators initiated an expansion that doubled its size in the early 1960s.

The air-cargo center on its own stood little chance of replacing New York City's once crowded docks as a source of employment or commerce. The labor-saving system of containerized shipping at the Port Authority's new Newark-Elizabeth waterfront doomed New York's waterfront culture and economy. At the same time, the air-cargo center, for certain types of high-value items, proved to be an important element in the maintenance of the New York metropolitan area as a central point in global trade routes as it had been for centuries. Until the 1970s, in fact, Idlewild's air-cargo operations surpassed in scale any other airport in the United States.

New York Congestion

By the 1940s, the New York metropolitan area had the most advanced and integrated system of high-speed parkways and bridges in the nation. This system was the result of decades of steady road building under the leadership of Robert Moses, the Regional Plan Association, and political leaders in both the city and surrounding counties. The growth of the parkway network, beginning in the 1920s, had set in motion an era of decentralization of population with long-term grave consequences for New York City—not to mention gridlock. In the 1940s, however, New York's leaders viewed the connection to these road networks as a positive element of modernization. While Mayor La Guardia saved the subways in 1940, mass transit was a notorious financial drain and, in many respects, a legacy of an earlier age. It should come as little surprise then that city leaders across the board placed a premium on automobile connections to the new airport. This singular dependence on automobile, truck, and bus travel to and from the airport, however, meant that all increases in number of passengers would lead to a greater flood of vehicles.[96] Foreshadowing decades of delays, the *first* scheduled outbound flight from Idlewild in 1948, bound for Chile, "took off 31 min. late yesterday because of the delay in the arrival of the coach carrying passengers from Manhattan."[97]

As a rule, airports across the nation lacked mass-transit connections to their new airports until the 1980s and 1990s. Most large postwar airports (Dulles, O'Hare, LAX) rose on vast parcels of distant land, far away from established urban neighborhoods: older mass-transit lines were in short supply or absent in these open spaces and new systems probably uneconomical in light of the suburban boom and the American preference for private cars. The United States heavily subsidized new highways, as opposed to mass transit; so highways, paid for by federal dollars, usually become modern airport connectors.

But New York faced a different situation from other cities in the 1940s. While motorcars had become very popular as a result of Moses's highway systems, the congestion on these roads was growing in tandem with their popularity. Depending on packed roads for shuttling passengers to timed departures was rolling the dice. The city itself, despite suburbanization, was also still the most densely populated in the nation, with the nation's most comprehensive mass-transit service including buses and streetcars. La Guardia's plan for public ownership saved the subway system in 1940 from the bankruptcy and dissolution that ruined so many other transit systems. Idlewild was located close enough to existing mass transit (both subways and commuter rail) to make transit a legitimate option.

The original site committee of city councilmen, in fact, found in 1941 that the *only* deficiency of the site was the lack of transit and rail connections.[98] Some early observers saw, however, that a connection to the Rockaway Branch line could potentially get passengers to Penn Station in as little as twenty minutes. An extension of the subway (the new IND line in Queens) to the airport was also discussed at the time.[99] A reporter from *Colliers* predicted that in the future airport "newly built railroads, subways and highways will converge on this former wilderness," but someone would have had to show some leadership for this to happen.[100] In spite of serious discussion of an extension of the Rockaway Beach line of the Long Island Rail Road (LIRR) for passenger and freight travel to Idlewild in the 1940s, political leaders failed to create an efficient mass-transit system between city and airport.[101]

Mayor La Guardia was a great advocate for aviation and highways, but new mass transit to the airport was not his priority. On a tour of the airport site in 1945, the mayor made excuses by pointing out the difficulties of linking the LIRR to the airport: "We've been negotiating for 2 and half years to build a spur right into the airport. Life is short and so are the terms of a Mayor, so we're going to build the airport up to the end of the rail-road." The man who rebuilt a city couldn't get this done? Then again, the privately held and financially troubled LIRR had no incentive to work collaboratively on a transit link.[102] In 1948, eight leading citywide civic orga-nizations mourned the lack of connectivity between Idlewild and the sub-way. The express lines of the IND Queens Boulevard (now the E and F subway lines) could have been extended along the Van Wyck, thus "the opportunity of constructing an open cut subway as a part of this express highway at greatly reduced cost is now apparently lost because the highway project was blueprinted without consideration of the airport's full requirements."[103]

Without a fixed rail connection, every passenger who came to Idlewild would have to ride on rubber wheels or helicopters (see below). And those rubber wheels had to thread a crowded city only partly relieved by the parkways and highways Robert Moses had spread across the city. This was just the beginning of decades of bad connections. Robert Moses bragged in 1935 that "you can ride from 92nd Street and the East River all the way to Kew Gardens and east on a genuine parkway without crossings or lights," but it was a different challenge entirely to link Kew Gardens in central Queens to Jamaica Bay.[104]

Moses extended what eventually became the Van Wyck Express-way, paid for by a combination of state and federal funds, from Queens Boulevard-Grand Central Parkway to the airport after the war. The new high-way was designed both as a connector to the airport and "to serve Queens as a whole, with traffic separations planned to reduce congestion in the Jamaica area." In retrospect, this dual use was a major error. In practice, the Van Wyck would never serve as a dependable, fast route to the airport.[105] The Van Wyck Expressway when it first opened in 1950 had six lanes and two parallel service roads, which counted as a large highway for its day. Officials predicted a 20 percent reduction in city-to-airport trip time for both cars and buses . . . on a good day.[106] Robert Caro colorfully describes how Moses ignored dire traffic predictions for the Van Wyck and refused to even carve out a future right of way for transit down the Van Wyck, despite the ease and comparative low cost for transit on such a route.[107]

Access to Idlewild also suffered from a local quirk in the regional road network. On paper, Robert Moses appeared to have created a fairly even distribution of highways linking Nassau County and Queens; Moses had essentially built out much of the system projected in the late 1920s by the

Regional Plan Association. Yet Moses refused to abandon the parkway ideal, of leisure drives through green parks, when the parkways had by and large become commuter routes through emerging suburban areas. As a result, Moses made traffic worse on the Van Wyck and limited efficiency in bus and truck service to the airport by banning buses and commercial vehicles from most of his parkways, including the Southern State (which connects both to the Van Wyck and the Belt), Belt Parkway, and the Grand Central. The Van Wyck Expressway, as the only highway to the airport that accommodated trucks and buses, developed a reputation in the 1950s for gridlock. The Belt Parkway also connected to Idlewild, but the Belt was a long, twisting, and dangerous connector to Manhattan that Robert Moses stitched together along the edge of Brooklyn marshes, waterfronts, and neighborhoods; it proved to be poorly designed as a dependable high-speed expressway. Many Nassau County commuters also realized that the shortest way from the South Shore of Long Island to Manhattan and the Bronx was to head north on the Van Wyck to the Grand Central rather than fight their way west on the Belt Parkway. Truckers loading up cargo had to find their way to their destinations either by slow surface roads or, like everyone else, by crowding the Van Wyck Expressway.[108]

Port Authority leaders were not deaf to the criticism and requested that Moses alter his policies. Port Authority chairman Cullman in 1947 made clear that "an outstanding need of a smooth functioning airport system was permission from the city to operate buses over the Belt Parkway. Robert Moses . . . has opposed airport traffic over parkways."[109] Moses, however, still viewed his parkways as "ribbon or shoe-string parks" whose aesthetic qualities would be destroyed should buses be allowed on them. He explained his resistance to the privately run Carey bus service to Idlewild by irrationally predicting worse congestion from buses than cars: "You can understand the difficult traffic problems that would arise if regularly scheduled trips at intervals of a few minutes were permitted over the parkway system to Idlewild Airport."[110] Yet tens of thousands of individual cars and taxis nevertheless congested parkways to and from the airport, and their numbers rose in tandem with explosive increases in aviation traffic.[111]

The airport's negative reputation for difficult access and egress solidified during the 1950s as more and more travelers found themselves stuck in traffic: "During the past few years many travelers have noticed that at times it has taken longer to drive from New York International Airport, at Idlewild, in Queens, into Manhattan than it has to make the flight from Boston to New York City." Carey passenger buses remained banned from the Grand Central Parkway, for instance, thus making their journey to the airport painfully slow on regular city streets like Woodhaven Boulevard.[112] The Whitestone Expressway, the interstate connection to the Van Wyck that finally allowed trucks and buses direct access from the airport to the regional road system, including the Long Island Expressway and the Whitestone Bridge, was not built until the 1960s as part of preparations for Moses's 1964–65 World's Fair.

Blaming Moses or Mayor La Guardia is an easy game, and they deserve their fair share, but the Port Authority's leaders such as Tobin and Cullman share equal blame for subsequent failures to link the airport to the mass-transit system. Early on, Port Authority officials envisioned the airport as elemental to the modernist reconstruction of the city and region around automobiles, buses, and trucks. Cullman in 1950 boasted that his agency was "furnishing the first modern terminal facilities in the port District for three of the most widely used forms of transportation, namely, the airplane, the suburban and long distance bus, and the over-the road truck."[113] In the 1950s, Tobin took no blame for the decline of mass transit as a result of the Port Authority's bridges and tunnels but described the collapse of mass transit and the rise in numbers of autos, buses, and trucks in the New York region as a "national and a world-wide phenomenon" leading to arterial highways and other infrastructure for vehicular traffic.[114] The original Port Authority airport proposal in 1946 called for "an intramural bus system" among future terminals that would connect to city-sponsored bus lines and the Howard Beach LIRR station. The Port Authority, in fact, created a bus system for intra-terminal connections and city links in the Terminal City plans carried out in the 1950s; yet the system was never very popular as passengers had to face additional transfers and negotiation of stairwells while loaded down with luggage.[115]

Provisions for the automobile received far more careful attention and planning from the beginning. By 1948, managers at Idlewild had already created two thousand parking spaces and envisioned room for six thousand total spaces in just a few years. They even created a monumental airplane overpass for a roadway entering the airport. The new airport was where the automobile from the city or the suburbs could be comfortably parked so that the businessmen or elite travelers could transition seamlessly and without urban filth, noise, and social diversity to the most modern and expensive transportation in existence.[116] Postwar European cities invested more heavily in communal transportation facilities, including rail-based mass transit, than their American counterparts, including New York.[117] A pioneering modern airport like that in Hamburg in 1929 had included both roadways and a tram line to get passengers right downtown, but it would not be until approximately five decades after its opening (in 2003) that JFK had a functioning rail connection to mass transit and, even then, the ride was a complicated one to Manhattan.

The lack of mass-transit connections to airports did not distinguish New York from other cities at this time, but the New York metropolitan area was more transit dependent than any other city in America. New York's ground congestion began to take its revenge on the ground traveler, as it would for decades. Travelers, who minutes before had been sailing comfortably in the skies at hundreds of miles an hour, suddenly found themselves creeping along jammed highways. Those without cars turned out to be easy prey for unscrupulous cabbies. By the 1950s it was well known that cab drivers took advantage of passengers at New York International seeking to travel to the suburbs. Cabbies as a rule turned their meters off outside the five boroughs, so it became a matter of negotiation; the cabbies frequently took advantage of their near monopoly on ground travel. Signs were posted at Idlewild to negotiate before setting forth to destinations. Welcome to New York!

New York Is Noisy Enough

At the 1948 dedication of Idlewild, massive bombers staged "the greatest exhibition of air power ever staged in one spot in peace time in history of the United States. . . . They dived in snarling formations out of overcast and simulated bombing and strafing, and their 'bombs' tore the earth in fiery bursts."[118] The thundering bombers, and even an experimental and very loud F-86 jet fighter, were surely less comforting to audience members from Queens or Nassau County, some of whom must have understood that these were not simply temporary displays but a frightening premonition of a noisy future for their neighborhoods.

The secret to the rapid growth of America's civilian aircraft industry was the ease by which airlines converted warplanes designed to drop a bomb or to ferry troops into comfortable and reasonably safe airships for businessmen and tourists. The Boeing B-377 Stratocruiser, after all, was just a converted Boeing C-97 Air Force transport plane. Almost all the technology that made possible the rapid rise of airports like Idlewild came from the trial and error and aviation research funded by the government during World War II. Planes became more dependable, more powerful, and faster. What lacked funding during World War II were deliberately stealthy airplanes. Powerful airplanes not only carried maximum destructive payloads but also served a critical role in terrorizing urban populations. Military bases may have been full of American citizens too, but soldiers and their families had no choice but to endure the noise aircraft generated. Almost as soon as the planes were reborn as civilian aircraft, however, the complaints began from a far less docile population of urban and suburban residents. Civilians did not sit quietly as a veritable civilian Air Force, engaged in a war to determine commercial supremacy, invaded their neighborhoods.[119]

It had already taken decades to add sewerage and smoke to the list of nuisances that the government had a right to regulate for the public order. New York, in fact, was coming off a particularly strong half century of regulation with new sewage-treatment plants, expanded parks, and electrified rail lines that made New York a much cleaner and healthier city. Unlike other forms of pollution that can be photographed, monitored through chemical analysis, or even smelled (and that are often rooted in one particular location), noise proved to be a particularly elusive pollutant that escaped detection. Noise pollution is also usually a subjective form of pollution: the standard of what constitutes noise pollution varies by individuals and societies, among other factors. The transition to a postindustrial society, however, generated office workers with a very low noise tolerance compared with the generations that had toiled in steel mills and machine shops.

Adding noise pollution to the list of environmental problems in the 1950s and 1960s demanded consistent activism and documentation in the face of a powerful and politically savvy aviation industry. Once the search began for quiet, it was inevitable that airports would be singled out for their contribution to regional noise pollution. Like highways, airports were now among the few sources of industrial-scale noise pollution left in American cities and suburbs. Suburban populations, rather than being passive in the face of environmental decline brought on by their own development, became surprising forceful in the fight for new environmental regulations in the 1950s and 1960s. This pattern of suburban environmental activism appeared with equal force in New York's regional suburbs.[120]

In the areas around Idlewild, the loud buzzing of propeller aircraft was so distinctive, so close, and so frequent that even the most elite and bucolic

suburbs, housing their share of air travelers, rose up in protest. Suburbanites since the nineteenth century had successfully zoned out other activities
they considered nuisances (stores, stables, and factories): they considered
tranquility a reward for success. Yet lucky urbanites recently escaped from
crowded tenements to the comparatively pastoral surroundings of southern
Queens and Nassau County suddenly found themselves sleeping and living
next to an aviation "factory" that was busier on a daily basis than almost
any military base in the world. In 1948, the very year the airport opened,
eighteen civic organizations representing, among others, neighbors in the
Rockaways, Rosedale, Laurelton, Springfield, St. Albans, and South Jamaica,
protested noise and low-flying planes.[121] The many complaints in Queens
from low-flying planes included claims that planes "skimmed" homes and
hospitals.[122]

The New York region's preeminence in air traffic thus created citizen
pressure, nearly from day one of operations, for regulation and identification of noise as an environmental problem. Residents, however, faced an
uphill battle on the legal front. Congress had made regulation of air noise
a nearly impossible task for local government because in 1926 it had
"granted a right of freedom of transit through the navigable air space of
the United States." Regulations defining "navigable" airspace proved weak
at best, setting a thousand-foot minimum over densely populated areas
and no clear agency for enforcement.[123] Sensing danger from an outraged
populace, the CAA quickly pioneered regulations in 1948 to limit low-flying
airplanes at both LaGuardia and Idlewild.[124] The system for Queens was
hailed as "the only traffic pattern of its kind in the country. We call it the
anti-noise pattern."[125] This initial system, however, ended as a result of
"unsafe air congestion" that the system created.[126]

Growing traffic over Queens and Newark kept the issue on the front
burner. In 1951, Queens borough president Joseph Mafera joined civic
groups in protesting low-flying aircraft and put pressure on airlines, Congress, the CAA, and the Port Authority.[127] The airlines, their pilots, and the
CAA (which directed the air-traffic controllers) agreed in 1952 to divert
additional airline traffic away from densely populated areas near LaGuardia
and Idlewild. More flights would fly in over Jamaica Bay as long as weather
permitted: this was the start of the preferential runway system.[128] By 1954
"preferential" areas such as water or meadows accounted for almost half of
the takeoffs and landings in the New York metropolitan area. The airlines
also claimed that they had moved training flights out of the area, reduced

low landings, and introduced steeper climbs over uninhabited areas all to reduce noise. The Port Authority hired sound engineers in a desperate bid to tame aircraft noise on the ground[129] and became a leading force behind the National Air Transport Coordinating Committee (NATCC). This organization gathered together the airlines, manufacturers, and airports in order to coordinate noise reductions in part to stave off government regulation.[130]

These preemptive actions by the airlines did not stop civic leaders from Queens and Nassau County protesting low-flying aircraft in 1952 to the House Committee on Foreign and Interstate Commerce. They made a radical and entirely unrealistic bid for the "closing of the big airports," including both LaGuardia and New York International, and proposed moving them to Long Island.[131] The Council for Elimination of Airports in New York City, the force behind the drive, claimed to represent fifty civic organizations.[132] The fact of the matter is, however, that local politicians were not much help in mitigating noise pollution in domains they did control. They did not restrict urban growth around the airport in the 1940s and 1950s when large areas of open space still existed. Instead, they allowed developers a relatively free hand in filling every possible block with housing. Hundreds of thousands of additional residents filled in around the airport, in the Rockaways, and in Nassau County during this era.

As politically unlikely as ending New York City area aviation might sound, calls for elimination of airports got a good bit of tailwind from both noise and many gruesome crashes in the early 1950s. A cargo plane, for instance, had plowed into Jamaica, Queens, in 1952. Advocates sought to have airports declared a public nuisance because they made "a considerable number of persons insecure in life or the use of property."[133] Antinoise advocates could also draw on growing evidence of noise as a serious threat to human health. The U.S. Air Force had by this time identified aircraft noise as a potential source of fatigue, nausea, and even tissue damage for those on the ground. The new jets in development even threatened noise levels between 120 and 140 decibels and would be "the loudest man-made industrial noise known up to now," even exceeding the rumble of B-36 Intercontinental bombers.[134]

The idea of closing New York's airports went nowhere, as did an attempt by the gilded village of Cedarhurst to set its own local limits. This affluent and well-connected town, regrettably positioned directly under major air-traffic routes at Idlewild, in 1952 created a thousand-foot limit on over-flying planes as an exercise of the police power that they believed

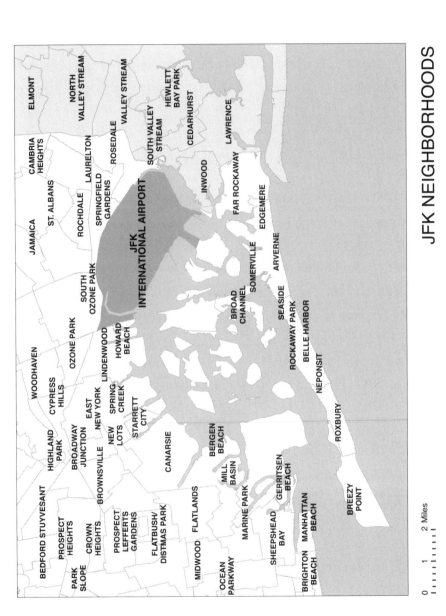

JFK NEIGHBORHOODS

FIGURE 10. Selected neighborhoods surrounding JFK. Minna Ninova.

FIGURE 11. Space for victory gardens in Forest Hills, Queens, illustrates the amount
of undeveloped land even in some of the region's most densely developed
neighborhoods, 1944. In time, these spaces filled in with housing, putting more
and more New Yorkers close to the airports. Howard Hollem, photographer. Library
of Congress Prints and Photographs Division.

protected health, safety, and well-being. This ordinance, however, was
struck down in 1955 by a federal court (despite the fact that it was quite
similar to a 1926 rule). The courts agreed with the CAA, the Port Authority,
and the airlines that local governments had no right to regulate airspace. It
was argued, with some cogency, that if local governments did successfully
gain this right from the federal government, it would destroy air commerce
in the United States. Local politicians were unlikely, for instance, to be as
lenient as federal officials with offending airlines.[135]

Howard Cullman defended air travel in 1952 but also positioned the
Port Authority as the defender of the little man: "I have no patience or
excuse for those who attempt to brush off the problems of planes over
populous areas by suggesting that 'the people got used to the railroads.'"[136]

Tobin shared the belief that the "social problem of aviation" impact would have to be directly addressed and was skeptical that jets could ever be successfully integrated into the densely populated New York area. Yet the Port Authority did not make any friends by encouraging Lockheed to establish at Idlewild "the biggest commercial overhaul base on the East Coast" that would bring even more planes into local airspace. Residents in Laurelton were particularly concerned about the noise from the constant warming up of engines. Port Authority leaders such as Cullman expressed concerns about noise, but actions spoke louder than words: economic growth first, quality of life second.[137]

The noise problem threatened to worsen with the dawning jet age. The Port Authority put a great deal of pressure on airline designers to design quieter engines, but there was no easy technological fix for what ailed those trapped below. Boeing, after all, "parlayed its military subsidized work on an Air Force jet tanker . . . into a running start on a civilian transport version" in 1953 and began testing it in 1954. What this meant in practice was that initial Boeing designers had paid more attention to speed, payload, and power rather than noise. Noise mufflers and suppressor systems, while initially greeted as the solution to jet noise, made less progress than hoped by the late 1950s because muffling devices threatened to reduce thrust too much for safe operation.[138]

Beginning in 1951 the Port Authority, realizing the substantial difference between jet and piston noise, put in place the following regulation for Idlewild that essentially prohibited all jet operations until 1958 in the New York region: "No jet aircraft may land or take off at any (Port Authority) air terminal . . . without permission." This "permission" was, however, contingent on airplanes meeting a 112-decibel standard that the Port Authority knew was beyond the capabilities of the early jets.[139] Restrictions in the most important air market in the world, even before the jets had been readied for civilian use, definitely got the attention of the airlines.[140] Airport officials at the time were worried because they "had only the military establishment's experience with jet fighters and bombers to guide us. The noise history of these jets had caused much apprehension to the residents surrounding the airport."[141]

These concerns did not stop airlines from ordering jets because of their obvious advantages in speed and (eventually) capacity. Pan Am even ordered three of the notoriously loud British-manufactured Comet III jets in 1952 to ensure that the company would remain at the forefront of

commercial aviation. A Port Authority official who traveled to Britain dis-
covered that Comet noise had airport neighbors up in arms in London.
Contrary to airline claims that Comets might operate successfully in New
York, they discovered that "if a Comet jet passed three times over the airports in the N.Y. metropolitan area, all airports would have to close."[142]
The Port Authority denied landings of the Boeing 707 at Idlewild and the
Comet III at any New York airport in 1955. This decision did not, however,
stop an airline like United that very same year from placing an order for
thirty jets.[143] These early skirmishes over noise foreshadowed decades of
protest and legislation, a great deal of it inspired by unhappy New Yorkers.

By the early 1950s New York's leaders had secured the city's leading
position in the booming postwar aviation industry. Defying the naysayers
and skeptics New Yorkers had reinvented their metropolis, if not their city,
for an entirely new era of transportation and trade. Airport promoters had
carved out space for an international-scale airport, constructed the basic
elements of that airport, found a competent and well-financed manager,
negotiated hard for sustainable contracts with the airlines, created space for
a new air-cargo industry, and linked the airport to the regional highway
network. The reconciliation of noise and environmental concerns, and the
matter of a transit link, remained unresolved, but these shortcomings were
not at the time considered to be major obstructions to a bright future for
the airport as a whole. On another level, it was clear that the airport was
already changing from a city airport, like LaGuardia, to a metropolitan-
scale institution. Its market, design, management, and environmental
impact already reflected the fact that such an enormous enterprise, and
both its benefits and downsides, could not be contained within the city
limits.

CHAPTER 2

Terminal City's Suburban Form

If an airport was judged on no more than the number of passengers and flights that it processed, Idlewild was a great success by the mid-1950s. In 1955, the Port Authority actually crammed 3.5 million passengers through the "shanties, the Quonset huts, (and) the cinderblock 'termporary' terminals" at Idlewild.[1] These shabby and overcrowded structures, however, hardly delivered on the Port Authority's promise of a great international terminal. Despite over a decade of grand plans and promises, travelers were hard pressed to find a decent meal, a clean bathroom, or even suitable waiting space. Celebrities and dignitaries arriving by luxury plane, who minutes earlier might have been tucking into lobsters and filet mignon, rarely lingered at the spartan airfield; ordinary civilians were not so lucky. It was supposed to be otherwise.

Designing a metropolitan-scale airport terminal system was a difficult undertaking for the simple reason that its designers could not draw upon the experience from other airports of a similar size. Nor could they accurately predict the growth curve for such a volatile and rapidly expanding industry. The Port Authority was thus forced to sponsor a risky and very expensive experiment in airport design. If their answer to the needs of modern air travel now seems dated or ill conceived—the "Terminal City" concept—it is only because we filter the outcome of that experiment through our modern eyes and passenger experience. A few more years of construction delay might have led to an entirely different design, and one that would have worked better for passengers and airlines in the long term,

FIGURE 12. The glazed eyes and boredom of stranded passengers often exceeded the excitement of the air age. This time it was as a result of dense fog, but delays became, and remain, a fact of life at JFK and other regional airfields, December 23, 1956. Courtesy of the Queens Borough Public Library, Long Island Division, *New York Herald-Tribune* Photograph Morgue Collection.

but those were not years that the Port Authority felt it could wait when so many competing cities were entering the aviation race.

The Terminal City's "unit terminal" system, with most major airlines each developing and running a signature terminal (seven terminals in total plus a shared International Arrivals Building [IAB]), appeared at the time to planners as the most practical, glamorous, and futuristic approach to meeting the needs of such a massive and complex operation. The Port Authority explained in 1954 that the unit terminal model won out because "the future traffic requirements specified by the airlines are so great that the only practical way of accommodating such volumes of passengers . . . is through several unit terminals spread around the periphery of the central terminal area." A central terminal was "discarded . . . because the walking distances [within the terminal] and building size involved became impractical."[2] Austin Tobin thought it critical that the maximum walking distance from parked car to terminal be no more than four hundred feet. This planning principle was similar to the suburban malls rising at the time, but one that would not be sustainable in the long term at Idlewild.[3] The plan also spread out the construction costs rather than erecting one massive terminal that the Port Authority would have had to finance and build on its own at one time. Finally, individual terminals allowed airlines to create a brand identity amid such a large complex.

The initial Terminal City plans in 1954 called for over one million square feet of terminal space to be divided among a shared IAB and many large unit terminals run by individual airlines. Such a grand airport, they estimated, would be able to process about one million passengers a month by 1965. In retrospect, they were conservative in their calculations. By 1966, 1.5 million passengers flowed through the various terminals per month.[4] The power of the Port Authority to charge fees and collect rents made possible such an ambitious program. By 1963, when the Terminal City complex was largely complete, in its first iteration at least, the Port Authority had invested $349.9 million in Idlewild alone, a far cry from the $42 million the Port Authority had invested in the airport by 1951.[5] To cover these costs and the debts accrued, the Port Authority charged rent to airlines for their terminals, demanded a share of concession profits (for example, restaurants and fuel), and charged airlines by weight for takeoffs, for use of the IAB, for porter service, and even for customs and baggage. While many of these charges were small, taken over millions of passengers and hundreds of thousands of operations, they added up to significant sums.[6]

While many critics in subsequent decades have condemned the unit terminal arrangement as illogical and inflexible, to planners at the time the scheme appeared to be a precise solution to a very complex problem. A special issue of *Architectural Record* in 1961 provides excellent diagrams illustrating the changing layout and the logic that led to the final design. Among the criteria Port Authority designers used to determine the final layout were total capacity (with the ability to handle a hundred plane movements per hour), passenger convenience, flexibility in long-term terminal use, and maximum leasable space for moneymaking concessions. By the early 1960s, the airlines and the Port Authority had, in fact, built the largest terminals that they could, with totals far exceeding the early square-footage projections. Some of the planned individual terminals were so big that if plopped down individually in a smaller city, they might have been mistaken for airports in their own right. The Eastern Terminal, for instance, debuted as one of the largest air terminals in the country, and it was just one of many terminals on site.[7]

The Port Authority's leaders and designers aimed for practical solutions, but they also drew inspiration from the clean lines and modernist plans pioneered in the era's modernist urban renewal projects, suburbs, and world's fairs. The Terminal City plan, by dividing the airport into distinct zones for individual airlines, supporting services, air cargo, parks, and parking lots, was modernist in conception (a planned community with expressways linking different urban functions). The custom-designed zones not only separated planes from people and planes from automobiles but different activities one from the other. The highways and service roads, not walkways, thus linked passenger terminals to runways, repair hangars, a hotel, parking lots, a bank, gas stations, government offices, and cargo facilities. This strict separation, paralleled in urban-renewal projects of the era such as Stuyvesant Town or the United Nations and emerging suburbs in the surrounding area, was new for an old city that once jumbled its transportation and commercial activities into crowded central districts. Terminal City was one of many important testing grounds for ways of untangling the historical city.

In terms of direct design precedents, the Port Authority borrowed key themes for Terminal City from recent World's Fairs, particularly the 1939 fair in nearby Flushing Meadow Park. This was the result, most likely, of the leadership of architect Wallace Harrison, who played a key role in planning for both Terminal City and the 1939 World's Fair. At the fair, Americans had gotten a taste for what a total modernist environment would look like: the careful arrangement of the pavilions one to the other and to the surrounding landscape; their streamlined, coordinated modern appearance shorn of most ornamentation; and the scale models of a perfect and highly autocentric urban future displayed within both the spherical Theme Center and General Motors' Futurama exhibit. At Terminal City, too, the Port Authority predicted that the arrangement of terminals would appear to the visitor "like jewels on a necklace" and the complex as a whole "would surround a landscaped area of parks and fountains." Early illustrations of the airport's control tower show people milling about landscaped grounds more typically found at a fair.

World's Fairs, on a symbolic level, were also an appropriate precedent because it was at these grand pavilions that technocrats in the employ of

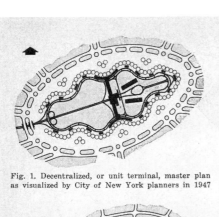

Fig. 1. Decentralized, or unit terminal, master plan as visualized by City of New York planners in 1947

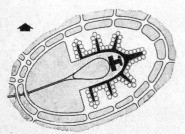

Fig. 2. Early 1948 version of centralized terminal building scheme developed by the Port Authority

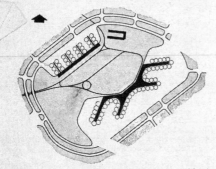

Fig. 3. Variation of the centralized scheme, with air cargo facilities added, developed by P. of N.Y.A. in 1949

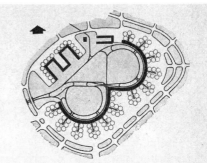

Fig. 4. Revised version of the 1953 scheme, made in an attempt to add more gate positions in the plan

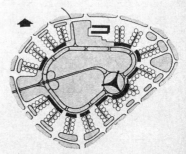

Fig. 5. Unit terminal scheme of 1954, with cargo removed to a position outside of the central area

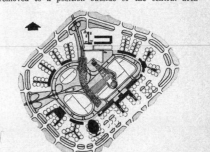

Fig. 6. Master plan of Terminal City, in all major respects, as finally conceived of and constructed

FIGURE 13. Changing design concepts for Terminal City. As the passenger projections, costs of construction, and aircraft size increased during the planning process, the options narrowed for the designers. Courtesy of *Architectural Forum*.

FIGURE 14. Austin Tobin presiding over the 32-by-40-foot Terminal City scale model during a press conference, January 30, 1956. The International Arrivals Building is in the foreground. Courtesy of the Queens Borough Public Library, Long Island Division, *New York Herald-Tribune* Photograph Morgue Collection.

FIGURE 15. Fountains and gardens (now replaced by parking ramps) gave Terminal City a festive air in 1957. Courtesy of the Queens Borough Public Library, Long Island Division, *New York Herald-Tribune* Photograph Morgue Collection.

major corporations such as General Motors encouraged the public to embrace the future despite potential risks associated with technology. The terminals at Idlewild, just like the fair pavilions, were also in the hands of a few of America's leading corporations: the major airlines. This arrangement transformed the various terminals and functional requirements into grand and reassuring experiences for a public that had some genuine concerns about aircraft safety.[8] Architectural historian Alastair Gordon recalled that the connections to the fairs and futurism were palpable for first-time visitors: "We glided along freshly paved overpasses and beneath the signs bearing candy colored numbers. The terminals were strung out like pavilions around the looping roadway, and it felt as if we were back at the fair. . . . This wasn't pretending to be the future; this was the future."[9]

Even though his earlier terminal plan had faltered, the selection of architect Wallace K. Harrison as the responsible party for the overall plan and coordination of the new Terminal City design aligned the project with major modernist urban-renewal strategies of the postwar era. Harrison played a leading role in Rockefeller Center in the 1930s; designed the Trylon and Perisphere at the 1939 World's Fair (housing the theme display); and achieved international standing as coordinator of design for both the United Nations and Lincoln Center. Harrison's exact role in the design of Idlewild is difficult to document, in contrast to his later terminal design at LaGuardia Airport (1964), but an article in a leading architectural journal of the time, *Architectural Forum*, listed his role as "design consultant and coordinator of exterior architecture for the entire project." The article gives him credit for "the roadway layout and building locations for the central area" and "the landscaping of the plaza and a large reflecting lagoon at the center." The Terminal City concept parallels his work in terms of the integration of various signature pavilions into a larger, isolated, modernist urban ensemble with formal gardens and generous walkways. Harrison, the unofficial "dean" of New York architectural practice at the time, lent establishment weight to the concept.[10]

More specific design coordination fell to Thomas Sullivan of the Port Authority, who became the leading architect-engineer to oversee the final design and coordination of terminal design by different architects. There is not a lot known about him, but Sullivan kept a paperweight on his desk with Daniel Burnham's famous dictum, "Make no little plans; they leave no magic to stir men's souls," indicating his awareness of the City Beautiful concept that Burnham promoted for American cities at the turn of the century. Sullivan compared the new Terminal City favorably to iconic New York landmarks of the era in an interview at the time: "For Sullivan, Terminal City is the World's Fair, Botanical Gardens and Empire State Building all rolled into one jet age airport and tourist attraction." Sullivan even believed that as an attraction, "when this airport is finished, Rockefeller Center won't have a chance." [11]

In this era, the airport quickly became as popular a sensation as an actual world's fair. Nearly 5 million visitors in the first year "came to see such sites as a world's fair might offer—the Fountain of Liberty, to take just one, with its 200 foot diameter, 900 odd jets and 6 min. cycle of color changes." Millions paid a modest entrance fee to go up into the tenth floor of the eleven-floor control tower. There they found the view "completely absorbing" and, if they overlooked the martial roots of all the technology surrounding them, were "likely to think of the world of tomorrow—a world united by the conquest of distance and, they hope, eventually by the conquest of conflict."[12] Others toured the airport in distinctive Flightseer vehicles and got up close to airplanes. Designers of the airport envisioned new democratic public spaces for both a new New York and a new America: "People would take outings of the airport, to watch planes land and take off, walk alongside the reflecting pool, and picnic by the fountains."[13] The airport, conceived to be as alluring a destination as Rockefeller Center or Central Park, featured 160,000 trees, shrubs, and flowers in the central International Park, which itself was "about as large as the New York Botanical Garden in the Bronx." Visitors roamed "gravel walks . . . further beautified by reflecting pools and fountains."[14]

Richard Rowe, general manager of JFK in the 1990s, fondly remembered, "It was a gorgeous airport. It was just starting out then as an international airport, but it was a beautiful sight to behold. The roadway system worked well."[15] The plan did not, however, endure as an attraction or even as a popular airport design. Why not? It did not take long for many other designers and visitors to question a concept that ignored the many provisions earlier designers had made for pedestrians in both World's Fairs and at Rockefeller Center. The designers of Terminal City may have set aside landscaped park space and encouraged innovative design, but they completely ignored pedestrian circulation within the airport, a tactic that would have never been attempted at these earlier planned venues. The excuse of the Port Authority for the lack of connections between terminals—that most travelers left from or entered a single terminal when they visited New York City, or transferred planes within one airline (reducing the necessity of interline transfers between terminals)—did not explain away the designers' lack of attention to such an important detail as connecting sidewalks for both visitors and employees. Nor did planners of fairs fail, most of the time, to establish pedestrian precincts or establish rail connections from city centers to their fairs.

Nevertheless, and despite its flaws, the grand gestures were key elements in asserting the enhanced role of an airport in the urban and national fabric. The Port Authority believed that Terminal City would be an "airport worthy of New York, the world's greatest city, and [would] be a beautiful and convenient aerial gateway to the United States."[16] As a model of New York's future and of global urbanism, the airport was also a model of the benefits of the rationalized modernist city. No longer did the corporations and people jockey for space and attention in a crowded midtown. Technocrats, planning carefully in advance, found space for

FIGURE 16. When Idlewild was a major tourist destination, visitors could ride the Fliteseer tram. Visitors paid only fifty cents for a twenty-minute tour, June 4, 1959. Courtesy of the Queens Borough Public Library, Long Island Division, *New York Herald-Tribune* Photograph Morgue Collection.

corporations and people alike in a highly regulated version of urban space. A journalist in 1960 realized that the airport was a model city:

> The downtown district is built, as modern city planners would have all our cities built, around a huge park bright with greenery and alive with the waters of pools and fountains. Around the oval park the resplendent new buildings glitter at the edge of 10 miles of highway and nestled up to them are parking spaces for 6000 cars. . . . This is certainly one of the few cities in the world where the 20th

century absolutely prevails—all the buildings made of the latest materials in new, imaginative designs, and created specifically for the comfort and easy movement of people.[17]

The Chapel Plaza, initiated in 1960, provides strong evidence of the peaceable, assimilated, suburban-style society envisioned by New York's postwar leadership. The Faith Chapel Plaza plans in 1960 intimately grouped modernist Protestant, Jewish, and Roman Catholic chapels alongside a reflecting pool. The synagogue, an equal member of such a trio, made a particularly bold statement and reflected New York's powerful and large Jewish community, which was undergoing rapid acculturation in Queens and the surrounding suburbs. Nestling a synagogue next to the Roman Catholic and Protestant chapels in this era was to some a "'symbol to the world'" of religious freedom."[18] New York senator Jacob Javits at the groundbreaking contrasted the suppression of religion in the Soviet Union with the groundbreaking of a temple "side by side with the Catholic and Protestant churches." Airport officials promised for the chapels "a beautiful and serene setting, relatively secluded from the bustling activity of the airport." What kind of serenity could be found at the center of Idlewild Airport even in 1960 is hard to imagine. Giving over such a large space to fountains, plantings, and chapels at the heart of one of the world's busiest airports, however, indicates that more than transportation was at stake: the airport was as much symbol as terminal. (The decorative water features, alas, did become a favorite place for waterfowl that spent a little too much time flying near powerful jet engines.)[19]

Terminal City reflected an edited version of the inclusive American dream. With the exception of the Puerto Rican migration ("the world's first migration by air" made possible by bare-bones service developed by Pan Am between San Juan and New York), Idlewild served as a largely upper-class entry and departure point to the United States.[20] There was, for instance, a notable alteration in the famous poem that airline administrators adapted from the Statue of Liberty. The calculated distance between New York past and present, and the poverty that had featured so prominently in the New York immigrant story, was indicated by the Port Authority's willingness to cut the reference to "the wretched refuse of your teeming shore" in a modernized wall inscription of Emma Lazarus's famous paean to the immigrant experience: "Apparently the airport operating Port of

New York Authority believes the omitted description no longer applies to the nation's immigrants, many of whom now come by air."[21]

Terminal Stories

The designers of individual terminals making up Terminal City aimed to impress visitors with a combination of dramatic flourishes, grand public spaces, and expensive finishes that conveyed the wealth and ambition of the airline corporations. For most visitors, the majority of their time at the airport was spent in one of these large, modern stations. For this reason, both the Port Authority and the airlines devoted millions of dollars to buying what was the best architecture and infrastructure planning then available.

The $30 million IAB, stretching the equivalent of eleven city blocks, was the closest thing to a central terminal at the airport.[22] The IAB served as a shared terminal facility for smaller, foreign-flag airlines (a miniature United Nations in itself) and the arrival point, with customs, for all international passengers regardless of airline. The IAB existed not necessarily because the individual lines wanted to share the process of foreign arrivals but because the centralization of customs officials and immigration reduced costs for the government. In the meantime, American lines handled their domestic travel and departing international flights in their own unit terminals. The IAB, smoothly designed by the leading corporate architectural firm of its day, Skidmore, Owings, and Merrill (SOM) (and now demolished), suffered so many renovations over the years that it is a challenge to understand the role it once played in establishing the tone and experience of Terminal City as a whole. Expansion and adaptation began even before the complex had been completed. By 1956, the designers added a third floor and expanded the planned wing buildings for the foreign-flag airlines from 310 feet each to 530 feet and 600 feet each (as the number of national lines expanded).[23] Behind the heroic scale of the complex was the powerful message it telegraphed to visitors. The *New York Times* caught the spirit of the massive complex when it opened in 1957, explaining that the IAB "is just what a European expects America to look like." The interior ethos of the airport reflected modernist corporate style, as its "large, high ceilinged, spacious and clean" spaces "could have been transplanted from some of the new Park Avenue and Madison Avenue office buildings."[24]

The glass curtain walls, adjoining parking fields, and streamlined profile of the IAB anticipate the pastoral, suburban office parks SOM and other firms would create for America's growing corporations, including the firm's Connecticut General Life Insurance campus (1957) outside Hartford. The analogues with shopping malls are even more obvious. The grand atrium of the IAB, festooned with a Calder mobile, also had its analogues in the new suburban shopping at Southdale (opened in 1956) that attracted affluent families in this era. Southdale's vast parking fields and climate-controlled interior spaces (carefully landscaped, festooned with public art and attractions, and highly policed) set a new standard for regional-scale shopping. Pioneering mall designers such as Victor Gruen, who designed Southdale, viewed their malls as more than just shopping places; they saw them as new, safe, and satisfying Main Streets for disorganized American suburbs. Socially, the new malls also filtered out the poor, nonwhite populations who might be found in traditional downtown shopping districts by the 1950s. The IAB's similar mixture of air conditioning, light-filled atrium, public art, shopping, comparative social homogeneity, and plentiful parking aimed to soothe affluent users. Although fulfilling different functions, the malls, airports, and office parks had a similarly corrosive impact on older cities. The new airports represented the future; the declining and dirty rail terminals were the past.[25]

Suburban lifestyles directly influenced the traveler's experience at the IAB. Customs officials and the architects at SOM admitted to adapting circulation systems of the supermarket and expressway age for the circulation of human beings and luggage at the IAB. In the customs area, for instance, visitors experienced "a fine example of our supermarket efficiency" at checkout counters.[26] Those flowing through the seventy-two customs checkout counters benefited as well from systems at the "nation's turnpikes—the fanning out of such highways into multiple parallel lanes at toll gates, to allow automobiles to go through them" at rapid speed. The customs officials pressed a button to move a conveyor belt just as a clerk would speed along groceries in a modern supermarket. Airplane hostesses also explained to arriving passengers that although skycaps were available, "self-serve" at the airport was the new standard. Luggage carts, "another refugee from the grocery trade," were also made available to travelers looking to navigate the vast complex. (They could scarce imagine that one day these innocent carts would become a key element in a sophisticated "Smart Carte hustle"—aggressive panhandlers "offering" baggage service to unsuspecting tourists.)[27]

For the various national airlines that rented space in the Wing Buildings, being part of such a complex had a more subtle meaning. Supporting

FIGURE 17. Customs inspection at the International Arrivals Building brought supermarket efficiency to airline travel as passenger numbers skyrocketed, December 29, 1963. Courtesy of the Queens Borough Public Library, Long Island Division, *New York Herald-Tribune* Photograph Morgue Collection.

a national airline in this era (and one that served New York no less), no matter the cost and how modest the schedule, announced to the world that a nation had arrived in the modern era. New York was by this time the world's capital city in terms of politics and finance, so aspiring nations had to be there to be in the game. BOAC (now British Airways) alone dumped $1 million into its section of the Wing Building. Representative examples of modern furniture and graphic design from home countries meshed with luxurious finishes such as teak and leather to create stunning interiors that demonstrated, at least to the elites passing through them, that these nations were fully modernized. The Wing Buildings functioned as showcases for national aspirations for design or aviation.[28] SOM also conducted studies of "passenger psychology, travel motivation, waiting room environment, and pedestrian traffic circulation" so that passengers in the IAB, comfortably distributed to the waiting areas of the various foreign lines, would be "catered to as people" rather than as cattle as in traditional terminals. Every element of modern planning was thus integrated into this once dazzling space.[29] The Golden Door restaurant, atop the IAB, offered a gourmet destination and views for both travelers and New Yorkers curious about the airfield.[30]

The IAB's streamlined structure may have included dramatic flourishes such as its central atrium, but it paled quickly in comparison to the "rhomboidal, curvilinear, parabolic, (and) rectangular" terminals of the airlines.[31] Unit terminals, unlike fair pavilions, served both practical and public-relations needs of the major corporation that operated them. The airport's general manager at the time clarified the importance of brand identity to the airlines: "Each airline's terminal was to be a living thing, reflecting the company's corporate identity."[32] Some of these terminals, such as those built by United and Eastern, proved to be useful to both brands and passengers and quite a good value, while others turned out to be less practical. The precedent for corporate identity through design had been firmly established in the early twentieth century with the Woolworth and Singer Buildings, but in the city center, signature skyscrapers struggled for attention. Not so at the airport. At Idlewild, the distance between terminals guaranteed a fair return on investment in identity, even if the particular message of the individual structures, in the hands of modern architects, remained more ambiguous. The fact that the Port Authority financed the unit terminals and then rented them to airlines, in proportion to the total costs, encouraged some airlines, such as Pan Am, to splurge on their designs to make a statement.[33]

The Pan Am terminal, for instance, included an expensive concrete "umbrella" that floated over aircraft gates. Functionally, this overhang made it more pleasant for passengers and planes, but it also gave Pan Am a distinctive and memorable gateway. The design, loosely borrowed from the German precedent at Berlin's Tempelhof, far exceeded in scale, ambition, and price tag any existing terminals. Pan Am was announcing its global might through scale and eye-catching design. The design of the terminal interior probably made a bigger difference to travelers: the terminal's oval shape reduced walking distances for all passengers. Designers separated passenger flows internally, with incoming passengers using the first level and outgoing passengers the second level; arriving and departing vehicles also benefited from separation on the exterior. Adjustments had to be made during the course of construction that reduced the utility of the umbrella; Boeing 707 jets were both larger and louder than the planes designers had planned for in the mid-1950s, and so had to be parked farther away from the building than planned.[34] The architectural drama did not come cheaply; the Terminal ended up costing $118 a square foot as compared with the more modest and equally successful terminal constructed by United for about $58 a square foot.[35]

The most famous and least functional unit terminal of this era was Eero Saarinen's TWA terminal. TWA president Ralph Damon desired to feel "the spirit of flight" in the new terminal and found just the architect to achieve that goal.[36] Saarinen, as many observers have subsequently noted, did not place a premium on function but "outlined two primary objectives for the project: first, to create a 'distinctive and memorable' signature building for TWA; and second, to 'express the drama and specialness and excitement of travel.'" At TWA, functionality and flexibility definitely took a back seat to architectural vision. This supremacy of design reflects the growing role of postwar architects in iconic projects. Saarinen was already making a name for himself on high-profile projects, such as the St. Louis Arch, but architects such as Louis Kahn, Le Corbusier, and Frank Lloyd Wright also received commissions for expressive, iconic structures in this era. The nearest equivalent to the TWA Terminal was Frank Lloyd Wright's stunning Guggenheim Museum, similarly famous more for its visual impact on museumgoers than its functionality.[37]

The Saarinen terminal quickly became an icon and was dedicated after many delays and Saarinen's untimely death in 1962. With its exterior allusive of a bird in flight or a stingray, the mostly concrete terminal included soaring interior spaces made possible by complex structural engineering, sculptural stairways, innovative graphic design, and glass curtain walls. These integrated features announced the new era in travel, and the terminal immediately grabbed the public's attention. Critics over the years have, however, found the space to be less successful as an actual airport terminal, lacking sufficient provisions for increased capacity, alternative circulation patterns, and separate departure and arrival areas for vehicles.[38] The terminal also proved to be an expensive vision of the future that cost about $100 a square foot.[39] A number of alterations were necessary over the succeeding years to improve functionality. To make space for 747s, for instance, the temporary concourse was replaced with a new structure, Flight Wing One, beginning in 1967, even though this new addition simply funneled more passengers into the comparatively small main terminal. In 1978, the roadway in front was reconfigured, with a freestanding canopy in the middle of

FIGURE 18. TWA Terminal model. The distinctive style of the TWA Terminal was a major success in terms of corporate public relations; as an airport terminal, it proved more limited. Its architectural quality has guaranteed its preservation, even though its final function remained undetermined in 2014. Balthazar Korab, photographer. Library of Congress Prints and Photographs Division.

the road, "to resolve arrival and departure airline passenger traffic congestion at the terminal facility." Saarinen clearly chose form over function.[40]

The TWA and Pan Am terminals defined the public's view of the airport, but less famous terminals proved more flexible, expandable, and useful for travelers in spite of their weaker symbolic value. The Eastern Airlines terminal unit, at one time claimed as the largest ever built for one airline, included separate driveways for departing and incoming passengers, glass curtain walls, interior ramps, electronic flight information boards, and mechanized baggage handling.[41] The oversized (317 by 23 feet), colorful, stained-glass curtain wall fronting the American Airlines terminal enlivened the bland but still functional unit terminal that separated arriving and departing vehicles and passengers on two levels. SOM's United Terminal also retained its crisp functionality for decades.

I. M. Pei's design for the terminal known as the Sundrome mostly presented visitors with open glass curtain walls surrounding a vast central hall

FIGURE 19. Aerial view of the American Airlines terminal, February 10, 1960. This terminal carefully separated inbound and outbound traffic and offered travelers "magic carpet" automatic doors, air conditioning, showers, and private dressing rooms. On its own, the terminal could process four thousand people per day, with a total of four million per year. A mosaic design enlivened an otherwise typical modernist box. Courtesy of the Queens Borough Public Library, Long Island Division, *New York Herald-Tribune* Photograph Morgue Collection.

(382 by 112 feet) and was one of the more pleasant and functional spaces at the airport for decades. None of these terminals proved expressive enough to merit conservation, and all have been demolished or are slated for redevelopment. On the other hand, the TWA Terminal has been designated as a historic landmark despite its limited functionality. Saarinen was on to something, at least when it came to his legacy.

The exciting Terminal City project, and launching of iconic terminal structures, overshadowed the fact that the crowded temporary terminal continued to be the face of Idlewild for many arriving passengers during the era of construction of both the IAB and the many unit terminals. This terminal was described at the time as "an unkempt bus depot" that at best was confusing, dirty, and poorly lit. Even in 1960, in part because so many terminals remained under construction, roughly half of all Idlewild travelers still used the temporary terminal. Within a few years, of course, all passengers would arrive or depart from the modern terminals described above, but for over a decade, New York International had treated passengers poorly. Despite the excitement of the Terminal City project, the reputation for poor service endured even as the new terminals came on line.[42]

Cracks in the Façade

Terminal City reflected the Port Authority's belief that aviation as an industry would always be organized as a series of profitable, large, vertically integrated transportation companies. Architects Harrison and Sullivan, and Austin Tobin as patron, did not fully appreciate what reorganization of the aviation industry might do to the carefully planned unit terminal system. Nor did they contemplate how to integrate the airport into the existing infrastructure of the aging and congested city that it served. Their ideas about the future were big and bold, but they were also painfully narrow and inflexible. The designers of the complex should have taken a closer look at the World's Fairs, most of which had included high-speed mass-transit connections to handle the millions of visitors. Even Robert Moses's 1939 World's Fair at Flushing Meadow had included a subway connection. Terminal City reflected an unhealthy obsession with a future entirely based upon motorized individual transport for the city and the suburbs.

Architects Sullivan and Harrison failed to plan for passenger movement within the Terminal City complex in anything but cars or buses. Despite frequent comparisons between the scale of the airport as a whole to Manhattan below 42nd Street, no one noted the lack of internal passenger circulation for such a sprawling complex. The only design idea that seemed to matter was the distance between a parked car and a terminal entrance. Once the closest lots got full, which was almost immediate from all accounts, the entire planning concept failed as a basis for such a large complex. Seven terminals and an IAB no longer represented the most logical way of organizing such a system for travelers.

The improvised internal bus system in operation at Idlewild was made to sound better than it actually functioned, as buses tried to thread their way through jammed terminal roads. The Port Authority brushed off concerns because "less than 10% of Idlewild passengers have to make such immediate connections because so many originate or terminate in New York or stay over in New York." It was true that only about a thousand people daily used the intra-airport service in 1959, but even that many unhappy people per day added up to hundreds of thousands per year! Ridership between terminals was also projected to grow in the coming years to five thousand daily—all of whom would have to endure torturous shuttle rides. The growing importance of more distant long-term parking lots also meant a growing traveling population dependent upon shuttle buses.[43]

For a so-called Terminal City, almost three-quarters the size of Central Park, the absence of speedy connection between terminals was glaring. The Port Authority did not even bother to provide a safe system of sidewalks connecting the terminals. Although it is true that Terminal City had a great deal in common with other airports built at the same time, most of which lacked transit connections, few airports needed transit more than Idlewild. New York's subway and rail systems might have been failing, but they were still heavily used. The terminal unit system's decentralized plan reduced distances for travelers within terminals, but it created enormous and dangerous gaps for pedestrians (both employees and travelers) between terminals. Perhaps it was too much to ask for the Port Authority to have envisioned a rail connector, but there are reasons to doubt their interest in traditional forms of transportation.

The Port Authority clearly had no trouble with certain kinds of futuristic transport. For instance, Tobin and other administrators promoted helicopters—an extremely dangerous, expensive, and loud form of modern travel—as a realistic, exciting, and futuristic solution to moving travelers among the region's airports and throughout the region. Helicopters, if implemented on a grand scale, would have reduced the need for other forms of mass transit and dependence on Moses's roads. Helicopters on a grand scale would also have enriched the Port Authority by driving a massive traffic to the heliports it created in Manhattan and at the various airports.

Indeed, helicopters could have reduced travel time to the airports by as much as 80 percent. Instead of a forty-minute slog from Manhattan to Idlewild, promoters promised the trip by helicopter would be a quick and thrilling eleven-minute ride. The civilian helicopter was only conceivable because the military industrial complex used government money to perfect the technology for civilian application: "Helicopters have had and are still getting extensive field tests in the Korean fighting. Larger and more dependable types of helicopters are being built." Helicopter promoters hoped that one day, "helicopters will be as big as boxcars and as dependable as wheelbarrows." It didn't work out that way.[44]

In 1951, the Civil Aeronautics Board (CAB), the federal agency that regulated airline routes and finances, approved a New York helicopter line and authorized New York Airways Inc. to provide the service connecting the three major commercial airports, Manhattan, and some of the suburbs. The company limited the service to mail cargo in the first year in order to test out the safety of the system (another of many federal subsidies that propped up aviation). The Port Authority headquarters already had a heliport in place and constructed another one on a pier in the East River that was integrated into the system.[45] Express mail service in helicopters began in 1952, linking LaGuardia, Newark, and New York International Airports.

In 1953, New York Airways started the world's first regularly scheduled civilian passenger helicopter service. The system, as planned, ran between the airport and regional destinations. The depth of subsidy is reflected in the mysteriously low fares. The first helicopters seated just four to seven passengers each, yet the rates were only five dollars between LaGuardia and Idlewild and ten dollars between Idlewild and Newark. These were comparable rates to those charged by a ground taxicab. In the first month, the system carried 123 people between Newark and New York International and made only a thousand dollars in passenger revenues. Airmail was still subsidizing the service as the system had not yet found firm financial footing: "The problem has been mainly to reduce the cost of operating the rotorcraft, which . . . remains a fairly complicated piece of machinery that has relatively high maintenance and repair costs."[46]

The airmail subsidy proved robust enough to keep the system growing, and passenger service grew in the 1950s, but it is unclear whether passenger service alone was ever profitable for New York Airways (the company closed permanently in 1978). Adventurous and well-heeled travelers could nevertheless by the late 1950s skip the traffic and ride in fifteen-passenger helicopters to heliports in Manhattan, area airports, and even Roosevelt Field Shopping Mall.[47] By 1960, New York Airways was expanding to multiengine, turbine-powered, twenty-five-passenger helicopters by Vertol and Sikorsky. New York Airways even placed an optimistic order for Fairey Rotodynes, experimental British vertical lift planes that rose like a helicopter, then used wing engines to reach cruising speeds of almost two hundred miles per hour. The Rotodynes program was cancelled as impractical and dangerous, and the planes were never delivered.[48] Helicopters accommodated only 2 percent of airport traffic in 1961, not enough to make much of a dent in ground traffic.[49]

The futuristic vision for helicopters as a regional traffic system stalled out in the 1960s despite continued support from interested parties. The Port Authority's futuristic pavilion in Flushing Meadow Park, at the 1964–65 New York World's Fair site, designed largely around the massive helipad on the roof, reflected the Port Authority's continuing fascination with helicopter travel. The highest number of helicopter passengers at the airport ever recorded was in 1966 when 448,909 passengers flew.[50]

The practical difficulties of ramping up helicopter service, however, became clear to Pan Am and other operators as they tried to make helicopters more widely accepted among travelers. Pan Am's own helicopter service from its Terminal at JFK to the roof of its headquarters tower at Grand Central started in 1965 in Vertol 107s (seating twenty-five each). The service lost money, and it was discontinued in 1968. A later attempt by New York Airways to revive service to the Pan Am headquarters building in the late 1970s was discontinued after just four months when a helicopter toppled over, killing four passengers just above Pan Am's roof in midtown. New York Airways ceased operations in 1978. A number of private charter organizations have offered expensive service to JFK since then, but total numbers hovered just around a hundred thousand per year. Today, only a tiny fraction of air travelers fly helicopters to JFK on an annual basis.[51]

Had helicopters scaled up as envisioned, swooping millions into the air above New York, the noise generated by these vehicles would have spawned many more noise complaints than airplanes. A practical answer to transporting passengers between airports and to relieving regional gridlock would not come from helicopter service, which remained a niche service for the adventurous, affluent, and time-pinched traveler. The contrast between the Port Authority's enthusiasm for helicopters versus traditional mass transit condemned decades of travelers to gridlock and did great harm to the reputation of the airport as a whole.

Paying for Speed

The effort to build a vision of the airport and Terminal City as a postindustrial landscape, free of the pollution of the industrial age, overlooked the ways in which the skies had been once again appropriated for industrial purposes. Living near an airport meant skies, backyards, and living rooms filled with the din of shrieking jet engines. Airports and airplanes had become factories for generating money, not just for defending democracy. Despite valiant efforts by the Port Authority to mitigate the impact of the jet age, neighborhoods in the surrounding region paid the price for speed.

The creation of the Terminal City complex coincided with the beginning of the jet age. Flight paths for those jets were a form of industrial infrastructure every bit as important to construct as the terminals themselves. The introduction of passenger jet service is another example of the transition of Cold War defense technology (such as nuclear power, plastics, silicon chips, and microwave ovens) into everyday consumer living, with a dramatic impact on quality of life. Travelers on jets enjoyed incredible improvements in terms of comfort and speed, but those living below the new jets did not view their overflights as a positive development.

The Port Authority trod a careful path with the emerging jet technology in the 1950s because the leadership understood how deeply embedded the airport had become in the urban fabric. The city's rapid growth in the districts surrounding the airport in the postwar era increased impact dramatically by adding hundreds of thousands of additional residents near the landing zones. The first attempts by residents to exercise some control over noise and their airspace revealed the lengths to which local communities would go to contain noise. The noise of the jets and their early reputation for crashes represented a threat to the restraint so far exercised by the airport's neighbors. The preferential runway system, in spite of a tremendous increase in piston engine operations, had staved off a general rebellion of communities in the area.

Yet New York had to enter the jet age if it was going to remain American's leading commercial city. The Boeing 707, for instance, could travel 3,500 miles at a speed of 550 miles per hour, significantly reducing the need for refueling compared with previous aircraft. Passengers enjoyed a smoother ride with less vibration and shaking; less turbulence meant reduced need for "barf bags" in flight. Jetliners also offered potential for greater profit on transatlantic and domestic flights because of their speed (if the airlines, of course, had been able to fill them to capacity). Ironically, the airlines were just starting to make money on their earlier, expensive bets on advanced piston aircraft such as Super-Constellations, DC-7s, and Stratocruisers, but within a few years, they would scrap this entire fleet for jets. While the British were first out the door with commercial jets, with dire consequences for the unfortunate passengers and staff on the ill-fated Comets (worst name for a product ever!), a safe and fast jet aircraft had a powerful economic logic for the long-haul flights Idlewild dominated. A full Boeing 707 jet, through a combination of multiple high-speed flights in a twenty-four-hour period, had the potential to make $100,000 a day. And it didn't even matter much that these early jets were fuel hogs or ran at less than optimal density early on because the cheap fuel they gulped barely factored into the profit model: 11.5 tons of fuel cost only $412 in 1958.[52]

The propeller aircraft of the immediate postwar era made enemies in the surrounding communities, but it was the shift to jet aircraft that everyone realized would be a much sharper acoustic nuisance. Boeing 707s, for instance, which derived directly from shrieking B-52 bombers and KC 135 air-force tanker planes, first had to have their noise suppressed at some level in order to meet any reasonable standard of impact in urban areas. At first the Port Authority appeared to be on the residents' side and placed limits until the late 1950s (beginning 1951) on the early jet aircraft. This had practical consequences. Before the Port Authority would allow operations, for instance, it required that noise suppressors be developed. Despite these restrictions, Pan Am in 1955 ordered twenty Boeing 707s and twenty-five Douglas DC-8s then under development.[53]

The Port Authority also helped pioneer aircraft noise control by commissioning a leading acoustic engineering firm, Bolt, Beranek and Newman, to undertake the careful study of jet noise. From their research, they developed a new unit of measurement called perceived noise decibel (PNdB) that "took into consideration such things as interference with conversation, interference with radio or television sound, disturbance of sleep and general irritation." The research not only used field measurements but also human subjects to test the difference between jet and piston engines. Jets, for instance, might produce decibel readings in the range of piston aircraft, but the perceived noise level (because of the higher frequency) could be worse than a propeller craft. Propeller craft might "rattle dishes," but the high-frequency noise from jets was far less tolerable.[54] A 102 PNdB reading for a Boeing 707 jet, for instance, was equivalent in impact to a 120-decibel piston engine, even miles away. Sound experts thus added about 15 decibels to a standard decibel reading to render a PNdB reading for jets. This standard revolutionized the field of noise pollution by significantly raising the bar for aircraft operators and manufacturers.[55]

Based upon these studies, the Port Authority set a limit of 112 PNdB for takeoff in surrounding communities, thus banning the new jets for most of the 1950s. Airline industry and manufacturers were obviously opposed to this formulation as a "discriminatory handicap on all jet aircraft."[56] The Port Authority set limits but knew it had to walk a fine line because there was "little chance of blocking the big jets." One critic determined that the Port Authority "had assumed a defiant posture on jet noise not expecting to keep out the planes but as a public relations device to ensure that, when they did arrive, the disturbance to communities and its community relations would be minimal."[57] In reviewing internal papers, this criticism is not entirely fair. Port Authority figures took a hard line with both airlines and manufacturers, particularly Boeing, in the run up to jet operations at Idlewild. The Port Authority needed jets to pay its bills, but it also had a lot to lose if neighbors revolted successfully. In New York's often volatile political arena, even a seemingly powerful and independent agency such as the Port Authority had to negotiate with customers and neighbors.

Civic leaders were leery of jet operations for good reasons. After an early test of jet noise made in 1957 by a French twinjet Caravelle in South Ozone Park, a number of leaders in attendance "appeared unanimous in the conviction that it was noisier than the planes that had preceded it."[58] The Port Authority, however, allowed demonstration tests for both the British Comet IV and French Caravelle jets, indicating its general belief that the planes would eventually meet standards because the companies had worked closely with the Port Authority to ensure that their planes *could* meet the standards.

The Port Authority still disagreed, however, in the summer of 1958, that even suppressor-equipped Boeing 707s could be tolerable for neighboring communities. This judgment, it must be noted, was independent of the relative safety and dependability of the 707 compared with other jets at the time. With its extensive use in military operations (Boeing developed the KC-135 jet, that became the 707, for the U.S. Air Force for fuel transport), the Boeing 707 was destined to be the most powerful and dependable commercial jet of the time. Douglas's jet aircraft, the DC-8, was still in the developmental stage, even though it was planned for a fast rollout. The Port Authority, however, knew that it might face many more lawsuits by aggrieved citizens who would demand compensation for loss of property value. One particular threat worried both manufacturers and airlines: the Port Authority might force planes operated out of New York to be lightly weighted to reduce noise, thus making them less profitable.[59]

Relations between Boeing and the Port Authority became adversarial in the 1950s. The Port Authority characterized the Boeing staff as "surly" and reported that Boeing president William Allen in private accused the Port Authority of having an "unprogressive attitude of simply being against jets." The Port Authority disagreed in light of the fact that Terminal City was planned with jets in mind.[60] Boeing went as far as to hire a public-relations firm to cast the Port Authority's regulations in a bad light and thus undermine public support for the jet limits. On the day of dedication for the Arrival and Wing Buildings of the IAB, Boeing claimed "complete success" for the suppression system without actually demonstrating this to Port Authority officials.[61]

The Port Authority, "one of the most noise conscious airport authorities on the world's trade routes," maintained its hard line.[62] Suppressors on the 707 reduced the noise level by five to six decibels, but these tests intentionally had not taken into account jet whine, heavily weighted planes, or difficult weather conditions in a staged demonstration near Seattle in 1958. Port Authority officials on their visit felt that the "crack test pilot" at the demonstration was able to finesse the test to tolerable levels by pushing the plane as high as possible, and not necessarily in a normal operation, over the noise monitor. Boeing officials, on their side, took issue with the PNdB methodology on the visit and challenged Beranek directly. Boeing knew its plane was louder than the Comet or Caravelle. Part of the problem for Boeing may have been the difficulties in adjusting the powerful KC-135 tanker from the military to the civilian arena.[63]

New York's resistance to jets was doomed. The newly created Federal Aviation Administration (FAA) may have been authorized in 1958 to regulate noise as one of its duties, but it was under pressure from both the defense industry and the airlines to do as little as possible. In addition, passenger safety and profits for airlines and manufacturers remained of paramount concern for the new FAA. The agency thus became the instrument for pushing acceptance of jets at Idlewild. Resistance to the Boeing plane, according to the reasoning among FAA officials, had become a matter of national interest as America's high-technology industry was at risk if Boeing proved unable to put its jets into commercial service. Tests of the Boeing 707 at Idlewild commenced in fall 1958 as a precursor to approval. The planes made a better, although not a perfect, impression on neighboring communities as a result of noise suppressors, and the Port Authority was given some credit.[64] Boeing and airline officials, on the other hand, claimed total success with noise suppression.[65] The head of the FAA on October 9, 1958, thus "requested" that the jet restrictions be lifted. Daily Atlantic service was in place by late October by Pan Am (which was in competition with BOAC in launching transatlantic jet service). Then head of the FAA, General Elwood Richard Quesada, considered the Port Authority regulations in place "artificial," "very unfortunate," and temporary.[66]

The Port Authority's leading figures doubted that the suppressors were sufficient to allow unlimited operations. Administrators also faced significant pressure from elected officials in Queens, Nassau County, and New Jersey. The Port Authority thus put in place protections for the neighborhoods over which these screeching behemoths would take off and land. As a result the authority expanded the preferential runway system that included over-water landings (and predicted that nearly half of all flights could land over water); sharp right turns to avoid communities whenever possible; and steep takeoffs and landings that included a power cutback and a minimum altitude of 1,200 feet over neighborhoods. The Port Authority claimed that early operations were in fact meeting noise-reduction targets by sending 63 percent of takeoffs over the water. In the authority's opinion, a "tolerable" level of noise had been achieved.[67] In 1959, the Port Authority added a 112 PNdB standard for noise in communities in the flight paths for both landing and takeoffs. The authority, however, could do no more than admonish airline executives and then perhaps file lawsuits (an expensive and time-consuming process against a well-armed foe) for noncompliance. The Port Authority also restricted nighttime jet operations, as was the case in much of Europe, defying FAA policy.[68]

Airlines also claimed to follow a voluntary policy, working with air-traffic controllers, that reduced neighborhood noise by having pilots favor takeoffs and landings over low-density areas (for most weather conditions). Many within the airline industry, however, including union leaders, felt that these noise restrictions still might compromise safety.[69] In 1959, for instance, "it was a noise abatement takeoff—low-power, sharp turn" that sent an American Airlines jet into Jamaica Bay.[70] Compliance varied greatly as efficiency and safety frequently trumped noise reduction. Summer months were particularly bad for noise as a result of the extra power required for takeoffs in hotter conditions, but noise was a year-round problem. The Port Authority singled out American and TWA for violations, with about 40 percent of all takeoffs from October 1958 to May 1959 in violation for these two airlines. These airlines openly chose safety and economy over noise reduction. Pan Am, on the other hand, went out of its way to reduce noise, which was evident in the low violation rate of just about 8 percent of Pan Am jets.[71] Additional reductions in jet noise in the early 1960s resulted from the switching out of turbojets with fanjets that produced more thrust with less noise.[72]

Surrounding neighborhoods and the activists who lived nearby took a far dimmer view of what had been achieved in terms of noise reduction. An antinoise leader explained that in 1958 the Port Authority had promised that there would be limited noise and "assured us that jet aircraft was no louder than propeller planes. They said it would fly no lower than 2,000 feet and not at night over residential areas. It took them two weeks to break their promise. There were two flights at the beginning, and, one year later, they were three minutes apart, bombarding Jet Alley with unbelievable noise."[73] It would be easy to dismiss complaints as a simple matter of *caveat emptor*, but as one lady explained, noise had come to them: "If we had known we'd have to live like this, we would never have come here. When we looked at the house, we didn't see or hear a single plane. There was a school nearby for our son, a shopping center at the end of the street, and the house was attractive."[74]

Signaling a willingness to move beyond legalistic or formal bureaucratic means, and reflecting New York's activist tradition, was a series of interventions by residents to take matters into their own hands. They put their legislators on alert by taking direct action. Caravans of residents from Valley Stream, Cedarhurst, Laurelton, Springfield Gardens, Cambria Heights, and Rosedale had delayed traffic around the airport in 1959 to protest jets at Idlewild.[75] Politicians, in turn, threatened night bans, construction to block access to the airport, limits on loads, extension of FAA regulatory power over noise, penalties for airlines that violate rules, and local noise limits.[76]

The airlines and the Port Authority won this early battle over jets, but in the long term, the citizen activists and their elected representatives would have their day. A new antinoise organization, Nassau Aircraft Noise Control Council, claimed that aircraft noise disturbed up to half a million people in Nassau County in 1960. This population explosion in areas with jet noise was the result of Moses's highway program and relatively unregulated suburban development in Nassau Country. The farm fields gave rise not only to Levittown but to hundreds of thousands of additional homes. In Queens, the story of population growth was much the same. The extension of the express subway lines through central Queens generated significant postwar apartment construction in neighborhoods such as Forest Hills. Even where the subway did not run, housing developments sprouted in undeveloped land in Queens, Brooklyn, and Nassau County. The result of this growth, in political terms, was a frightening increase for the Port Authority in the number of anti-airport voters.[77]

Under pressure from civic groups, the Port Authority experimented with new landing and takeoff patterns in 1959. The Port Authority even extended a jet runway into Jamaica Bay to reduce noise over communities. Flight controllers gave directions to pilots to turn over Jamaica Bay after taking off over Howard Beach, rise to two thousand feet, and then finally go over Queens. Administrators also banned right turns over frustrated middle-class Queens communities such as Ozone Park, St. Albans, Laurelton, Springfield Gardens, and Rosedale.[78] Even the FAA's General Quesada would acknowledge in 1959 that "the public is becoming offended, damaged and hurt by the noise of modern aircraft. . . . Producers of planes and jet engines must give greater consideration to noise abatement." These concerns resulted in an expanded role for the FAA air-traffic controllers at Idlewild in regulating noise on takeoff and landings..[79]

Metropolitan Engine

The airport represented a threat to domestic tranquility, but there was no denying that JFK had become a major economic force in a city struggling to maintain its industry and population. By the late 1950s the two airports in Queens had become the borough's greatest single industry. As the president of the Queens Chamber of Commerce modestly put it, Queens had become "the airline capital of the world." The powerful influence of the airports, he predicted, would also preserve "our position as the best borough in the city in which to live, work, and play."[80] Indeed, Queens may have shared in the city's industrial decline on its western edge near Long Island City (just across the East River from Manhattan), as factories closed down or simply left their warehouses and vertical lofts for greener suburban pastures; but Queens as a whole had also become the seventh most populated county in America, with a population of 1,809,578 in 1960. Queens was primarily a comfortable, middle- and working-class residential suburb of single-family homes and brick apartment buildings. Developers added thousands of new housing units every year in the late 1950s and early 1960s in Queens and neighboring Nassau County. Home values and population swelled during this time, even as much of the rest of the city was in decline. Queens was the kind of place where Jews and Italians fleeing East Harlem and East New York, increasingly inhabited by African Americans and Puerto Ricans, found a home, greater social exclusivity, and a middle-class job.[81]

The airport contributed directly to this prosperity and new housing development. According to a study commissioned by the Port Authority, "builders are meeting no more buyer resistance in these areas than in other sections of the borough," and the study also pointed to rising home values near the airport at the time as proof of the positive influence of the airport.[82] To calm the aggravated souls in Queens, the Port Authority in about 1959 made a brochure with some specific facts they felt mattered: Queens housed 8,900 airport employees and, among other expenses, these employees spent over $14 million in Queens food stores.[83] Garden apartment complexes, such as Fresh Meadows in Queens, as well as apartment buildings across the region in Long Beach, Forest Hills, Kew Gardens, Lynbrook, and Atlantic Beach, aggressively advertised their apartments, cocktail lounges, air conditioning, and proximity to airport employees in Idlewild's internal newspaper, *Aviation News*. The manager of the Somerset, Steven, Syracuse, and Stuart Arms apartment buildings in Kew Gardens, for instance, mixed social and practical appeals: "Naturally with all these buildings within a block or two of the Q10 Bus to Idlewild, there is little room for doubt that we have a greater proportion of your fellow employees in one or more of these fine, up-to-date buildings."[84] The airport employees' demand helped generate income and additional jobs in these areas. The Forest Hills Inn and other Queens hotels (including newer ones around the airport, such as the Holiday Inn, Riviera Idlewild, and Skyway Hotel) profited from short stays as did many restaurants and bars.[85] The airport was thus a key element in the economic prosperity of thousands of families at this time, even if the noise drove some of them batty.[86]

The director of aviation for the Port Authority, John Wiley, in 1957 provided a vivid description of the ways in which the airport was globalizing life in Queens: "Today, a typical Queens family might think nothing of vacationing in a distant city or foreign country that before the air age was as remote as the valleys of the moon. Clothes that were in a Parisian designer's salon a few days ago are in a store in Queens today, and an engineer who will drive home along Queens Boulevard tonight might be working on a hydroelectric project in Chittagong next week." The airports made it possible for Queens residents to contribute to and partake in "the material and cultural wealth of the entire world."[87]

The connection to the airport, in this telling and in reality, was making New York more cosmopolitan by bringing affordable travel and exotic imports to a larger percentage of New York's regional population. The Grand Tour, or latest dress, was no longer the preserve of the wealthy but could be enjoyed by the middle class as well. The value added by air cargo and travel to apparel design and manufacturing, a New York specialty, is illustrated in this fascinating description of globalized existence in 1961: "A leading department store shipped American-made garments from New York International Airport on Tuesday night to be photographed against local background. The scenes were for a telecast appearing the next Sunday. Not only were the scenes shot, but the clothes were back in New York on the day before the telecast to freshen them for a fashion show on Monday."[88]

The growing global power of the American fashion industry based in New York City in the 1950s and 1960s—including design, production, and style magazines—received a boost from the global reach of Idlewild. The city had for decades been the apparel production center of the nation, but editors such as Diana Vreeland at *Vogue* in the 1960s not only shared in the dynamic European fashion scene with greater ease because of jet travel but could now dispatch models and photographers to the most exotic locales by simply putting them into a taxi for Idlewild. New York could thus serve not merely as a production site but as the center of a more cosmopolitan, globalized fashion culture that suffered no disadvantage because of its distance from Europe.

The multiplier effects of a variety of different airport-related businesses, on the other hand, were calculated in the billions. The region, including New York City, collected billions of dollars in benefits because of business travel, air cargo, and tourism. In this era New York also benefited from a concentration of airline executive and maintenance functions in Manhattan, including those of American and Pan Am, the world's leading global airline. A Port Authority administrator reminded increasingly frustrated Queens and Nassau residents that in spite of all the noise, commercial aviation was the "only major industry in the New York–New Jersey Metropolitan Area which is still growing at a rapid rate."[89]

The airport and the service industries benefiting from it provided a bright spot in an otherwise dismal industrial picture for the city. New York

FIGURE 20. Mr. and Mrs. Sidney Goldwag of the Upper West Side return from their trip to Israel and Europe with shopping treasures, August 20, 1960. They were described as a "new breed of traveler" who "boards a transatlantic flight, as though he were taking the subway to work." The jet age brought the exotic within reach. Courtesy of the Queens Borough Public Library, Long Island Division, *New York Herald-Tribune* Photograph Morgue Collection.

City in the 1960s was in the process of ceding its longtime role as the nation's leading manufacturing district. The New York region, and particularly its suburbs, had continuing strengths in certain high-value products, such as aerospace, electronics, and pharmaceuticals. Long Island, for instance, was at its height during the 1950s and 1960s in terms of aerospace production. A company such as Grumman enjoyed lucrative defense contracts for jet fighters and the space program. On the whole, however, the region would lose hundreds of thousands of manufacturing jobs during the postwar decades, and New York City absorbed these losses first.[90] The city was particularly hard hit as even many of the remaining industries in the region shifted to lower-cost suburban locations astride highways and new subdivisions.

Idlewild thus had a growing role to play not only in Queens but also in the region as a whole as it made its painful transition to a postindustrial service economy. An emerging bright side in the New York economy was the spectacular growth of business services: "The slower growth in employment associated with manufacturing production has been more than offset by expansion in wholesale trade, finance, insurance and real estate, and . . . as the headquarters for the administration of large manufacturing and mining enterprises."[91] The 1950s in Manhattan generated one of the great office construction booms, with the city adding acres of modern glassy floor space in Manhattan that in turn housed the country's most impressive concentration of Fortune 500 headquarters, such as Union Carbide and U.S. Steel. In 1955, for instance, New York City counted 1,200 headquarters for companies with $1 million in assets or more. At the same time, many of those corporations that left the city center simply migrated to nearby suburbs (General Foods in Westchester County, for instance) and set up vast office and research parks that still relied upon excellent national and global air service.[92] By the early 1960s, for instance, Westchester, Nassau, and Fairfield Counties had similarly high ratios of business trips to population as Manhattan.[93]

Observers, such as economists in the employ of the Port Authority and the Regional Plan Association (the metropolitan area's most powerful voice for long-term planning), understood that the growth of the nation's best domestic and international air service renewed New York's competitive advantages in business services. The vertically integrated postwar firm with national and global reach, ensconced in either a glassy Midtown tower or pastoral suburban office park, needed excellent transportation and air-cargo service. According to the Port Authority, "Comprehensive air service, supported by three major airports . . . has contributed significantly to an even greater centralization here of American management, financing, insurance and industry." Management scale in New York far exceeded regional needs: "These responsibilities involve extensive commerce with and travel to and from distant divisional headquarters in markets." Headquarters of major retail chains benefited from air travel as did the pharmaceutical and Cold War electronics-aviation industry that could ship its high-value cargoes anywhere in the world in just a day.[94]

Idlewild, then, both influenced and matched the changing modes of the city's economy. It may be that the design of Terminal City, with its large, isolated, and inflexible terminal units, misjudged the future of air travel, but the presence of this massive global airport (along with Newark and LaGuardia) began the process of establishing New York's competitive advantages in the global economy. While projected by the Port Authority as a futuristic suburban node astride an aging city, the airport would soon take its proper place as a key element in New York's regional leadership in the new cutthroat, globalized urban order. Crowded with people and products zooming around the world, Idlewild was not recognizable as a model for the American future, but a large part of New York's future was being built there.

CHAPTER 3

How the Other Half Waits

The public excitement surrounding the Terminal City project dissipated all too quickly in the 1960s. At almost the same time that the airlines took possession of their shiny terminals, the reputation of the airport began its sharp descent. The futuristic designs could not compensate for a growing set of problems, which, in retrospect, became permanent fixtures of JFK's identity. The 1960s turned into an era of jammed roads, skies, and terminals. The affluent population of the metropolitan area and travelers from around the globe continued to crowd into the airport despite these shortcomings, maintaining JFK's importance in national and global travel routes, but no amount of Port Authority public relations could overcome the disturbing fact that the much-vaunted planning of the 1940s and 1950s had faltered. JFK was unable to handle, at least in a very efficient or comfortable manner, the consequences of the national 1960s jet boom. The overwhelming success of the aviation industry was in many respects too much of a good thing for airports like JFK.

It is not an accident that wrecking balls in 1964 leveled New York's grand passenger terminal, Pennsylvania Station, just a few years after the dedication of both Terminal City (1955) and the Port Authority Bus Terminal (1955). Lacking the deep government subsidies of highways and airports, railroad corporations could not compete with airlines (which every year grew faster, cheaper, and more reliable), trucking companies, coach lines, or the private automobile. Rail lines serving passengers and freight shippers collapsed in the face of new competition. By 1955, in fact, "long-distance railroad passengers apparently had been reduced to or near a nondivertable hard core."[1] Bad decisions plagued railroad management, but airlines and airports enjoyed both consumer preference and extensive government subsidies the railroads had long ago lost. Dying rail giants like the Pennsylvania Railroad thrashed about selling assets, such as Penn Station, to stay afloat. Penn Station—neoclassical, centrally located, and intimately linked to transit and surrounded urban decay—was the opposite of Terminal City with its decentralized, sprawling, modernist, auto-oriented character.

The fast and nearly complete collapse of intercity passenger rail and steamship travel created its own set of problems as passengers flooded into airports like JFK for domestic and international travel. By 1963, for instance, airlines alone accounted nationally for "more than half of all common carrier intercity passenger-miles involving trips of over 100 miles."[2] The overwhelming bias in U.S. public policy for highways and aviation in the postwar period blinded most Americans to the potential benefits of a healthy, if necessarily subsidized, system of intercity rail that could have reduced pressure on airports, as was the case in Europe at the time. The airlines had captured a wide band of the most profitable travel segments from business to leisure. The average bread-and-butter passengers for domestic air travel in the 1960s were still middle-aged, college-educated men making frequent trips for business, but growing numbers of women, couples, and young people could now hop jets not only for domestic destinations but also for Europe, the Caribbean, Africa, and even India. JFK's global airlines did so well in this era that they also sank the once-proud ocean liners that had previously dominated global passenger routes.[3]

Airlines and airport operators thus found mainstream success to be a double-edged sword. The mass popularity of aviation finally made profits for airlines and airport operators (airports counted for 45 percent of the Port Authority's gross income of $242.8 million in 1969), but the financial returns obscured a crisis both on the ground and in the air.[4] The airline's successful defeat of older forms of transportation was not the unalloyed success airline executives had envisioned. The masses of people proved to be disruptive to even an optimistically designed terminal system like JFK.

Jets in the 1960s regularly dropped over 100 passengers per flight in the IAB, roughly double the figure compared with that of planes from the 1950s. A Boeing 707 could deliver in one pass 180 passengers, and a single 747 by the 1970s could deliver over 350 passengers. These same jets could also make more trips in a day than the planes that had come before. Jets

FIGURE 21. The introduction of the Boeing 747 set off a wave of reconstruction—and bankruptcies—that affected JFK and the airlines on site. Arthur Tress, Documerica Collection, National Archives.

shifted JFK's regional status dramatically as airlines took advantage of the metropolitan area's most extensive and advanced runway system. By 1954 the airport already handled 31 percent of regional air travel, but by 1964 JFK accounted for 64 percent of regional traffic.[5] Terminal City as a whole by 1967 thus barely handled its 20 million annual passengers,[6] far exceeding even the most optimistic forecasts made in the 1950s. America and the world had simply gone crazy for air travel, consigning both passenger rail lines and oceangoing freighters to the dustbin of history. The combination of rising incomes, hefty federal subsidies, improved aviation technologies, and cheap fuel created and sustained America's aviation boom.

The first "Black Friday" on June 7, 1963, revealed in the starkest possible terms the limitations of both New York airspace and runway capacity. Maximum departure delays on that Friday reached almost two hours at JFK. Even the Port Authority acknowledged that there was a major problem.[7] June 7 was also a record operations day for the airport, with 3,700 takeoffs and landings. Defying the most basic logic of operations, the air-lines tried to squeeze twelve airplane departures into one 6:00 P.M. slot.[8] The system worsened by mid-decade. Newark International was actually the worst in the nation in terms of total percentage of late flights in 1965, but both O'Hare International and JFK were known for very long delays of up to two to three hours during peak season. As the leading national air-ports, their delays scrambled the national air network.[9]

The odd form of regulation practiced by the government made conges-tion that much worse. The government strictly regulated many elements of the carrier routes and aircraft safety, but federal officials only weakly regu-lated airline schedules. The airlines made the congestion situation worse by overloading peak times in order to secure the biggest chunk of the most profitable time slots, the so-called rush hour, that was popular with both business travelers and those bound for Europe (where nighttime noise lim-its frequently mandated a morning arrival). JFK's parallel runways, because of space limitations on the site, were not actually far enough apart to allow for simultaneous operations that would have allowed controllers to better manage this many operations. Chicago's widely placed parallel runways, for instance, could clear a hundred operations per hour versus only about seventy per hour at JFK.[10]

In 1960 the Port Authority started work on an extension of a long run-way (known as 4L-22R) into Jamaica Bay. This expansion was designed specifically to reduce the noise of airplanes in surrounding neighborhoods by allowing planes to reach higher altitudes over Jamaica Bay before head-ing out over those neighborhoods, but it also stood to boost operations by allowing for more operations with less noise. The Army Corps of Engineers quickly issued dredging permits for the 3,550-foot extension into Jamaica Bay. There was no environmental impact statement required (as the system did not at that time exist), and quick construction yielded a runway 11,400 feet long. By 1964 the extension was complete and, as predicted, signifi-cantly boosted operations. The Port Authority likely wished it had done more expansion at this time because this extension did not offer enough of an expansion to alter the fundamental congestion problems.[11]

Austin Tobin and airport administrators realized that the problems at the airports threatened the region's long-term viability as the nation's lead-ing international aviation hub. They began a new wave of initiatives to alleviate crowding, most of which failed to address the issue. The first order of business was the low rates for landing rights by general aviation craft. At

JFK in 1967, for instance, general aviation accounted for 30 percent of flights: "Horses and bicycles are barred from our parkways, but their aerial equivalent has the right by federal law to use up a giant Kennedy runway with a flivver plane carrying just a pilot." The Port Authority raised fees for general aviation in the aim of reducing congestion during peak times. That these flights were often for elite travelers on business jets made it politically easy to reduce their numbers.[12] The 1970 Port Authority Annual Report stated that 75 percent of general aviation traffic had shifted to nonduty runways as a result of the flight limitations and new fees.[13]

These well-meaning attempts at capacity control did not unravel the overscheduling and crowding at JFK or at other area airports. The Port Authority and regional leaders thus spent millions of dollars in the 1960s on a desperate and ultimately fruitless search for a fourth regional airport. The addition of a jet port would have been the biggest contribution to stuffing more airplanes into the region, but it was too hot an issue in the 1960s and 1970s. Environmental activists, buttressed in some cases by a number of potential airport sites that threatened the calm in wealthy neighborhoods, stopped all these expansion plans on the grounds of either noise or environmental destruction. Wetlands, or at least those adjoining wealthy neighborhoods, no longer always counted as marginal, dispensable land as they had when JFK had been constructed in the 1940s.

The limits to growth experienced at JFK International also inspired a series of bizarre environmental proposals. Some of the highlights include a "Wetport" that would have been located on an artificial island resting somewhere between Port Jefferson, New York, and Bridgeport, Connecticut, in the middle of Long Island Sound. The Wetport was trumpeted because it would reduce aircraft noise on either side, thus allowing for busy airplane traffic, while passengers still could zip on high-speed rail to Manhattan or planned hotels on the shore. Proponents even envisioned superfast hydrofoils that would take passengers directly and rapidly to Manhattan.[14]

Another Wetport, to be built in the Atlantic Ocean off of the Rockaways, was envisioned as a vast complex nine miles long to replace all the current airports in New York. A massive breakwater, which could also serve as a new harbor and site of a nuclear power plant, would have protected the airport. Each of the twelve runways would have been thirteen thousand feet long. Proponents envisioned massive barges to transport fill to the spot where a combination of floating and anchored facilities would rise.[15] Local opposition quickly coalesced against the Rockaway plan as "a frightening monstrosity, a gargantuan ecological imbroglio" that would destroy the quality of life in the Rockaways. Critics pointed to the million passengers per day that might stream through it, and the sewage from up to 150,000 employees. The plan was never more than a glimmer in the eyes of a few visionaries.[16]

The failure to expand JFK or develop an alternative airport in the 1960s meant that the congestion problem remained unresolved in either the short or long term. According to Leonard Victor, who covered JFK in great detail for the *Long Island Press*, the airlines in the late 1960s remained "fiercely competitive" and caused the "bottleneck themselves when they schedule flights at the most popular hours (i.e. 20 flights to leave right at 6 pm) thus creating delay." Airlines made congestion even worse by running many planes out of JFK and other major airports at only 50 percent capacity just to keep their grip on profitable routes.[17] As a result of crowding and its national impact, the CAB in 1968 limited flights during peak hours (3:00 to 8:00 P.M.). The only other airports under this high-density rule after 1968 were LaGuardia, O'Hare, and Washington National.[18] The CAB also excluded New York as a target area for new transatlantic service to cut back on the already congested skies above New York.[19]

The air-traffic problem in the New York region was compared to "trying to funnel the ocean into a bathtub." About one-quarter of all aviation passengers in the United States at some point found themselves squeezed uncomfortably through New York airspace. Aging radar systems, designed for a simpler time, forced greater separation in the name of safety. Lack of simultaneous operations set tight limits on total operations per hour. Use of preferential runways at JFK made matters worse because "jets must land and take off from a runway that keeps ear-warpage to a minimum in neighboring heavily-populated areas."[20] Air-traffic controllers in the region were overwhelmed and overworked; as a protest they began to demand the three-mile separation set by federal safety regulations at some of the peak arrival and departure times, even though in general practice such a rule was more loosely enforced. In practice, this separation meant more delays.[21]

The challenges of operating JFK began to alter the airport's role in national aviation from that of being both an important domestic and international airport to being just a leading international hub.[22] Tobin went as far as to demand that the federal government force changes to relieve the overscheduling at JFK if the airlines could not do it themselves.[23] In 1969 the FAA placed even more restrictive limits, with only eighty landings and takeoffs per hour total of all flights (a stretch in itself for JFK controllers). The results of such limits had a double-edged result: the skies partly cleared over the airport, but the limits also cut into JFK's dominance.[24]

The year 1968 marked the beginning of declining growth for the New York region's air market. Air travel increased 11 percent nationally, but New York's growth was only a paltry 3 percent. The reasons for the slowdown included the New York region's slower growth compared with that of the South and Sunbelt along with the larger total share of air travel to begin with and the longer and faster journeys made possible by jets; but aviation experts considered congestion in the air to be the primary factor. The Port Authority's frank acknowledgment of these problems in its notoriously upbeat annual report indicates the severity of the problem.[25] In 1970, for instance, while overseas flights at JFK rose a strong 10 percent, domestic travel continued its decline by about an equal amount.[26]

The airlines, having partly created the multihour waits by tight scheduling and low-density flights, now gazed fondly on greener pastures. The process of decentralizing international travel out of New York had deeper roots than just crisis. Long-range piston aircraft, beginning in the 1950s, had opened new Arctic routes from Europe to Chicago, Los Angeles, and other new gateways that competed with New York. Longer-range jets had then accelerated this process in the 1960s.[27] By the late 1960s, however, it was well known that "the carriers [were] casting about for likely substitute airports in other cities to serve as gateways for foreign travelers" because of New York air and ground congestion. Airports in Washington, Philadelphia, and Miami were already thought to be gaining from "diversion" of flights. In truth, airlines mostly added new flights at these airports rather than actually diverting journeys out of New York. Boston and Philadelphia experienced tremendous increases in 1967, for instance. Pan Am executives visited Philadelphia because "customers balk at having to circle JFK for 30 minutes to 90 minutes before landing, then face transportation delays getting into Manhattan or other destinations."[28] The fact that airlines would put planes in the sky knowing they would circle for a long time also reflects the comparatively low cost of jet fuel at the time.

Ignoring the problems of congestion and endless delays preserved quality of life in many neighborhoods surrounding the airport, but avoidance or deferment of tough decisions did spell problems for New York's central role in the nation's air network. Perhaps it was inevitable that New York would have to share air travel with more of the country, but the loss of dominance was accelerated by airport design and contextual limits of the New York metropolitan area.

Rebuilding Terminal City

Saddled with a Terminal City design it could not easily replace, and incorporating millions of dollars of accumulated capital investment, the Port Authority and airlines in the 1960s and 1970s twisted and stretched the once futuristic complex while still extracting enormous profits. World's Fairs were great places to visit, but they were temporary installations; designing an airport around the idea of individual pavilions, as the Port Authority had done, made updating and accommodating growth complex and expensive. Constant expansion and renovations not only undermined the customer experience inside terminals but also wiped out the festive atmosphere in the name of practical considerations. An ad hoc expansion of Terminal City, starting in 1966, extended the complex from 655 to 837 acres to accommodate new roadways and taxiways demanded by the growing scale of the jets in service.[29] In 1974 the Port Authority ripped out the Fountain of Liberty and flowerbeds in front of the IAB in order to expand the parking lots.

The debut of the Boeing 747 in 1970, the largest commercial passenger plane of its day, at first breathed new life into JFK. Pan Am's Juan Trippe in 1966 made a pace-setting order for twenty-five of the advanced, high-capacity Boeing 747 craft under development. Each plane cost about $20 million in 1966 (about $141 million each in 2012 dollars). Trippe made this big bet because he viewed the future of global air travel in rosy terms based upon his past success. He believed wide-body (two passenger aisles) aircraft would help relieve air congestion, although not necessarily ground or terminal congestion, at major hubs such as JFK. Pan Am, in fact, initiated 747 flights on the popular New York-London route in 1970, and other airlines in the years to come followed with their own service from JFK to global cities.[30]

By 1971 the IAB alone had doubled in size to accommodate both more planes and the new Boeing 747s entering service at JFK. Alterations to the IAB, in the name of capacity, included cheap and unpleasant windowless airside extensions to the Wing buildings. Eight Plane-Mates, variable-height mobile lounges, added even more capacity to the IAB by delivering passengers, in a fairly uncomfortable fashion, to planes waiting at more distant apron gates. Many unit terminals, some of them ultra-modern just a few years before, also faced dramatic restructuring. The challenge on the ground posed by 747s was daunting. Airlines had to stretch and twist terminals that had been built for another scale of aircraft entirely.

In order to accommodate 747s at Pan Am's distinctive umbrella terminal, for instance, designers added temporary walkways at higher levels; shuttle buses (Plane-Mates) with hydraulic lifts were also employed to handle up to 360 people that might arrive on a single flight. A massive addition to the terminal in 1968, in a fan shape, made it six times larger. The redesigned terminal could now hold six 747s or ten standard jets at one time and could process an astounding three thousand passengers per hour.[31] These changes undermined the symbolic value of the Pan Am terminal, to say the least: "Dramatic architecture was out and the fan was clad in dull brown bricks with ugly smoked-glass windows."[32] Architectural historian Thomas Leslie provides a wonderful description of the disorientation created in the new Worldport: "One might, for example, disembark from an arriving plane, descend into the basement customs area by escalator, walk halfway around the building to collect luggage, and then walk back to the sub-level arrivals roadway in almost the exact same position as the aircraft one had just left." As a result, "the new building was forced to employ an extensive graphics program to route passengers through a functionally efficient, though experientially labyrinthine, series of spaces."[33] The TWA and American Airlines unit terminals also underwent major expansion to accommodate the new 747s.

The Port Authority's judgment on the Terminal City concept was on view for all to see in the 1960s when it rebuilt Newark International to reflect best practices at the time. At Newark, the Port Authority now offered parking for eight thousand cars (with space for expansion), and separated departing and arriving traffic throughout. Above all, the designers dispensed with individual unit terminals; the Port Authority clustered the terminals and airlines together in shared international and domestic terminals so that passengers could more easily transfer from one airline to another.[34] Newark International reopened to great applause in 1973, although even these planning changes did not allow it to avoid the air and traffic congestion that defines the New York region.[35]

Meanwhile, the short-term result of ambitious reconstruction at JFK was a construction hell that in certain terminals lasted for decades. The Port Authority tried to mitigate some of the inconvenience with additional skycaps, "Golden Girl" passenger aides, and helpful signs directing passengers through the mazes, but constant and annoying construction damaged the airport's already tarnished reputation. Nor did these renovations address the scale of the congestion that passengers faced on their way to and once inside the airport. Even the Port Authority had to concede in 1969 that "airport patrons still face discomfort and inconvenience during peak hours of heavy traffic volumes because of congested terminal, parking and ground transportation facilities." Such a concession in an annual report by the Port Authority reflected the seriousness of the crisis.[36]

Within JFK, transferring passengers risked life and limb if they declined to wait for the internal bus system. A travel expert in 1961 reported that the big problem was that the airport, like the idealized American kitchens of the time, had been "designed by men who usually never go into them."[37] An exasperated visitor, one of many, shared her frustration: "It is quite obvious that the designers of John F. Kennedy International Airport had only contempt for pedestrians and made things as difficult as possible for them." With her children and husband in tow, she had the misfortune of making a terminal change: "No provision is made for pedestrians between terminals in the way of sidewalks, overpasses, underpasses or anything else. . . . It is almost an impossibility to cross the road, even at crosswalks, without being run over by some driver who pretends he is a fly boy, too." The thousands of passengers now changing terminals, a situation once written off as unimportant in the decentralized design of Terminal City, were miserable.[38]

Driving a car within the airport's road system was not necessarily any more satisfying. One might see desperate passengers "abandon their cars and leg it across the grassy verges to terminal buildings" in order to make their flights.[39] Traffic backed up for miles in the high summer season because of the heavy traffic and poor design of the internal road system. Rebuilding the internal road network appeared to be the only solution to untying these knots: "The idea is to end the chaotic conditions that developed at Kennedy Airport last summer when streams of cars approached . . . parking lots either unaware that they were full or hopeful that spaces would soon become available." Administrators discussed creating a three-level loop that would include space for trains, cars, and passenger concourses (a system that would only be more or less implemented four decades, and many traffic jams, later).[40] The jets contributed to gridlock on the connecting highways because their greater speed created a "peaking of air travel coinciding with the peak load on highways for regional home-to-work travel."[41]

The growing space for parking over the decades reflected the Port Authority's automobile preference (motor-vehicle tolls from the region counted for 31 percent of the Port Authority's income in 1969).[42] The steady uptick in parking at the airport did not necessarily keep pace with demand, but its scale does reflect the emphasis on the automobile: in 1954, 6,000 spaces; in 1962, 6,700 spaces; in 1968, 9,200 spaces (all figures approximate). After 1970, the Port Authority, having exhausted open space in Terminal City, began the design and construction of multilevel parking areas. The focus on automobiles realized the aim of making JFK a modern, auto age institution. By 1961, nearly 80 percent of airport users arrived by private automobile while only about 15 percent arrived by bus service. Taxis composed only about 5 percent of arrivals. Nassau County, blossoming as an automobile suburb, now outpaced Queens and Brooklyn as a destination for travelers. In order to make driving even more functional for suburbanites, the Port Authority initiated long-term parking in 1962 at just a dollar a day.[43]

The reliance of consumers on automobiles, taxis, and the low-performing, low-quality, privately run Carey bus service provided plenty of justification for Port Authority leaders to ignore mass transit: "The low volume of potential traffic is illustrated by the fact that in 1965 the Carey" bus services "to and from John F. Kennedy International Airport averaged less than 4,000 passengers per day in each direction, out of more than 22,000 airline passengers that move through this airport each way on an average day." The report argued that bus service still remained "the superior mode" for mass transit and listed twenty different connection plans over the years, including hydrofoils and rail: "These studies have come to discouraging conclusions; they fail in the test of potential travel time advantages, passenger convenience, or physical or economic feasibility."[44]

In light of the growing popularity of today's AirTrain service (initiated in 2003), these studies might have failed to capture New York's unique character and density; driving is just miserable in New York, and getting to one place or another is often much easier by transit. Austin Tobin had, under pressure, assumed management of the short but vital passenger railway linking sections of New Jersey and Manhattan (the PATH [Port

Authority Trans Hudson] system, formerly known as the Hudson tubes), but it was no secret that Tobin deliberately avoided the high losses associated with the management of mass transit. Tobin only accepted management of what became the money-losing PATH system in order to secure the necessary political support for the Port Authority's development of the World Trade Center project, which was developed and owned by the Port Authority. Tobin exacted a legal promise, a covenant, from New York and New Jersey in 1962 that the Port Authority would not be forced again to assume money-losing mass-transit operations.[45]

Futuristic ideas began to percolate around the Port Authority that some experts believed would somehow relieve the traffic pressure. Included in this grab bag was an experimental bus rail vehicle that would operate on roads and tires at the airport but then turn into a railroad car that could speed into the city on an existing railroad line. The bus-rail combination, as described in 1967, would be "fitted with steel wheels that retract when it is operated on highways. Rubber-tired rear wheels provide the driving power when it runs on the railway." Such a system would allow for the bus to circulate around the terminals and then enter the city on rails. As absurd as this contraption sounds, and perhaps to deflect attention from its inaction on mass transit, the Port Authority actually sponsored a prototype vehicle. It literally ran into problems in the winter: the rubber skidded on the icy rails and the project was abandoned.[46] This failure was by no means the end of the pressure for a rail link. In 1968 the idea of a twenty-minute ride from JFK to Manhattan by rail resurfaced, but Tobin did not follow through.[47]

Governors Nelson Rockefeller of New York and William Cahill of New Jersey were both known for their promotion of mass transit as a solution to gridlock and environmental problems in the region. Rockefeller and the New York State Legislature, for instance, created the Metropolitan Transportation Authority (MTA) in 1968 to renew and coordinate the region's failing mass-transit systems. Like many outsiders, Rockefeller and Cahill viewed the Port Authority's multibillion-dollar portfolio as a potentially rich source for mass-transit upgrades in the region. The legislatures of the two states in 1971 passed a law directing the Port Authority to create rail access from Newark and JFK Airports, thus avoiding an open-ended commitment of the Port Authority to mass transit that many believed would violate the 1962 agreement. The resignation of Austin Tobin in December 1971, however, reflected his displeasure over political pressure to use Port

Authority funds for additional money-losing mass-transit activities (and to place any limits on his power).

After Tobin's departure, the Port Authority in 1972 (with more pro-mass transit board members, including MTA chairman William Ronan) planned to expand the PATH system to JFK and Newark, using a mix of Port Authority funds and federal and state grants. New Jersey's resistance to funding its portion of the project eliminated the federal grants and doomed the plan.[48] When airport rail transit in 1973 again seemed to be gaining traction and a system had entered the planning phase on a high-speed rail link and internal circulator system for JFK, it was the intransigence of Queens politicians who this time scotched the idea by demanding local stops in Queens.[49] Gaining regional cooperation, as usual, proved difficult to secure.

Port Authority bondholders proved to be the biggest stumbling block in the long term. Many investors remained convinced that mass transit would damage their investments in Port Authority bonds made under the terms of the 1962 agreement. After New Jersey and New York repealed the 1962 covenant in 1974, bondholders sued the Port Authority. The U.S. Supreme Court, agreeing with the investors about potential financial damage and rejecting the argument that public welfare demanded the Port Authority invest in mass transit, upheld the 1962 limits in a 1977 decision. Their decision ended the legal and political push, which had been gaining steam, for greater Port Authority participation in regional mass-transit issues. The rail-mass transit link for JFK would not be in service until 2003 and then would be paid for out of aircraft passenger charges rather than Port Authority revenues.[50]

The failure of a transit connection condemned JFK passengers to four more decades of bad traffic. While a few hundred thousand passengers eventually navigated a slow A train subway ride to a shuttle-bus circuit at JFK (beginning in 1978), nearly all travelers threaded the roadways in one way or other to catch their flights for many decades to come. The Port Authority, with its eye to dominant metropolitan patterns of auto mobility in the postwar era, overlooked the potential of mass transit to better serve New York City.

Goodfellas at the Airport

The reputation of JFK International suffered from an additional oversight on the part of its planners. The airport's promoters genuinely hoped that their new port facilities would avoid the notorious disorder that beset New York's waterfront. Within a few years of the start of major air-cargo operations, however, the founders of the airport faced an uncomfortable reality. They had made few if any provisions to defend their new airport against urban disorder, and had created an open, decentralized facility on a suburban model; yet the corruption had come to them. Gangsters, it turned out, could drive on modern parkways just like anyone else.[51] The city's legacy of corruption and theft crept into the futuristic hangars and terminals. New York's neighborhood culture thus influenced the reputation and operations of JFK for decades.

New York's waterfront docks had long ago earned a reputation for crime and disorder. The Mafia by the 1940s, in fact, had infiltrated the longshoreman's unions on the waterfront. Their henchmen made off with stolen cargo that they could fence with little risk and at great profit. New York City as a whole in this period was famous for the Italian and Jewish gangsters nurtured in tenement districts such as Little Italy and East New York, neither of which was really that far from the airport. The new airport cargo system was simply too delicious for gangsters to resist, especially in an era of containerized, oceangoing shipping cargo that reduced the opportunities for graft by mechanizing and reducing human labor at the docks.[52]

The Port Authority managers had many years when they could have controlled crime problems at JFK instead of allowing them to fester and grow. During the 1950s, for instance, air-cargo security was pretty well nonexistent, and enterprising criminals figured this fact out very quickly. In 1952, for instance, robbers filched $35,000 in cultured Japanese pearls. This was the third theft of cargo in a month. Police also suspected there was extensive smuggling of diamonds through the airport: high-value, small-sized cargoes were hard to catch in customs.[53] According to author James Kaplan, even by the 1950s, "the airport had become a vast, slack Goodie bag, with larceny going virtually unchecked. Cash, gold, jewelry, watches, fur coats: if it looked good, it walked, and there was little the shippers could do about it except to pay fat insurance premiums—and report as little theft is possible, to keep the premiums from going any higher." That no one seemed to be watching, or even to be that concerned, made easy work for criminals.[54]

Because no Port Authority planners had thought an ultra-modern operation like an airport would ever be subject to old-fashioned criminal organizations and so refused to take seriously the crime problem at the airport in the 1950s and 1960s because it did not affect the Port Authority's bottom line, very few provisions had been made for security even into the late 1960s. A reporter in 1968 who took a tour with a truck company owner "drove with him in a private car through unguarded gates into freight areas where a variety of cargo was piled in the open. . . . The visitors wandered for more than an hour . . . without being asked to identify themselves."[55] Any firm with such a laissez faire system by the docks would know what to expect.

By the late 1960s it was well known that the mafia—the "Goodfellas" so vividly portrayed in Martin Scorsese's classic historical drama—was still filching diamonds, stock issues, and even American Express travelers' checks. Valuable paper documents, the lifeblood of the city's global corporate system, could also be valuable to criminals. Five men, for instance, were arrested in 1970 for stealing stock certificates with a value of $1 million from a mail pouch at JFK.[56] Many believed that only the expansion to the airports of the Waterfront Commission of New York Harbors, which had been used to rein in mob activity at the docks, would be sufficient to stem the tide.[57]

Capacity problems undermined airport security in an obvious way. The air-cargo business had grown so rapidly that there was often not enough secured space for all the materials offloaded from the growing cargo holds of arriving planes. Trucks zoomed in and out of the area, and managers sometimes had to resort to temporary canvas tents to hold cargo. In 1969 alone, there were "545 reported cases of theft (including 38 hijackings on roads outside the airport) with losses totaling $3,387,317." Stolen goods could be easily fenced and redistributed in a big city like New York. The Mafia called the shots through, among other means, its control of the Teamsters Local 295, which in turn dominated the airfreight trucking industry. Mafia leaders, as was their custom, found jobs for their members or associates at the airport, even if they had criminal records that made them unreliable hands. The airlines and truckers claimed that they were powerless against such a well-oiled racketeering organization. The airlines themselves had been in part infiltrated by this criminal enterprise: "Many racket connected employees in the airlines' own cargo terminals engaged in the wholesale pilfering of goods spilling from broken shipping cartons or in the snatching of entire packages."[58]

The Port Authority for many years reported a low loss rate in cargo, but it was well known to law enforcement that many firms failed to report crimes. Instead, they had just started calculating a certain loss rate as part of doing business at JFK. By the late 1960s, the reputation for crime was not only public news but also potentially damaging to the health of the Port Authority air-cargo business. The Port Authority finally organized an airport security council to coordinate screening of workers and to develop accurate record keeping for cargo.[59] For the first time, all the employees who worked in air-cargo areas had to wear identification badges and were now monitored by closed-circuit television systems. The Federal Bureau of Customs oversaw an armed patrol division created in 1973 to crack down on hijackers and other thieves.[60] Perhaps even more important, large air-cargo operators such as Pan Am built enormous and modern new facilities in the 1960s that were better secured and more efficient. The accumulated investment in facilities for air cargo and the cost of theft to shippers demanded a new attitude. Electronic sorting systems on conveyor belts and containerization of air cargo reduced the number of hands on packages, a crucial change for reducing theft.[61]

In spite of new energy and resources, crime reduction came slowly. In 1971, for instance, a reporter could say with confidence that "John F. Kennedy International Airport is still mob town, USA . . . trucking rackets, hijacking, mail thefts, flagrant pilferage, loansharking, illegal gambling and other crimes are still flourishing despite a record number of investigations by local state and federal agencies." He recounted that there were still "mob 'spotters,' some of whom are employed at the airport . . . [who] are trained to detect valuable cargo no matter how it is disguised. They tip off the racketeers in charge of arranging steps and hijackings." Coordination of a lot of the crime rested with gangster Harry Davidoff: "A short, squat, beer barrel of a man with an explosive temper, he has a police record dating back to 1933 that included convictions for burglary, extortion and gambling" and deep connections to Murder Incorporated. He was still in charge of a "paper local," Local 295, where he worked industriously with his associates in various organizations to skim cargo and place criminals.[62]

Despite regular declarations of victory by the Port Authority, the crime problem continued. In 1973, for instance, "more air cargo may be stolen at the New York–New Jersey airports than throughout all the rest of the country together, and that the losses of cargo to theft at the New York–New Jersey airports can reasonably be estimated to exceed $10 million per year."[63] Sealing JFK's reputation as deeply corrupt was the gruesome Lufthansa robbery, memorably dramatized in Scorsese's *Goodfellas*. The 1978 heist, made possible by insider information, involved an estimated $6 million in cash and jewelry and led to a wave of murders as the ringleader covered his bloody tracks.

The airport's reputation for security, despite major upgrades in day-to-day operations, had certainly hit rock bottom. The influence of urban social patterns on the shape and reputation of the airport damaged the city's national standing in such an important business. Locating the air-cargo business at the airport did not prove sufficient insulation from urban crime. It would not be long before many shippers found greener, and safer, pastures.

The Port Authority created JFK International with the best intentions and the most modern planning philosophies of its day. Its aim was no less than the creation of both a great airport and a new landmark for the New York metropolitan area. The speed with which this vision dissipated, in spite of so much expense devoted to the achievement of ambitious goals, was remarkable. The airport's designers had underestimated the scale of the jet age, had overemphasized space-age solutions for practical ones (helicopter versus mass transit), and had taken for granted the airport's isolation from urban crime. There was no shortage of vision at the Port Authority in the 1950s; in retrospect, what seems to have been in short supply was an accurate appraisal of the real nature of the New York metropolitan area.

CHAPTER 4

Neighborhood Battles

The Port Authority, and Austin Tobin in particular, would have dramatically expanded runways at JFK International in the 1960s to a scale commensurate with its growing operations if not for the airport's location in a metropolitan area experiencing a major awakening about environmental quality. The notion of growth at any price, which arguably had been in force in the 1940s and 1950s, no longer held sway among all urban or suburban residents and their political representatives in the 1960s and 1970s. Environmental concerns of many types—wildlife protection, open-space preservation, water pollution, and noise pollution—dovetailed in resistance to the Port Authority's plans to expand JFK into Jamaica Bay.

By dint of the airport residing in a beautiful, if degraded, coastal Jamaica Bay location, surrounded by increasingly dense urban populations, limits came from residents and concerned parties interested in both ecological and human impacts. New Yorkers who cared less about human welfare would fight the agency if they filled marshland, while those who did not care much about animals and nature would also fight expansion, even if they lived at a distance, to try to minimize their exposure to jet noise. These opponents, from average citizens to Governor Nelson Rockefeller, stalled expansion even if it meant damaging one of the few growth industries in the New York region. To top it all, the Port Authority had become a major polluter of the bay in its own right. No longer were Port Authority leaders the impartial brokers, if they ever truly were, who could negotiate in good faith on environmental issues.

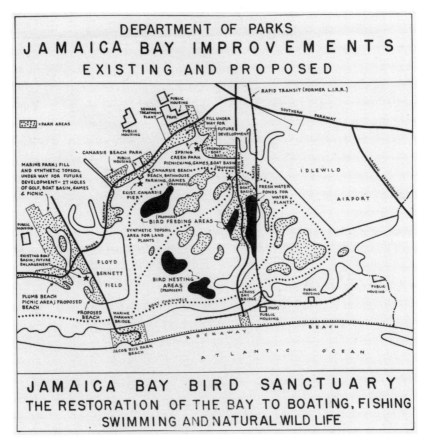

FIGURE 22. New York City Parks Department plans for the transformation of Jamaica Bay into a wildlife refuge. New York City Parks Department. Courtesy of the Queens Borough Public Library, Archives, Illustrations Collection—Jamaica Bay.

Robert Moses, as an environmentalist, laid the groundwork for the Port Authority's looming battles over noise and expansion. By the 1950s, Moses had gained control over many of the bay's island and marshes as part of his long-term vision of establishing an emerald necklace of parks around Jamaica Bay. His vision of a vast, regional-scale park, as described by a reporter in 1954, remains both alluring and elusive:

Commissioner Moses pictures the completed project as an expanse of clean, blue water, dotted with sailboats and fishing craft. Around the edges of the Bay will be wide stretches of white sand, with thousands of bathers enjoying themselves . . . . Back of the beaches will be playgrounds and parks, with large parking areas. Also included in the project will be large housing developments, schools and shopping areas, around the north side of the bay.

More than just a recreation and residential space, Jamaica Bay would become an ecological wonder where nature and man would live in harmony: "The marshy islands and sandbars out in the Bay will become the home of vast colonies of nesting birds and thousands of ducks, geese and other winged creatures."[1]

Moses's most extensive and ambitious plans, such as a miniature Jones Beach in Jamaica Bay to take advantage of the warm, calm waters, did not come to fruition; but he did realize many other interventions, including public beaches in the Rockaways, nature reserves in the bay, and vast middle- and low-income housing projects for thousands of residents. The success of these efforts would in the long term begin to tighten the circle of opposition around the airport, both its expansion and its daily operations, by making the bay worthy of defense.[2]

Moses admitted that Jamaica Bay "has been a pet project of mine for many years. In fact, I regard Jamaica Bay as the greatest recreational area of its kind of any city in the world. We still have some pollution problems, but we are keeping after them."[3] Moses anticipated correctly that "the creation of a few fresh or brackish water ponds in some higher marshes will attract ducks and other species of water fowl." Moses established the Jamaica Bay Wildlife Refuge in 1953 to augment the natural landscape. A joint effort of the MTA, the Department of Parks, and the Department of Sanitation, construction workers used fill (dredged at the same time as fill needed for the dike supporting the new Rockaway subway line that crossed the bay) to create freshwater ponds that could support a wide range of plant and animal species.[4] A dedicated park employee hired by Moses, Herbert Johnson, is credited with a green thumb that in just a few years turned man-made ponds and marshes, with new grasses and plantings, into popular refuges for a great variety of migrating waterfowl on the East Coast flyway. New Yorkers might not desire to swim in Jamaica Bay, but waterfowl were not so discriminating. The birds so loved the area that by the late 1960s a winter survey identified 30,000 various waterfowl stopping over as they migrated.[5]

Even more remarkable and dangerous politically for the Port Authority were the thousands of local birdwatchers enthusiastically documenting the renewed importance of Jamaica Bay for the East Coast flyway.[6] A gentleman wrote to the New York City Transit Authority out of gratitude: "A remarkable show which can only be properly seen from your trains as they cross Jamaica Bay is under way this Fall. Between Broad Channel and Howard Beach on that new pond which some genius conceived are thousands of ducks. . . . Whoever conceived this deserves a medal." It was Robert Moses who conceived it, but creating a pond for waterfowl near one of the world's busiest airports would not earn encomiums for Moses in the long term. He would even regret his contributions to the environment and argued within a few years that sections of the marsh he had helped restore should be sacrificed to the airport in the name of commercial supremacy. Once other New Yorkers, however, realized the significance of possessing such a vast and lovely combination of parks and natural space, there was no going back. Nature became an additional pressure point on the Port Authority.[7]

Water quality became a major environmental issue in Jamaica Bay because almost no one had taken seriously stewardship of the marshland. The city tolerated illegal sewer connection to many neighborhoods in southern Queens; these drains dumped untreated human waste directly into the bay. Even in the late 1960s, the entire Broad Channel neighborhood lacked sewers for the three thousand year-round residents.[8] Stormwater pollution control plans reduced water pollution in the 1960s, but sewage plants still discharged hundreds of millions of gallons of moderately treated sewage water into the bay annually; more disgusting was that these plants frequently overflowed during rainstorms and dumped untreated waste directly into the bay. Dredging in the bay by sand and gravel companies and JFK-related construction projects impeded natural circulation from the bay to the ocean. Continued garbage disposal at so-called sanitary landfills on the bay's edges were never as tightly controlled as one might hope, and solid waste frequently blew into the bay's marshes and waters. In sum, the bay's perilous condition had its roots in many non-airport sources.[9]

The environmental damage by such sources for a long time appeared to be the major culprit in the bay's decline, but the airport also began to take its toll. The airport had, in essence, removed thousands of acres of productive marshland that would have helped sustain species and clean water. The extension of a runway out into the bay in the early 1960s added further to the bay's circulation problems. The fuel storage "tank farms" on the edges

FIGURE 23. The tank farm at JFK that fueled planes but also polluted sections of Jamaica Bay, 1973. Arthur Tress, Documerica Collection, National Archives.

of the airport had been created in an era of industrial optimism and limited regulation, but now they began to be viewed by neighbors more as a problem than an asset. By 1957 the tank farm, run as a concession by Allied New York Services, held almost seven million gallons of fuel and cycled through fourteen million gallons per month in peak season. By 1961 the tank farm held almost eighteen million gallons, and by 1969 could hold thirty-two million gallons. The fuel was brought in tanker ships, pumped into the tanks, offloaded onto trucks, and then finally pumped into the planes. By the mid-1960s, an underground system of pipes controlled by a sophisticated computer system for fueling planes replaced the trucks.[10] The major tank farms made profits for the Port Authority and local firms.

Those lucrative tank farms also leaked. Even worse, JFK officials looked the other way as employees nonchalantly dumped petroleum by-products into the ground and waterways. A longtime manager confessed in the 1990s, "Years ago, when aviation fuel was very cheap, once we'd filtered out water, we just throw out the waste fuel—the sump. The product was

FIGURE 24. One of many landfills that may have fed gulls but also undermined Robert Moses's arcadian vision for Jamaica Bay, 1973. Arthur Tress, Documerica Collection, National Archives.

so cheap, and the volume so large, that it just didn't pay to save it." The Organization of the Petroleum Exporting Countries (OPEC) oil embargo of 1973, designed to punish the West for its support of Israel, initiated a worldwide economic retrenchment. When jet fuel went from 13 cents to 40 cents a gallon, the staff "started recovering oil and selling it."[11] The cumulative pollution, however, became too obvious to hide. Polluted creeks near the airport, for instance, earned a reputation for their sterility: "The area adjacent to JFK airport in the southwest corner contained excessive amounts of petro-chemical discharge and noxious sediment" that rendered the area sterile and anaerobic and thus reduced "bottom organisms used as waterfowl food."[12] Naturalists found that crabs and oysters had largely disappeared.[13] Extensive oil around houses in Howard Beach came to light when "it was noticed that the pilings supporting the homes were saturated with the jet fuel, requiring the hosing down of the pilings with high-pressure hoses."[14]

FIGURE 25. Old fishing shacks at Hunter's Point near the airport surrounded by polluted water and noise pollution, 1973. Arthur Tress, Documerica Collection, National Archives.

Local politicians on all sides began to demand remediation. Republican congressman John Wydler of Nassau County, after viewing the pollution around Bergen basin, reported that "one of the scientists on the tour had worked on the serious oil spill last year in Santa Barbara channel in California and pronounced Jamaica Bay as foul from oil spillage as waters off California."[15] By 1970 this pollution became the focus of a lawsuit as the growing environmental movement began to flex its muscles. State Attorney General Louis Lefkowitz, a moderate Republican, filed a complaint against the Port Authority over jet fuel and oil spillage that had created "large, ugly, obnoxious and foul-smelling oil slicks." Jamaica Bay activism was part of the growing awareness of the environmental costs of the postwar, energy-intensive culture of consumption that even those outside the counterculture began to question in the 1960s and 1970s. The New York region's loss of thousands of acres of wetlands to development, the destruction of much of the Meadowlands, and the expansion of Fresh Kills landfill in once productive salt marshes made the preservation of Jamaica Bay all the more pressing.[16]

In spite of damage, and partly because people still avoided it, Jamaica Bay remained ideal for migrating birds traveling along the Hudson Valley, Long Island Sound, and Atlantic Coast flyways. The bay was one of the few hospitable habitats in this urbanized metropolitan region where birds could rest, sleep, and eat with little human interference. Robert Moses's efforts to create an arcadian refuge astride the airport had not exactly come to fruition, but the popularity of the marshes and ponds with waterfowl indicates that he had achieved something significant. Efforts by the New York City Parks Department made Jamaica Bay Wildlife Refuge even better, including the planting of specific trees and bushes that improved habitat. A 1968 aerial survey over the course of a year found 30,970 total waterfowl resting at one time or another in the bay.[17]

The Battle for the Bay

Enter the Port Authority. Having lost the battle to open another Jetport in the wetlands of Morris County, New Jersey, Tobin and the airlines now sought to create a modern, parallel runway configuration at JFK in order to add capacity.[18] Airline officials, in particular, wanted new extensions into the bay because new runways would allow their planes to remain higher over towns on descent and takeoff. The net effect would be a "diminution of noise levels" that would loosen "preferential runway rules and make for increased traffic." There were some benefits to total capacity as well, with the most ambitious extensions adding thirty-five movements at peak hours to the seventy-four movements then possible. One version of the plan included dramatic extensions into Jamaica Bay, and the second plan basically envisioned the filling of much of the entire bay. These plans hit some major turbulence.[19]

The New York activist spirit had expanded its focus on social-welfare issues and fighting urban renewal to include quality of life and environmental ambience. The Sierra Club, a leading environmental organization, opposed expansion because of its impact on recreational fishing, charter boats, and hunting. An organization calling itself the Jamaica Bay Council in the 1970s promoted use of the bay for recreational and natural purposes. An ad hoc organization known as Jamaica Bay for the People stood firmly against airport expansion on the basis of noise and environmental impact. Other groups mentioned as opponents at the time included the Jamaica

THE DEVELOPMENT OF JFK

Source: Port Authority and Regional Plan Association

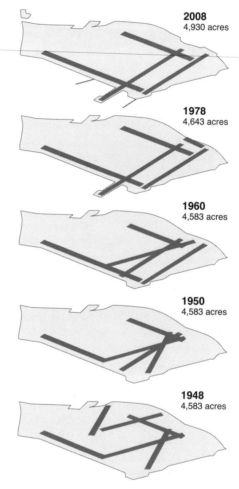

2008
4,930 acres

1978
4,643 acres

1960
4,583 acres

1950
4,583 acres

1948
4,583 acres

FIGURE 26. The redesign of JFK's runways over time, including the expansion of only one runway into Jamaica Bay in the period between 1960 and 1964. The Port Authority eventually achieved a parallel configuration and very long runways able to handle the world's largest jets, but it was unable to add additional runways that could have boosted operations. Courtesy of the Regional Plan Association.

Bay for the People Committee, the Parks Council of New York, the Linnaean Society of New York, the Green Ribbon Panel, the Save Jamaica Bay Committee, and the Council to Stop the Expansion of Kennedy Airport. A dramatic 150-boat, five-mile-long flotilla demonstrated solid resistance to airport extension.[20]

Leading civic leaders of the era lent their support to the cause from the local to the state level. August Heckscher II, New York City's park administrator and a passionate environmentalist, equated the extension of runways into Jamaica Bay "to the Everglades issue in Florida where a great National Park has been menaced by an airport which is going to be built nearby."[21] New York mayor John Lindsay also opposed Kennedy's expansion.[22] And Republican governor Nelson Rockefeller, a committed environmentalist, joined the fight against the extension of runways into Jamaica Bay. Additional public officials from Brooklyn, Queens, and Nassau County (state legislators, congressmen, and local officials) crossed party and county lines to throw up roadblocks to the airport expansion. This collaborative environmental effort was one of the metropolitan-scale success stories of the era and contrasts with the effective attempts by suburbs to isolate themselves in other respects from affordable housing, integrated schools, and social-welfare programs. The fight against environmental damage to the bay was one of many environmental issues that catalyzed suburban environmentalism, including air and water quality, but the resistance to Jamaica Bay's degradation appears to be one of the few environmental movements that successfully spanned suburb and city.[23]

The crystallizing power of the environmental movement can be read in the report by the National Academy of Sciences (NAS) commissioned by the Port Authority to provide a more objective analysis of their expansion plans. Under tremendous pressure, the Port Authority decided that it would be better off shifting the final decision on expansion to a panel of qualified scientists, social scientists, engineers, and other technocrats. The Draft Environmental Impact system in force today was not yet in place, but the NAS report qualifies as an innovative and early exploration of this type of multivariable analysis that evaluates different scenarios and impacts within the context of the city and region. Critics of the expansion believed that the NAS study had insufficient numbers of environmentalists involved—dismissing its members as "a community relations man, economists, psychoacoustic expert, political scientist, urban planner, lawyer," and the like—but in the long run, critics were wrong to worry. These experts demonstrated impartiality in their review, although a number of their suggestions, which would theoretically allow for airport expansion and environmental protection, turned out to be unrealistic.[24]

The authors of the NAS report, *Jamaica Bay and Kennedy Airport: A Multidisciplinary Environmental Study* (1971), acknowledged that Jamaica Bay was "impaired," but like Robert Moses before them, they believed that for millions of potential visitors it was "an irreplaceable asset in its size, its ready accessibility, and its ecological viability. Nothing similar to it is to be found in any other major city of the world."[25] They catalogued the numerous ways in which previous airport expansion, inadequate sewage treatment, and unregulated urban growth had compromised the environment. The authors, however, placed much of their emphasis on the sins of the Port Authority:

> It is beyond contention that the construction and operation of Kennedy Airport has adversely affected the ecological viability of the bay and the environment of millions of people within earshot of its air traffic. The taking of 4,500 acres of marshland and the dredging of Grassy Bay for airport fill destroyed one sixth of the original bay area. Air pollution from aircraft and airport-generated ground traffic, as well as oil pollution from airport activities, has affected all forms of life both above and below sea level. Above all, the whine and roar of jet planes has cast a noisy pall over areas far removed from the bay, and they are very nearly unbearable in the communities close by.[26]

The study authors believed, with some justification, that the scale and the number of runways at the airport were just two of the many factors impeding efficient airport operations. They firmly believed that eliminating remaining general aviation would significantly reduce congestion at peak times. This elimination alone, they argued, would equal 70 percent of the gain to be had from adding runways. The report also condemned "wasteful overscheduling of air-carrier flights" that "results from the regulations imposed upon airlines and the gross underpricing of peak hour capacity."[27] They envisioned vertical-lift aircraft and jumbo jets relieving projected increases of the future. In sum, they contended that the so-called airport crisis was a management problem incorrectly framed as an infrastructure crisis.

Facing both political and scientific resistance, Austin Tobin announced in 1971 that he would follow the recommendations of the NAS. The airport would not, after all, be extended into Jamaica Bay because of the excessive damage that would be caused to the ecology of the bay. In 1972, in order to protect the bay and with leadership from the Regional Plan Association, the park was integrated into the National Park Service's Gateway National Recreation Area that includes parks in the Rockaways, Staten Island, and northern New Jersey.

An odd dissent to the overwhelming consensus on environmental management came from Robert Moses. He felt that the resistance of activists in New Jersey to accept a fourth jetport in their swamps meant that the region needed "Kennedy runway extensions in the Eastern one third of Jamaica Bay as a temporary expedient." He downplayed the inevitable destruction that would have ensued had the plans been carried out: "The statement that the integrity of the game refuge we established in the face of so much indifference and opposition would be destroyed is grossly exaggerated." Aviation and the commerce it generated for the region, Moses contended, trumped migrating birds. Marginalized by his political enemies and unwilling to embrace a more combative form of environmental activism, his opinion carried little weight.[28]

Hitting the Sound Barrier to Growth

Noise pollution would have been a much less severe problem if politicians had taken responsible growth positions in the 1940s and 1950s. Politicians could be counted on for statements of outrage over noise and pollution, but they and their predecessors had exercised no restraint on residential development that might have reduced the problems in the first place. The regional vision that had inspired the airport, public beaches, and surrounding parkways made few inroads in the regulation of new housing and commercial development vis-à-vis aviation. New York's zoning laws separated residential, industrial, and commercial uses in eastern Queens and Nassau County, creating a typically suburban landscape both within and outside city limits, but these laws were not sensitive enough to respond to long-term threats to quality of life around the airport. The importance of building "middle-class" enclaves, particularly within the city limits, permitted a great deal of residential development right in the path of aircraft operations.

Noise around JFK would have been less of a problem if the city and Nassau County in the 1940s had rezoned neighborhoods under major flight paths to reduce or at least restrict population growth. When the airport was first established, Queens still had large undeveloped areas. The South Shore

0 5 10 Miles

1930
1950
1960
1970
1980
1990
2020

URBAN AREAS 1930-2020

FIGURE 27. The density of the population around JFK grew drastically from the 1930s to 2000. With adequate planning, provisions could have been made to restrict urbanization, at least in corridors, near the airport. Such steps were not taken, with consequences for noise pollution in the decades to come. Minna Ninova.

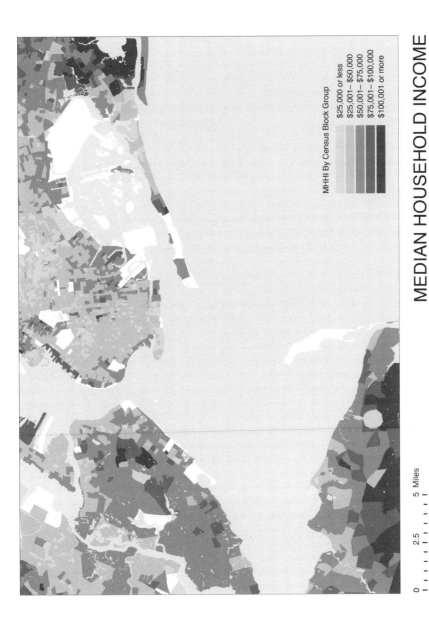

0   2.5   5 Miles

MHHI By Census Block Group

$25,000 or less
$25,001– $50,000
$50,001– $75,000
$75,001– $100,000
$100,001 or more

MEDIAN HOUSEHOLD INCOME

FIGURE 28. Income levels among the populations living around JFK in 2000. The dark areas of high income in the right-hand corner are the "Five Towns," such as Cedarhurst and Lawrence, but communities with a great range of income levels surround JFK. Minna Ninova.

of Nassau County also had "little villages," and the Rockaways were "isolated." All these same areas, however, as a result of very limited controls
on developers, by 1960 were "heavily populated" and no longer could be
considered "a buffer zone of empty land over which airplanes could fly
without worrying about noise." Moses's parkway systems opened up every
area of Nassau County and eastern Queens to suburban-style development
while the city's massive investment in the IND subway system (from the
1920s onward) created new clusters of high-density housing in Queens.[29]

Single-family or duplex homes mostly filled in the open land of southern Queens and Nassau County, but even high-density developments rose
near the airport in the postwar era. Tall structures were banned early on
within two miles of the airport, but it was not hard to find large areas of
open land outside that limit but within earshot of the airport in which
to build high-density complexes or towers. The two-mile range had been
established for airplane safety, not civilian peace.[30] Inevitably, some of this
growth came in areas near the airport or in the line of flight paths: "The
buildings of new multiple dwellings—skyscraper apartment houses and tri-
plex houses—is proceeding at a fast pace in areas of Queens and Brooklyn
that are aligned perfectly with the runways of Idlewild and LaGuardia."[31]

In the 1960s there were still thousands of additional publicly sponsored
low- and middle-income projects planned within earshot of the airport in
Brooklyn and Queens or its major landing and takeoff routes. Rochdale
Village (five thousand cooperative units alone) and other great accumula-
tions of public and middle-class redevelopment towers added tens of thousands of new residents to the area. Robert Moses, in particular, saw these
new developments as a means to upgrade districts, whether it was marshes,
an old racetrack, an abandoned airport, or rotting Rockaway cottages. As
one report glumly noted, "It is apparent that a great deal of unrelated planning is currently underway in Jamaica Bay."[32]

Calls for a land bank of vacant property for industrial use or rezoning
large parcels for industry near JFK got nowhere in the early 1960s. Land was
just too valuable to owners both for future residential development and as a
source of future tax revenues for a cash-strapped city.[33] Talk of creating a
home-free zone in the Rockaways, the densely populated barrier island in
Queens, to reduce noise also went nowhere. FAA administrator Oscar Bakke,
for instance, recommended air corridors cleared of homes (purchased from
residents) in Nassau County to reduce noise, but the proposal failed to excite
much interest.[34] The NAS report from 1970 acknowledged that while no one

in 1947 could have predicted the impact of the airport, "The present situation is a result of improvident actions of City officials, airport authorities, and land speculators, and it exacts from nearly a million people a daily penance for the sins of oversight of public and private planners."[35]

If airport operations had only harassed the sleep of poor people, the Port Authority could probably have eluded strong opposition. During this time, New York's poor neighborhoods, once full of stables, factories, and workshops, became the sites of similarly unpleasant facilities including highways, waste-transfer stations, and bus depots, what is today called environmental racism. Administrators faced little organized resistance and were able to build all these facilities, as minority communities remained focused on survival issues related to disinvestment, employment, and housing. The force for noise regulation at JFK actually came from the middle- and upper-class neighborhoods pummeled by flight paths. The builders of Lindenwood Village in Howard Beach, for instance, placed 25 six-story buildings for 2,400 families right under the airport's flight paths—where it remains today. Howard Beach boomed in the 1950s and 1960s, changing from a partially undeveloped area into a neighborhood of densely developed, single-family homes, two-family units, and apartment complexes right next to the airport. More people, of course, meant more aviation impact on ears. Howard Beach may have had a reputation for housing airport workers, but middle-class activists from Howard Beach and neighborhoods like it did not hold back in their criticism of noise pollution.[36]

Nassau County was also not to be trifled with. Cedarhurst, for instance, was "an El Dorado of country clubs, yacht harbors and houses selling for a nice, round figure of $500,000. . . . These big houses on their broad green lawns will knock your eye out." Neighborhoods like Cedarhurst and nearby Lawrence originated as elite Protestant enclaves, but by midcentury they were populated by an increasingly diverse group of socially ambitious and upwardly bound Protestant, Catholic, and Jewish families in newer subdivisions that replaced sprawling estates. The ritzy "five towns" area as a whole (Cedarhurst, Lawrence, Woodmere, the Hewletts, and Inwood) had grown by twenty thousand residents between 1945 and 1964. New subdivisions of split-levels and ranchers, such as Sutton Park and Brookfield Estates, sold out, at high prices, even before they were completed. Yet as these successful migrants reached their golden shore, the noise of the city they had tried so desperately to escape followed them into their bedrooms, living rooms, and disturbed backyard barbecues: "Local residents contend that jet aircraft approaching and taking off from JFK International Airport . . . are wrecking their sleep and giving them nervous fits." Days in the five towns were concluded by the rush hour at JFK. Residents of the Five Towns were easily able to raise $50,000 for their noise abatement committee.[37]

The jet age aggravated the noise problems. Housing that once seemed out of the range of aircraft noise had been "moved" to Jet Alley. Jets were loud and impressive, just as they were meant to be, according to reporter Leonard Victor of the *Long Island Star*: "The jets using Idlewild . . . are blood brothers of those military planes. The commercial jets, right down to their noisy motors, were based on the knowledge gained from the military designs."[38] In the dawning era of the jet age, 1959, Queens civic officials protested about aviation noise to the FAA, but this industry-dominated federal agency refused to take action. The political tide began to shift in the early 1960s. Members of the House Committee on Interstate and Foreign Commerce, for instance, came to hear resident complaints from Queens and Nassau County. The FAA assistant administrator felt compelled in 1961 to tell thirty civic leaders that the aviation "program can only be sustained if the political problems on the local level can be resolved" and admitted slyly that "when voters bark they are responsive." It would take a few more years, however, before the activist bite was as big as its bark.[39]

Frustrated by lack of rapid political action, citizens had first sought relief through the courts. Over eight hundred Rosedale property owners, for instance, sued the Port Authority in 1961 for loss of market value that they believed was the result of planes that dipped below 500 feet as they roared over their neighborhoods. The Port Authority, in turn, sued the airlines in case the property owners won." As multiple cases like this worked through the court system, the Port Authority's leadership grew uneasy about developments on the federal level. In a major lawsuit, *Griggs v. Allegheny County* (1962), the Supreme Court decided in favor of citizens who suffered property damage as a result of airport operations. The court ruled that a "homeowner is entitled to compensation from an airport operator if low flying planes make his home unlivable." The Port Authority expected a "deluge of suits" after this ruling; in the end, however, the courts protected airports from major liability by making the bar for "unlivable" so high that few residents were able to receive compensation.[40]

The Port Authority, in light of these growing challenges, now had a direct incentive to shift the blame for the failings to the airlines. As far as they were concerned, just about everything that could be done had been done in terms of reducing impact by means of after-market aviation systems, such as turbo fans, suppressors, and so forth, as well as airport management systems, such as longer runways, preferential flight paths, and special aerial maneuvers. Further improvement, they believed, would only come from brand-new planes built to a higher standard. Port Authority administrators began to demand that the FAA factor in noise before certifying new aircraft for passenger service. According to the Port Authority's counsel, this would address the "final gap" in noise regulation that would finally bring forth "quieter planes."[41]

Even as the Port Authority put pressure on the FAA and aircraft manufactures for their failures, they trumpeted the record they had painstakingly compiled. In spite of record numbers of operations at JFK in 1963, for instance, noise complaints actually declined by 40 percent, with particularly steep declines in Rosedale, Howard Beach, and South Ozone Park. Complaints in the five towns also took a major fall between 1961 and 1962, dropping from 472 to 86.[42] The Port Authority linked these improvements to their having commissioned ITT Corporation to create the "world's first automatic aircraft sound monitoring system." The system, installed in neighboring areas, relayed a graphic trace of the noise and location of violation for planes that exceeded 102 to 103 perceived noise decibels (PNdB). A Port Authority staff member of a sound crew office then checked these traces against a visual identification of departing planes. The Port Authority then sent "violation letters" for planes exceeding the 112 PNdB level. Serial violators were warned and, in a limited number of cases, sued by the Port Authority. Even in these suits, however, an arrangement was made with the airlines for "corrective action." As proof of the effectiveness of the system, a Port Authority official claimed, "between 1959 and 1964, despite jet take-offs having increased more than twelve-fold, there was a 40 percent reduction in the actual number of noise violations."[43]

If the situation was improving, why were residents in the flight paths resorting to legal and political action? The director of aviation admitted that protest was shifting out of frustration from individual complaints to group efforts: "They have sought relief as individuals and have not found it. Now they are organizing to seek relief." And the simple reason was that "112 perceived noise decibels is far from quiet." The sheer number of aircraft movements cut into whatever noise reduction the Port Authority achieved on individual takeoffs and landings. More people in the region, more flights, more jets—the Port Authority had, as he admitted, reached a point of "diminishing returns" in terms of their own regulations. The fact that noise had become redefined as a nuisance gave activists a new power in struggles over regulation.[44]

The airlines, of course, felt that they were doing all they could to mitigate noise while still preserving passenger safety. Many airline executives insisted that pilots made every effort to reduce noise, even braving "annoying tail and cross-wind components if it will cut noise on approaches."[45] Airlines directed their pilots over Flushing Meadow and flew higher over populated areas in order to reduce noise. The FAA in 1961 also allowed for the use of other runways to take some of the pressure off of Rosedale, Laurelton, Valley Stream, and Elmont. Pilots took routes over Floyd Bennett Field and along the Jamaica Bay shoreline to reduce noise in Springfield Gardens and Ozone Park. Higher altitudes over Elmont and Rosedale also seemed to help.[46] The FAA backed up the airlines and sent individual monitors to convince local officials that progress was being made.[47] The FAA also made threats, which were pretty unbelievable, about moving all jet operations out of the New York region.

Some citizen advocates begin to suspect that the Port Authority and FAA simply shifted airplane operations to minimize noise over the squeakiest wheels: "When one particular area raises a ruckus about the noise situation, flight patterns mysteriously are changed so that another area must bear the brunt of the noise. This, we feel, is no solution."[48] Residents in Lawrence and the Rockaways complained in 1961 that shifting planes away from Elmont, Rosedale, and North Valley Stream increased noise over their communities.[49] Pressure from Rosedale in 1961 sent more planes over Howard Beach. In 1962 Brooklyn civic groups in Canarsie, Mill River, Flatbush, and East New York reported that reduction of noise for Queens residents had increased jet noise for residents in these other areas.[50] Inwood residents claimed that reductions in noise over Long Island neighborhoods in the late 1960s made their lives worse.

The Port Authority had, in fact, long ago acknowledged that it did shift operations based upon noise complaints. Complaints and the Cedarhurst lawsuit in 1952, for instance, resulted in the opening of a new parallel runway that had been "held in reserve." This new runway "permitted a division of flights between the Cedarhurst area and the communities to the South. This, in fact, is typical of most operational changes in that taking flights away from one area results in putting them over another."[51] Thus, shifting noise was frequently a zero-sum game for the region. The Port

Authority by 1972 even put in place a computerized system to more fairly distribute aircraft operations and promised to limit continuous jet traffic in one area.[52] Officials nevertheless admitted that repeated instrument landings in times of poor visibility over a few concentrated and densely populated areas remained a thorn in their side because the "full flaps" on approach and more thrust created additional noise.

Congestion in the skies contributed to the perception of an airborne war overhead. The holding patterns for JFK over much of central Long Island and northern New Jersey were extensive and often crowded with planes waiting to land. The low cost of jet fuel likely contributed to this problem; airlines, as they frequently do today, could have delayed flights inbound for New York instead of stacking them up above the city. There were eleven holding patterns over New York City for all airports, and five just for JFK. Although the planes circled high above the cities and suburbs, and contributed little to air and ground noise, it did raise the sense among many residents that there was no escaping airport traffic and the pollution related to engines burning tons of jet fuel (a form of kerosene). Residents had reason to be concerned about a parking lot in the sky as the industrialization of urban air space just got worse each year.[53]

The fundamental weakness in achieving politically acceptable noise levels rested in great measure on the distributed responsibility for aircraft operations. The Port Authority operated the airports, airlines hired and supervised pilots, the CAB determined airline routes, and the FAA supervised the system as a whole. The FAA, aligned with the airlines, viewed New York as a troublesome node in a national system. Local concerns about noise had to be secondary to operational efficiency and safety. The FAA may have been charged with the responsibility for noise in 1959 under the Federal Aviation Act (1958), but the FAA always placed a much higher emphasis on safety and airline efficiency rather than noise. FAA officials admitted in 1964 they had never actually punished pilots for noise violations in the area because to do so might endanger passenger safety as it had sometimes in the past.[54] The FAA administrator, Najeeb Halaby, in 1961 even denied responsibility for noise: "My agency doesn't monitor jet plane noise because you don't bother to regulate the noise of railroads or buses."[55] Both the FAA and the airport administrators admitted that it was always "safety first, noise abatement second."[56] The thousands who did complain about noise to the Port Authority in the 1960s also received the calculated message that the FAA was the responsible party for "movement of all aircraft in the New York Metropolitan area, including direction and altitude."[57]

The Port Authority continued to position itself as a broker with the best interests of both airlines and residents in mind. The Port Authority, for instance, sued Delta Air Lines in 1964 for violations of noise restrictions for night flights.[58] The Port Authority, however, was always eager to declare victory over noise and was reluctant to admit that even a few hundred nonconforming flights over one or two neighborhoods in the course of the year were sufficient to disturb the sleep and mental well-being of thousands of already cranky New Yorkers. The Port Authority reminded the public that New York remained the nation's international travel hub, with "five out of six trips from the United States to Europe . . . through the Port of New York" and "three out of every four of these trips were made by air last year." Aviation had become the largest industry in Queens, and a jet ban would be urban suicide: "The Metropolitan area of New York would 'die' without convenient, efficient air transport service." They were not exaggerating.[59]

The Port Authority had on its side the fact that land values, as calculated in a 1960 study, actually increased around airports, even though some residents claimed economic damage. The neighborhoods growing around JFK, in fact, were some of the emerging middle-class districts of the time; even elite neighborhoods in the five towns subjected to increased noise had not lost the cachet that made them valuable. Being close to airports had its value both for travelers and as a place to live for the thousands who worked at the airport. To many residents, however, such points rang hollow. What did it matter if land values remained solid when you could not get a decent night's sleep?

With the tide of air transportation politics running against them, residents were forced to become more sophisticated in their approach. In 1963 the town of Hempstead funded a Joint Village-Town Committee for Aircraft Noise Abatement headquartered in Lawrence. The $35,000 budget gave them the funds to hire a professional firm, United Acoustical Engineers, who then came to the Five Towns to map sound in preparation for new laws and lawsuits.[60] The firm provided expert testimony in support of a Town of Hempstead airplane noise-control law that sought to set a 92 PNdB limit for planes over its airspace. These acoustic experts in 1964 effectively demonstrated in the courtroom the noisy reality of work and family life for many residents: "When a technician pressed a button, there was silence at first, and then a roar filled the courtroom, followed by a pause, another crash of sound, another pause, and finally . . . a deafening thunder until the aircraft passed out of range." These intrepid experts had visited homes, country clubs, and marinas to test the noise levels experienced by residents. Scientists for the town had found that 79 percent of takeoffs and 90 percent of landings violated noise limits in spite of the Port Authority's and airlines' many claims of progress. The distance between these figures and those of the Port Authority raised questions about the claims of progress over the past decade.[61]

Yet even this sophisticated monitoring could not undo federal rules or make jet noise disappear. The U.S. Court of Appeals for the Second Circuit struck down the Hempstead law on behalf of the Port Authority and the airlines based upon interference with federal flight patterns and procedures. The court found that planes under such a regulation would have to fly too high in order to be in compliance with town laws, and such high approaches would reduce both safety and commerce. Supporters of the Hempstead law nevertheless claimed partial victory. They believed, for instance, that the congressional law giving the FAA more power over noise resulted from their activism.[62] The Supreme Court, on appeal, actually endorsed the regulation: "The ordinance is well and properly written, based on well proven evidence and for a good and just reason—the welfare and health of the people, and that a problem existed from which the people were entitled to mitigation." But the justices still had to admit that federal law and regulation preempted those of local areas when it came to air rights.[63]

The larger versions of existing planes, or stretch-outs, in the mid-1960s threatened to undermine any modest progress on aircraft noise. These longer planes, which had to strain more on takeoff to handle their heavier loads, were even more likely to exceed the Port Authority's 112 PNdB limit for surrounding neighborhoods. The Port Authority expressed its opposition to stretched versions of the DC-8 and Boeing 727; resistance that manufacturers believed hurt their marketing of the plane. The Port Authority was of the opinion that the manufacturers and airlines bore primary responsibility for aircraft noise because Port Authority officials believed that airplane manufacturers did not prioritize noise issues in the design process. By this time, the FAA began to take the side of the Port Authority because of the growing national resistance to this type of pollution. Tobin believed that the population was so stressed that "some militant civic groups are planning to adopt civil disobedience tactics at airports."[64]

Representatives of the affected neighborhoods in the U.S. Congress began to introduce bills to regulate airplane noise. Joseph Addabbo, Ozone Park's representative, for instance, pushed for a federal bill on noise limits because, in his words, "I believe that an age which makes it possible for airline passengers to sleep . . . as they cross the country should also allow the citizens in their homes to have an uninterrupted night of sleep."[65] In 1968, as a result of this constant pressure from activists in Queens (and elsewhere in the region and nation), Congress passed the aircraft noise-control bill (Public Law 90–411) and President Lyndon B. Johnson signed the legislation. Public Law 90–411 gave the FAA extensive control over noise levels at any time in flight and the ability to ground planes that failed to meet standards. The law, however, left in place the ability of state and local governments who operated airports to set permissible noise standards for operations. Port Authority officials welcomed the new law—and internally took a lot of credit for it as well.[66]

The passage of this legislation, while often overlooked in environmental history because of its technocratic and administrative complexity, was in every way as momentous as the Clean Air and Clean Water Acts of the 1970s. The ability to observe improved air and water quality since the 1970s has made clean air and water laws more familiar to the public, but these early restrictions on noise pollution were equally important for the nation's environmental quality, particularly for millions of residents besieged by noise surrounding airports. In fact, Public Law 90–411 was an important precursor to this expansion of federal regulatory power, with one major caveat: enforcement.[67]

Many citizen activists remained skeptical. Nassau County activists, for instance, claimed partial credit for the legislation but felt that giving FAA administrators responsibility for enforcement was "tantamount to placing a hungry fox in charge of the chicken coop."[68] Resident activists understood full well that the passing of the law did not mean that the FAA would actually take their side: "The FAA has created nothing more than a long and expensive timetable. The FAA has shown much interest in the air industry and very little for those it for whom it was created to protect."[69] The impending arrival of jumbo passenger planes threatened to erase any progress that had been made. The early rules the FAA issued in 1969, for instance, did not apply to aircraft already in service or to the new Boeing 747. There were many planes in operation that would not meet even a reasonable standard of noise control.[70]

The FAA finally set a lower noise recommendation in 1971 but only applied the level to new DC-10s, L-1011s, and 747s entering service after 1972. Activists understood how light this regulation was even for these new planes: "Even with these new jet aircraft the 108 EPNdB [effective perceived noise level] noise level applied at only one moment of the aircraft's life time." Basically, the noise level was only checked at certification trials, "operated under the most fortuitous circumstances and in the hands of the most skillful of test pilots."[71] The only genuinely good news was the 1971 debut of the DC-10, the first aircraft designed to meet the law. Sidney Leviss, Queens borough president, was excited enough to announce that its arrival "is the first major breakthrough in aircraft noise reduction." To many, including Port Authority officials, the design decimated the notion that large jets had to be loud.[72] In other good news for the area, the new 747 certified on December 1, 1971, was 25 to 40 percent quieter than the original 747 designs.

After two decades of fighting and some progress, it was difficult for residents to be upbeat about their chances for reducing jet noise. Improvements in sound reduction, and those planned for the future, were balanced by more plane operations per day, noisy aircraft grandfathered into longer service, shifting flight paths, and noisy instrument landings. The NAS, for instance, found that "about 700,000 people live in areas near Kennedy Airport that are subject to a noise exposure greater than NEF (Noise Exposure Forecast) of 30. About 120,000 of them lived in homes subject to an exposure exceeding NEF 40, which should be considered tolerable only for commercial usage" in noise-proof buildings. About 280,000 students tried to study and learn in schools in areas with an NEF of 30; some teachers found that they had to use a "jet pause" during their instructional hours.[73] One New Hyde Park resident "had once suffered 52 straight hours of traffic" over his home.[74] Noise reduction was clearly uneven, and the degree to which one appreciated progress had much to do with the precise location of one's home relative to the airports busy runways. The lack of federal regulation, the explosive aviation industry, and weak local land-planning controls combined to reduce the quality of life for hundreds of thousands of New Yorkers—even in some of the region's most attractive neighborhoods.

The airport's neighbors may have remained dissatisfied with the level of noise regulation in the 1970s, but they had scored major victories that in time would begin the slow process of reducing harm from the airport. Not only had the expansion plans stalled out, but also the Port Authority now faced a permanent obstacle to expansion in the national park at its door-step. Residents, their political leaders, and their allies in other cities had also succeeded in passing national legislation that in the decades to come would reduce the noise levels of aircraft using JFK and other airports in the United States. These were no small victories and reflect the power and sophistication of the people and leaders in the New York metropolitan area.

New York's most ambitious effort at urban reinvention, JFK Interna-tional, reached its national height in the 1960s, but it began to stagnate as a beleaguered population organized to demand quality of life over creative destruction. Had the Port Authority and local officials more aggressively limited growth, proposed more creative solutions to expansion (such as expansion on the land rather than the water side of the airport), and improved the transportation network (including mass transit), the outcome might well have been different. When it came to destroying marshes for runways, the city said no. And when it came to destroying peace and quiet for growth, they also declined the offer. The postwar urban growth machine, from this perspective, had finally met its match in the New York metropolitan area.

CHAPTER 5

Decline and Disorder

Kennedy was once the premier air gateway to North America: now it is really no more than a very busy, very difficult entrance to a very busy, very difficult city.
　　—Paul Goldberger, 1990

JFK International in the 1980s and 1990s reflected the "dual" metropolis in which it was located. An elite sector of plush supersonic Concorde and business flights across the Atlantic and a booming international trade in tourists and luxury goods contrasted sharply with an airport landscape of poorly maintained terminals, drug-addicted hustlers, and sullen airport employees. JFK had yet to recoup the glamour of another era: perpetually under construction, its massive, crowded, and crumbling unit terminals had become grand monuments from a future that had quickly come and gone. It was in this era, in particular, that the subjective passenger experience of the airport, at least for anyone but the elite, became so miserable that any objective accounting of the many underlying strengths of the airport became difficult.

JFK International's most famous tenant, Pan Am, became a symbol for both the problems in air travel and JFK in particular. Pan Am had barely wrapped up its expensive terminal expansion for 747 jumbo jets when it had to face the bills for both construction and the jumbo jets. The recession and energy crisis of the early 1970s made it impossible for Pan Am to fill the planes' seats sufficiently to recoup the fuel costs of massive 747s in the transatlantic trade. The introduction of the wide-body craft may have saved JFK in the 1970s and 1980s by adding more passengers with fewer aircraft movements, but arguably the planes ruined the airlines that made the greatest investments in them.

Pan Am entered a long era of decline because of its big bet on large aircraft, which were difficult to fly economically, and its expanded terminal. Difficult economic times compounded bad corporate strategies (i.e., buying National Airlines for domestic routes), tougher competition after deregulation of the airline industry in 1978, and an expensive maintenance space for wide-body jets established at JFK in 1971 and unique in the Northeast. That particular repair facility added six thousand jobs and a payroll of $80 million, which was a major boost for regional industrial employment, but the high labor costs of the New York region added to the airline's financial problems.[1] Pan Am would eventually become a bankrupt relic of the postwar industrial model that had been built upon protective regulations, limited competition, high profit margins, generous pay, massive fixed costs, and cheap fuel.

Pan Am was not the only airline to suffer during this period. The recession and fuel crisis of the early 1970s cut back on air traffic nationally. Airplanes designed and built in the era of cheap oil turned out to be ill-suited to the straitened circumstances of the early 1970s and were difficult to run at profitable levels: "In 1973, the embargo raised the price of jet fuel from $.13–$.40 a gallon, putting a whammy on the airlines from which they still haven't recovered."[2] Growth in passenger numbers stalled in 1973–74 at JFK and did not resume their upward climb until 1976.[3] Many airlines in the country eliminated routes and employees, but an estimated 10 to 25 percent of the approximated seventeen thousand layoffs nationally came from the metropolitan New York area. Aviator-rich neighborhoods, such as Lloyd Harbor in Huntington, home to many pilots, were hit hard.[4]

The 1970s recession and a new emphasis across party lines on free-market competition forced a reassessment of the government's commitments to social and regulatory regimes both in New York and the nation as a whole. The large "legacy" airlines, such as Pan Am and TWA, that occupied the expensive unit terminals at JFK had prospered in an environment of regulation and protection in everything from routes to labor, and had made major investments in the best and most expensive aircraft of the day. They had also made very generous deals with their unions during the profitable 1960s to keep their planes running without disruptive labor issues. President Jimmy Carter's deregulation of the aircraft industry in 1978 in response to growing public pressure for lower fares and greater competition therefore bode ill for New York.

The legacy lines' massive debts from capital investments in planes and buildings, luxury service, and high labor costs became disadvantages in competition with new, low-cost airlines at less crowded, more affordable airports. Airlines had added additional costs by competing more over service quality than price (because prices were more or less fixed by the government), leading to better service and food in order to attract customers, even if these extras cut into profits. Deregulation, however, "permanently ended the genteel old days when high fares were fixed by fiat, and the airlines, like members of some kind of gentleman's club, were only nominally in competition with each other."[5] According to T. A. Heppenheimer, a leading expert on the airline industry, between 1938 and 1978 federal officials not only kept airline mergers to a minimum, but "no major airline had ever gone bankrupt; the CAB's fares had seen to that." When smaller airlines did fail, federal officials had usually folded them into healthier lines in order to maintain service. Deregulation ended the well-mannered bankruptcy.[6]

In a time of growing airline competition, JFK desperately needed upgrades if it was to regain its leadership, but the decentralized terminal unit system from both a physical and financial standpoint inhibited renovation: "Kennedy's headache began more than a decade ago" because "deregulation meant carriers could use a new generation of long-range aircraft and twin jets to open a slew of new international gateways on both coasts and in the heartland, bypassing JFK."[7] Complicated real-estate and industrial park investments rather than day-to-day transportation management distracted the Port Authority in the 1960s and 1970s from JFK. The airport, in addition, was now a steady source of capital for new projects regardless of customer satisfaction. The fact that the Port Authority lacked the power to expand the airport or its runways probably made top officials less interested in its future prospects, which now appeared dimmer.[8]

Airlines at JFK judged that many business and tourist travelers destined for New York would continue using JFK no matter how decrepit the facilities. The willingness of cities elsewhere to invest aggressively in new, multi-airline facilities allowed surviving airlines low-cost national growth even as revenues could be banked from steady service at an aging airport such as JFK. JFK's distantly separated unit terminals, high labor costs, crowded skies, and reputation for unpleasantness gave airlines a free pass: "New York's tarnished image among travelers," lack of mass transit, "as well as clogged roads, poor connections between terminals and long lines through customs" provided a justification for limited investment.[9]

The nation's fastest-growing airports, such as Atlanta's Hartsfield, usually had access to more land, lower-cost labor, more or better configured runways, clearer skies, and better connected terminal space (central terminals with extensions), and they were designed or redesigned to accommodate the demands of the hub-and-spoke system. Carriers now gathered passengers from across the country at smaller destinations in their hubs and then loaded them densely into outbound planes to final destinations. At Hartsfield, for instance, three out of of four passengers stayed inside the airport because most were bound for points beyond Atlanta; underground passageways, people movers, and moving sidewalks eventually whisked passengers across the terminals and past stores eager for their dollars.[10]

JFK was poorly suited to function as a hub not only because of its unique terminal unit system but because New York regional air operations remained clogged in spite of efforts by federal and Port Authority officials to reduce packing.[11] Because of the demands of many business travelers and others to travel at the end of the workday, restrictions on noise in Europe where many planes were bound, and the fact that three airports operated in close proximity, New York's regional airports bogged down at peak times. Large airports in other parts of the country were usually located far away from other airports because there were fewer cities (with their own airports) in the immediate vicinity.

The antilabor stance of President Ronald Reagan's administration only made the situation worse. Overworked and stressed air-traffic controllers at the Westbury, New York, air-traffic control center faced an even worse quality of life after Reagan fired 11,000 striking air-traffic controllers across the nation in 1981. It was difficult enough to recruit new controllers in New York because of the high cost of living and extremely stressful work; more planes for fewer controllers did nothing to help the situation. An airport with chronic delays made a very poor hub in a system that demanded nearly every passenger transfer at least once.[12]

The legacy airlines' solutions to the deregulation crisis varied and included one or more of the following elements: bankruptcy, mergers, labor cutbacks and nonunion labor, and shifting of high-cost service and maintenance functions to lower-cost regions. At the same time, surviving airlines

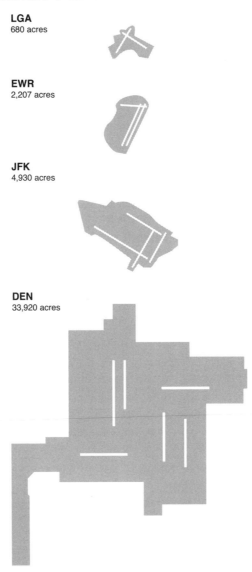

NEW YORK'S AIRPORTS COMPARED TO DENVER INTERNATIONAL AIRPORT

Source: Regional Plan Association

LGA
680 acres

EWR
2,207 acres

JFK
4,930 acres

DEN
33,920 acres

FIGURE 29. JFK International was a large airport for its day, and quite large compared with Newark and LaGuardia, but it is comparatively small when held up against enormous new fields such as that in Denver. Courtesy of the Regional Plan Association.

maintained their profitable routes in New York City, further taxing old terminals. While there had only been 46 airlines in the United States before 1976, that number grew to 270 in the early 1980s, but then fell back down to 69.[13]

In the era of deregulation of the 1980s and 1990s, the following corporate restructurings damaged JFK's global status and made renovation and upgrades unlikely: Pan Am went bankrupt in 1991; TWA moved to Westchester in 1987 and subsequently went bankrupt; Eastern moved to Miami in 1976 and later went bankrupt; and American shifted to Dallas-Fort Worth in 1979. Northwest took over the Eastern shuttle, and Delta took on the Pan Am shuttle. New York's Cold War-era defense aviation industry on Long Island also collapsed in the 1990s.[14] Were it not for New York's market power and location astride transatlantic routes, New York's traditional aviation sector might have contracted even more.

JFK remained the hands-down leader in New York for international travel, with over 17 million passengers in 1987 (compared with about 6.5 million passengers in 1967) on a remarkably similar number of planes (77,299 movements in 1967 vs. 85,553 movements in 1987).[15] Despite greater efficiency brought by 747s, in the 1980s, JFK continued to lose its overwhelming share of American international traffic, dropping dramatically in that decade from handling 38 percent of all international traffic (already much reduced from the 1960s) in the United States to 32 percent by 1990. This decline took place in spite of a significant absolute increase in passengers at JFK in that same period of almost 5 million and continued leadership in transatlantic travel. Americans were still flying abroad, but more and more of them were avoiding New York.[16]

JFK also faced regional competition in the growing domestic and international service at Newark, which by 1990 was growing more rapidly than JFK. People's Express, for instance, a bold attempt at cut-rate pricing and service in the new deregulated marketplace, made Newark its East Coast hub in 1983. Although Continental absorbed People's in 1987, Newark continued its steady climb as both a domestic and international airport. Annual domestic airline plane movements at JFK slipped from a high of 262,343 in 1967 to 108,725 in 1987, whereas both Newark and LaGuardia each handled over 260,000 movements in 1987 and steadily increased from there. This was not simply a matter of more passengers on larger planes at JFK, as in international travel, because JFK was still handling about the same number of domestic passengers in the 1980s (fluctuating between eleven

million and thirteen million) as it had in the 1960s, but LaGuardia and
Newark were each handling over twenty million domestic passengers by the
mid-1980s.[17]

The fading role of JFK in domestic routes resulted from a number of
sources. Newark and LaGuardia usually offered faster commutes to Manhattan; many companies now had expanded headquarters in New Jersey.[18]
Continental Airline's massive hub at Newark, in particular, reflected that
airline's pioneering embrace of the hub system, aggressive pricing, and lean
operations that would undercut the other legacy lines such as TWA, United,
and American at JFK. By 1999, for instance, Continental moved over seventeen million passengers through Newark alone (more than eight times its
closest competitor there). Some critics of the Port Authority believed as
well that the Port Authority was shifting its profits from JFK and other
airports to subsidize chronic money losers like the PATH system and Port
Authority Bus Terminal, making the airports of the region less attractive as
a whole to passengers.[19]

For these complex reasons, and despite some bright spots such as Continental, the New York region's importance in the national aviation picture
declined. Other cities captured the lion's share of new hiring in the still
growing aviation sector. As proof of this, *Newsday* reported that "airline
employment in the city has dropped in the past two decades while nationwide it has doubled." Airport employment in Queens, including LaGuardia
and JFK, dropped from 57,000 in 1970 to 52,000 in 1991; nationally, aviation employment jumped from 352,000 to 750,000. Even flight attendants
and pilots resisted living in the New York area because of the city's reputation for high crime and expensive living. These temporary residents
crowded into bare bones "crash pads" in neighborhoods like Kew Gardens
in Queens near the airport while maintaining their permanent residences
in lower-cost cities or towns on their routes. Dry cleaners, bars, and restaurants made some money, as did landlords eager to subdivide their homes
and apartments, but temporary residents like these did not contribute at
the same level as had unionized, well-paid employees (including pilots)
who made New York their home in an earlier time.[20]

New York could ill afford to lose so many middle-class jobs. The region
as a whole experienced a growing gap between the income of the college
educated and everyone else. The aviation industry employed many highly
educated and trained individuals, but also large numbers of less well-
educated folks who nonetheless had earned high wages for supporting such

aviation activities as air cargo, airplane maintenance, and catering.[21] Pan Am was the biggest loss in 1991 because of the large number of employees who actually lived in Brooklyn, Queens, and Long Island and the high wages and benefits the company offered its unionized employees. Delta, which took over the major Pan Am routes, was not unionized to the same degree (primarily pilots) and quickly reduced Pan Am staff. Experts at the time calculated that three thousand jobs were lost in addition to many service contracts essential to the local economy. "Because the carrier was headquartered in New York, it purchased much of its supplies and equipment locally, pumping tens of millions into the regional economy."[22] Only the overseas employees of Pan Am managed to keep their positions in the 1990s and only because of labor protections that existed in other countries.[23]

JFK's downward mobility continued in the 1990s. Between 1991 and 1999, the airport slipped from seventh to fourteenth busiest American passenger airport. During this same time, Newark (led by Continental) grew 46 percent; Los Angeles International grew by 41 percent; and even crowded O'Hare grew by 23 percent. JFK and LaGuardia grew at a rate of only about 16 percent, albeit on a larger starting base than many other airports in the country. By the 1990s, JFK was a large, international airport, but it was no longer the dominant player it once had been. A sure sign of the decline was the Port Authority's habit of lumping together its combined New York aviation figures for the three airports in order to illustrate the region's continued national leadership.[24]

Social Darwinism: The Breakdown of Order at the Airport

Disorder of many types within the airport underlined the slipping status of the airport as a whole. Administrators at JFK International found it impossible to isolate the airport from the aggressive urban disorder infecting the city at the time. The tourists and affluent travelers (from both the surrounding city and suburbs) in the 1980s often encountered the "real" New York at JFK without venturing into the city's disordered neighborhoods. Most outsiders picture the New York renaissance as dating from the 1980s, and the city did rebound as a hub of global finance, tourism, and gentrification, but these years included the seamier crack epidemic and crime wave that engulfed the subaltern city.

The declining terminals were one of only many unpleasant experiences faced by passengers at JFK. The declining quality of the interiors resulted from long-term financial problems of the airlines and a resistance on the part of the Port Authority to commit necessary funds to upgrading the IAB. The moldering landscape might have been acceptable if crime and other forms of social disorder had not accompanied the decay. The "broken windows" of aging terminals sent a strong message of tolerance for criminality. In 1998, for instance, Volunteers of America outreach workers began working with what they claimed were hundreds of homeless citizens living in waiting areas and bathrooms around New York City airports. JFK, in particular, was so notorious that it ended up becoming the setting for a feature film starring Tom Hanks, *The Terminal*, about a homeless migrant who takes up residence at the airport. While the Port Authority always denied that homelessness was a major issue, even administrators had to admit that New York's terminals suffered from the ills that also beset the city and its people.[25]

The many hours that luggage lingered in JFK between long connection times, for instance, created wonderful opportunities for pilfering. The problem of Mafia-driven crime was in part replaced by low-level crimes of opportunity. It did not help that this was an era when lower-paid contract laborers, as opposed to long-term employees, played a growing role in luggage handling. The Port Authority in 1984 alone admitted to $2 million in stolen luggage and pickpocketing, but one federal official thought it even higher. Officials reported 4,277 crimes at Kennedy and 900 arrests in that year alone. Even if an arriving passenger gathered his or her luggage successfully, risk remained. Self-service baggage carts created opportunities for "hundreds of freewheeling hustlers to retrieve the wagons for their $.25 return fee" and took to "cruising the terminals, stealing baggage from the carts and fleecing passengers with a host of confidence schemes." According to the authorities, and widely featured in *The New York Times*, the hustler problem could be traced "to the large number of homeless people, some of whom live in the airport, and to the spreading crack addiction in neighborhoods near Kennedy." These criminals even earned a sobriquet, "Smarte Carte Hustlers," in deference to their skill. Hustlers perfected many schemes: returning carts for the one-dollar deposit, acting as unofficial porters, collecting taxi fares to nowhere, or just stealing luggage. Skycaps, the unionized and official porters at the airport, estimated that there were between three hundred to four hundred hustlers operating at the airport;

Skycaps also reported violent attacks by hustlers and loss of income as a result of both the Smarte Carte system and the actions of unregistered porters. After making their money, hustlers sometimes took taxis out to Rockaway Boulevard in South Ozone Park, scored crack, and then smoked it in airport parking lots. Port Authority administrators were quick to point out to a reporter that in the fifty-five cities that adopted Smarte Cartes before New York, no similar crime problems had developed. Yet this high level of criminality at JFK persisted into the 1990s.[26]

Outrageous episodes reported in the papers over the years highlighted the daily chaos. Unscrupulous taxi drivers contributed to this drama—for decades. Weekend taxi shortages in 1970, for instance, created opportunities for "unlicensed Gypsy drivers, who charge outrageous rates."[27] In 1979, 422 cabbies were suspended at JFK and LaGuardia after a five-month crackdown when they were caught red-handed overcharging or refusing to take passengers.[28] Dispatchers were arrested in 1983 for taking kickbacks from cabbies for long-haul fares.[29] Hustling cab drivers in 1989 still often forced people into cars, sometimes took passports, airline tickets, and luggage until paid a certain amount: "When Port Authority police try to drive hustlers away by cracking down on illegal parking and loitering in front of terminals, hustlers became increasingly bold, worked in gangs, and used walkie-talkies to coordinate pickups and to monitor police movement." The hustlers were in essence running a kidnapping scheme that involved driving people around (and threatening their lives), all while demanding large sums of cash. Even today the Port Authority posts a warning to arriving passengers that they should avoid unregulated taxis.[30]

Driving a private car to the airport was not a silver bullet for avoiding crime. Long-term parking was a potential bonanza for criminals as cars became sitting ducks in poorly secured parking fields. In long-term parking, for instance, in just the first nine months of 1985, 73 cars and 489 car parts were stolen.[31] As one security officer reminded a reporter, "You have to remember that there are about 35,000 parking spots out here." It was hard to monitor all those spots, particularly as individuals could walk freely among the cars while posing as a car owner, airport traveler, or employee, simply looking for their vehicle.[32]

The Port Authority had taken some steps over the years to improve security. By 1980 there were 270 Port Authority police officers, 700 federal agents (including customs, postal, Drug Enforcement Agency, and Federal Bureau of Investigation), as well as 1,000 private security officers at JFK whose aim was to tame the urban disorder: "We've got the same problems out here that they have any place—thefts, people passing bad checks, car strippers, pickpockets, sick people."[33] Not exactly anyplace, to be sure, but certainly this kind of behavior aligned with 1980s-era New York City. And it was not that simple to crack down on crime because "you hit the hustlers heavy, and you risk seeing an increase in pickpockets, baggage thefts, parking lot break-ins. It's a delicate balance."[34]

There was also the matter of narcotics traffic. JFK served as a major port of entry for cocaine; financiers and crack addicts alike needed cocaine in the 1980s. Customs officials estimated that 90 percent of cocaine zoomed past authorities. A certain percentage of this illicit cargo took a more unorthodox route into the country, one made possible by the increasing speed of jets in the era. Human "mules" swallowed cocaine in Colombia, sometimes up to two pounds, and then were forced to excrete it on arrival. West African couriers, on the other hand, usually swallowed only heroin. This traffic became the subject of a motion picture, *Maria Full of Grace*.[35] In 2003, for instance, "145 drug mules were intercepted at New York's JFK Airport (38 women, 107 men)." With the airport's enormous volume of global traffic, it is not a stretch to imagine that the traffic actually intercepted is still only the tip of an enormous criminal iceberg.[36]

Illegal imports of other kinds also slid through JFK. Knockoffs and other gray market-manufactured clothing and handbags, sporting fake designer labels and styles that violated trade restrictions, were known to be coming through JFK from Asia. Customs officials did their best to identify the knockoffs, which became a major business on New York's sidewalks, but the volume of cargo and luggage at JFK meant that catching much of this material was difficult. According to customs officials, "Most fraud doubtlessly evades detection. On a good day, Mr. Pfeiffer and his 4 colleagues see perhaps 5 to 10 shipments. 'It's like standing under a spout spewing grains of rice and trying to catch them. . . . We're so understaffed it's ridiculous.'"[37]

JFK had by this time developed the reverse image of the new urban district sought by its promoters in the 1950s. The airport was no longer a great exhibition of American know-how and ambitions. The schemes and corruption administrators hoped to inoculate the airport against had lodged firmly into the daily operations of this supposedly secluded and thoroughly modern facility. The airport was losing its share of international travel, and its claim to global leadership in world aviation seemed to rest primarily on Atlantic routes fed by New York's unique role in global tourism and business. No one considered it particularly beautiful either. The once glamorous terminals, poorly maintained and crowded, had lost much of their luster. Its unique unit terminal system staggered to support the still heavy traffic. Delays echoed out from the crowded airspace. Travelers struggled to get to and from the airport. Asking New Yorkers to appreciate the airport's strengths was a difficult proposition for the Port Authority in this period.

CHAPTER 6

Resilience of a Global Hub

JFK International was slipping as the nation's global hub, and so was New York as the nation's dominant industrial and financial region, but neither the airport nor the region in which it was located fell as far as many had predicted. New York changed a great deal, but the metropolitan area bestowed gifts upon JFK that leaders in other cities only dreamed of. While the city's aviation sector was hit hard by deregulation, JFK proved resilient in large measure because highly lucrative sectors of the New York economy came roaring back in the deregulated 1980s. JFK took the first major hits from the initial era of deregulation, losing many legacy carriers and highly paid middle-class employees, but the airport continued to benefit from deregulation in key areas.

New York City's near bankruptcy in 1975 and its growing social problems convinced some experts that New York's future depended upon "planned shrinkage" of the city's generous services and neighborhoods to focus resources more wisely. As factories moved to the suburbs or Sunbelt, the Bronx burned, unions marched for higher pay, the middle class decamped for whiter suburbs, and the graffiti-covered subways lurched and screeched through their tunnels, it was easy to lose faith in the city's resilience. The financial and social crisis in New York City obscured the metropolitan area's underlying strength. Continued economic strength remained in pastoral suburban office and research parks, suburban downtowns and malls, and affluent suburban neighborhoods. Within the city, all was not lost either. The city's high-rent Midtown skyscrapers and luxury districts enjoyed continued popularity. A new era of immigration began refilling many working-class neighborhoods. Government policies, while reduced in scale, contributed to urban health. The large public payrolls maintained middle-class employment on a grand scale; the city's affordable housing policies (public housing and city-funded renovation) helped maintain the city's population base; and Mayor Ed Koch's administration policies encouraged private investment and fiscal conservatism.

Many dimensions of life had changed, however, in the metropolitan area. The New York region polarized in the 1980s into a successful "dual city," defined, as New York had been for most its history, by extremes. The collapse of the New Deal labor system, suburbanization, and deindustrialization divided New York society again into much more clearly defined groups of highly educated workers in the FIRE (finance, insurance, and real estate) sector in Manhattan and the wealthy suburbs facing off against low-skilled workers in declining factories or growing, low-paid service industries. The Manhattan of luxurious living and global enterprises, and leafy Westchester and Nassau suburbs of office parks and plush schools, existed at a remove from the still gritty city filled by a large working class, mostly immigrant or minority, struggling day-to-day for survival. The older white middle or working class either decamped for white suburbs, retired to warmer climates, or bitterly clung to a few white, "defended" outer borough neighborhoods and the remaining unionized public-sector or construction jobs. Immigrants had started to revive many city neighborhoods, and many filled professional positions; but their existence on the margins helped undermine the formal labor relations and big government of the New Deal era that had temporarily modulated inequality in postwar New York.[1]

The restructuring of the financial services industry contributed to inequality by generating extraordinarily high salaries for a comparatively small number of employees. Financial deregulation gave rise to such creative financial activities as junk bonds, hedge funds, merger and acquisitions, collateralized debt obligations, and derivatives in the New York region. Global financial activity among interconnected urban hubs, such as New York, London, Paris, Tokyo, and Hong Kong, also supported very profitable traffic, particularly in business class and Concorde service. New York's financial elite grew rich as they circled the globe making deals and pitches. The New York-New Jersey region added 650,000 jobs between 1977 and 1984; of these, an impressive 200,000 were in Manhattan alone, most of these in the FIRE service sector, such as banking and securities. Wall Street in 1985 still accounted for more than half of the world's equities markets.[2]

Gloomy predictions that global telecommunication and suburbanization would destroy all central places such as New York thus proved dead
wrong. The resilience of the New York region, even with its high labor,
taxes, and housing costs, came as a surprise to many experts but not all of
them. Columbia University sociologist Saskia Sassen predicted that select
global cities like New York and London would continue to flourish because
of the knowledge and capital requirements demanded by global and inter-
nationalized firms: "The more globalized the economy becomes, the higher
the agglomeration of central functions in a relatively few sites, that is, the
global cities." Manhattan may have lost its preeminence in American business life, yet even in the 1980s it still had the greatest concentration of
headquarters for transnational firms in the world.[3] Business services had
become critical not only for New York but for the nation. In 1990 alone,
the United States exported $120 billion in business services.[4]

Out in New York's suburbs, too, the luxurious corporate headquarters
of global firms such as Pepsico and IBM also relied upon excellent air connections out of New York's regional air system. Eventually hedge funds
and other financial services corporations in Connecticut added to suburban
wealth and commerce. These high-paying jobs not only preserved the
cachet of elite neighborhoods across the region, and gentrified areas such
as Park Slope where the business class reinvested in decayed neighborhoods, but these positions helped maintain global business travel and overnight delivery at the region's major airports. With so much personal wealth
in the suburbs, families traveled a great deal, and very far, for pleasure as
indicated by the exotic locales chronicled in the *New York Times*.

The financial firms both needed JFK (and LaGuardia) and helped keep
the two dated airports competitive. Business travel accounted for about 40
percent of JFK's traffic and 60 percent of LaGuardia's passenger base, and
was very profitable for airlines because of the high prices paid for last-
minute and business class travel.[5] A survey in 1979 found that "more than
half of all firms in the region consider air passenger service 'important' or
'very important' to their businesses. . . . Nearly half of all firms in the
region consider air cargo services 'important' or 'very important' to their
businesses." Firms from abroad with offices in New York reported that it
was crucial to have quick transportation back to their home countries and
was "one of the most important reasons for locating their businesses in
New York." These foreign companies accounted for 8 percent of New York
City's total employment and 15 percent of its banking employment.[6] In

1985, the region's airports offered 1,800 nonstop flights per week to 79 overseas cities (mostly at JFK) and 15,000 nonstops to 81 American cities (spread among the region's airports). An impressive 60 percent of all American transatlantic travel still passed through JFK alone.[7]

Above all, New York remained a goliath in business services. *Five of the six largest accounting firms, eight of ten advertising firms, and seven of the top ten management consulting firms were still headquartered in the New York region.* And these firms had employees who had to move quickly around the nation and the globe: "To function effectively in an integrated global economy, these firms must have quick and easy access to, and be accessible from, every corner of the world."[8] Air travelers tended to be high-status individuals in fields such as management and administration and had higher annual incomes and greater education than the population as a whole. Despite the challenge of reaching JFK and the inevitable flight delays, the number and variety of global destinations accessible through JFK bestowed competitive advantages for time-sensitive deal making and communication. In 1999, for instance, JFK hosted, on average per week, 141 direct flights to London, 55 direct flights to Paris, and 31 direct flights to Tokyo. A traveler, in fact, could choose every week from among 84 different direct international destinations.[9]

New York's reemergence as a tourist destination gave the city's airports an additional boost. The important role of the tourism industry in New York City's economy offered growing and lucrative business that kept JFK a leader in transatlantic travel. New York's airport administrators admitted in 1980, "we have much more competition with additional cities in the Midwest and in the Sun Belt being granted gateway status, but Kennedy will remain the premier, international airport because New York will remain the Number One attraction for both the tourist and business traveler."[10] Foreign students, who also flooded into the colleges in the New York in an era of a weakened dollar, helped support the same global routes.

New York's creative class, including pacesetting figures such as graphic designer Milton Glaser and flamboyant Mayor Ed Koch, had the talent and audacity to rebrand New York positively after decades of bad press. Glaser designed the famous "I Love New York" logo in 1977 that government (including the Port Authority) and private organizations promoted. New York as a renewed center of global entertainment and media also helped generate desire for a taste of the real item. Woody Allen's appealing New York characters and sophisticated conversations, glamorous sendups of

Wall Street financiers, and yuppie television series such as *The Cosby Show* and *Seinfeld* replaced New York's rough image with images of comfortable homes, charming people, and well-off families.

The transformation of New York into a tourist mecca was not a natural evolution but was the result of choices on the part of New Yorkers. The Koch administration's assertion of control over urban systems in the 1970s and 1980s, such as subways, and the market-driven gentrification of neighborhoods such as Soho, backed up the rebranding campaign by making the traveler's experience in New York sweeter. Extensive public-private redevelopment at Times Square and Bryant Park reached a critical mass in the 1990s as the rough edges were pushed to the background, replaced by a family-friendly landscape of tightly-controlled public spaces, bright lights, theaters, eateries, and trinket shops. For travelers, it became easier again to love New York.[11]

For the affluent international travelers visiting New York, JFK was often the worst part of most tourism packages. Few could imagine that a decade or two ago people once visited JFK to catch a glimpse of the future. Almost 60 percent of those who used JFK arrived for nonbusiness in 1985, but the pleasure only started once you left the airport.[12] The importance of the tourist trade grew at JFK over time. In 1999, for instance, 25 percent of passengers at JFK arrived on business, whereas 75 percent came for nonbusiness.[13] International passenger numbers at JFK increased from 13,614,290 in 1986 to 17,931,734 in 1999.[14]

Just as important in maintaining global routes at JFK was the restarting of New York's immigrant tradition in the 1960s. The airport had welcomed Puerto Rican migrants in the 1950s (and some Eastern Europeans on flights run by the International Committee for European Migration), but immigration restriction had temporarily ended New York's role as gateway to America.[15] The Johnson administration's lifting of immigration restriction in 1965, however, not only restarted the cycle of immigrant life in New York's neighborhoods, but it also created further opportunities for international travel at JFK. As a decentralized, loosely controlled, and crowded airport boasting daily destinations around the globe, JFK became the unheralded Ellis Island for immigrants. The customs facilities at JFK, with its "shiny walls and sharp angles of a fast-food franchise," lacked the drama of Ellis Island, but it was now playing the same role for a new generation.[16] After 1965 many immigrants from Asia, the Americas, Africa, and Eastern Europe could now afford to fly in comfort at a greater speed to their new lives. Instead of losing further population, New York as a city and region picked up speed as chain migration (family members sponsored migration of their relatives) generated thriving immigrant enclaves. During the 1980s, about eighty thousand immigrants a year came just to New York City; and in the 1990s, more than a hundred thousand arrived each year.[17]

Many immigrants settled into manual work, including driving cabs to the airport. Yet the city also welcomed the middle and upper classes from the Dominican Republic, Jamaica, and China. These newcomers often brought administrative or professional skills with them and helped restore economic vitality to neighborhoods across the five boroughs. The immigrants did compete with some groups in skilled areas such as construction, but they also opened new businesses, sent their kids to public and private schools and colleges, and generally aided in the revival of the city and many suburbs. By 2012 immigrants owned 31.2 percent of all New York City's businesses.[18] Immigrants in the New York region also enjoyed ethnic-identified stores, professional services, and religious institutions that reduced the sense of isolation from their coethnics and home countries. New York's mostly legal immigrants arrived by a comparatively expensive plane flight, with some papers, and were attracted by opportunities for education and work in well-paid fields in an economy emphasizing services (in both cities and suburbs) as well as manual fields.[19] Between 2000 and 2005 the percentage of immigrants with some college education entering New York was 52 percent.[20]

Not long ago, for instance, primarily native-born, white residents dominated affluent suburban Westchester County. That county in 2013, however, features a population that is 44 percent minority. Some of these changes have to do with growing working-class Hispanic and African American populations in the county's cities (such as White Plains and Yonkers), but the county's educated, highly skilled immigrant population, which could probably live anywhere, is also growing rapidly and changing the face of success in nearly every Westchester town. The same is true in Nassau County, southern Connecticut, and large areas of northern New Jersey.

The precise role of JFK in creating this diverse profile of immigrants, as compared with other "pull" factors in the region, is difficult to determine. Nevertheless, the large number of direct flights from around the globe to JFK, with increasingly moderate fares, encourages immigrants to both come to New York and stay there because of the ease of visiting and trading with the sending country. For the immigrants who have settled in New York, the airport's extensive global service supports important personal, financial, and cultural links to such home countries as the Dominican Republic and South Korea. In 1999, for instance, the Dominican Republic was the sixth most popular international origin from or destination out of JFK and Seoul was twelfth. These tight connections to the sending country helped maintain excellent service to the Caribbean, Asia, and Eastern Europe.[21]

The immigration story of the New York region and JFK is mostly one of legal or documented immigration, but illegal or undocumented immigration is also a small but important part of the story. In 2014, New York's immigrant population is estimated at 10 percent undocumented, a very low percentage compared with other major immigrant destinations in the United States. JFK from the 1970s to the 1990s became a comparatively easy entry point into the United States because it combined two classic New York characteristics: high volume and administrative laxity. Tolerance of illegal immigration took place because there was simply nowhere to place those who arrived without documents or those claiming political asylum. In one month in December 1992, for instance, two thirds of the nine hundred people released into the community with court dates never showed up again:[22] "Kennedy, more than any other airport in the country, has been flooded by travelers with forged papers, tampered passports, or no passports at all who walk off their planes and ask for political asylum." With just two hundred beds in detention centers, few could be held (in contrast to LAX, for instance, where a concerted effort was made to hold undocumented arrivals).[23] JFK, for instance, became an important point in an international smuggling operation connected to China.[24] Those arriving from Europe had an even easier time; large numbers of migrants from Ireland, Poland, and Italy overstayed their tourist visa in the 1990s. There was little chance of being caught in New York until the late 1990s (when a larger detention center was built). *In the New York region in 1995, the Immigration and Naturalization Service had only fifteen agents to investigate fifteen counties that held twelve million people.* This number of agents did not represent much of a threat to undocumented immigrants.[25]

During the decades since 1965, countless immigrants have certainly benefited from the global airport in their midst. The region, in turn, has profited from their contributions to economy and culture. It is true that immigrants would likely find their way to New York in any case, but a globally connected airport made a major difference in restarting and sustaining the region's immigrant engine. Many cities around the country, such as St. Louis, are trying to reposition themselves as gateway cities in the hopes of renewing their population base through immigration. Based upon New York's success in this area (and that of other gateways such as Los Angeles and Miami), there is reason for hope that immigration can play such a role in urban revival.

A Subsidized Penthouse in the Sky

An additional and controversial sign of the continuing economic strength of the region was the establishment in the 1970s of the fastest form of passenger service ever attempted. The Concorde (supersonic transport, or SST), shortening the trip from London to New York to just over three hours, represented a potential windfall for the city and region in the 1970s. A Manhattan advertising executive on the French Concorde for its first flight on November 22, 1977, bragged that the cost of high-speed travel was "only $140 more than first class on a regular jet," conveniently overlooking that a first-class ticket in this time was far beyond the reach of average Americans pinched hard by the recession. A reporter from the *Daily News* along for the ride reported that "time passed quickly for the 100 passengers on each plane. Champagne and other drinks flowed like jet fuel. Food never stopped coming during the flight. Aboard the French plane were canapés, liver Pate, lobster, lamb filet, pastries." This epicurean ride across the Atlantic now could be made in as little as three-and-a-half hours thanks to government subsidy.[26]

The Concorde was routed to New York at this time because the plane's operators, Air France and British Airways, knew full well that metropolitan New York had the wealth and travel volume to support this new luxury service. The service would theoretically endow New York with tremendous competitive advantages at the top levels of the global order. New York had businessmen, politicians, celebrities, and wealthy travelers with the treasure to pay stratospheric prices for supersonic travel. Other rich Americans would travel to New York just to take the plane. The long-term failure of the Concorde, however, had as much to do with the unique characteristic of the New York region. A dense urban region, with strong activist tradition, turned out to be surprisingly hostile territory for disruptive technology.

The Concorde program was one of the last gasps of the big government, modernist projects (paralleling similar efforts in the space program or nuclear technology) but with a postmodern twist. Even though the SST absorbed enormous French and British public funds to create and operate, it was a government-funded program that, unlike most social democratic programs in housing, health care, and social welfare, had wealthy people as clients. The rich people on the Concorde still paid a lot for the seats, but the real operating costs were externalized to communities and to government taxpayers. The Concorde became a notoriously ridiculous undertaking after fuel costs skyrocketed in the early 1970s. What began as an international effort that would bolster French and British technological prestige, bridge oceans, and bring people closer together ended up highlighting the growing gap between the rich and everyone else. The success of the 747 more or less doomed the Concorde program; airlines had no use for, and no money left, for a tiny (about 120 passengers per flight), gas-guzzling, and super-fast aircraft.[27]

The pressure for the SST program came from the highest levels of government in both the United States and in Europe. In an era of good feeling, the Nixon administration in 1973 promised to push at all costs for the SST's right to land in the United States despite the certain uproar over their environmental impact. The SST was a showpiece of postwar European cooperation every bit as important to European governments as America's trip to the Moon. America had abandoned its own SST program because of complexity, costs, and environmental impact (and we had already landed on the Moon), but Europe clung to the program as an outstanding example of European engineering. Marcel Cavaille, French secretary of state for transportation, demanded, in an interview, "We'll cease the battle when we win . . . over the faint bubbling of iced Perrier water in good scotch."[28] The Concorde absolutely had to come to New York to tap the rich vein of first-class passengers the Europeans knew could pay the premium for superior flight speed. Yet New York City was in a sense attracting trouble by its centrality to the global economy.[29]

The Concorde's problems started long before the first flight. In 1975, an environmental impact statement offered a number of troubling findings for the New York region. The report's authors had discovered that the sound generated by the Concorde would be distinctive and would be perceived as louder than other planes. In fact, it would achieve four times the noisiness of a 747 and would be eight times as loud as the DC-10. Many more people than before would now live in areas subject to high noise levels. Nor was the SST defensible from an energy perspective. In an era of growing criticism of petroleum in terms of air pollution and oil spills, Concorde fuel consumption was shockingly bad. A completely loaded 747 with 375 people aboard gulped 65 gallons of fuel per passenger for a transatlantic trip, yielding a gallon-per-passenger-mile rate of 0.021. This was bad enough, but the Concorde on a similar journey would use 190 gallons of fuel per passenger while racking up a gas-guzzling 0.063 gallons of fuel per passenger mile.[30]

Under pressure supplied by British, French, and American political leaders, the Environmental Protection Agency (EPA) nevertheless approved Concorde operations in 1975 on a limited basis. At one point, EPA officials asserted that the Concorde sound impact was basically indistinguishable from the Boeing 747 when operating at subsonic levels, which it was required to do over New York.[31] Residents sprang into action. Even the Queens Chamber of Commerce stood against the FAA because of the small number of people that the Concorde served as opposed to the massive noise disturbance: "The Queens Chamber is not opposed to technological progress advancement but we must insist on progress that does not have serious environmental consequences. And we must oppose a program that endangers the continued successful operation of Kennedy International."[32] Sensing the power of local opposition, and standing to gain little from SST operations, the Port Authority put a ban on Concorde operations in 1976 that held for only about one year.

Massive motorcade protests in 1976 and 1977, filled by mostly middle-class and very angry residents from surrounding communities aimed to cut off the airport by clogging its roads. The number of participating cars slipped over the course of 1977 from over a thousand to a few hundred as it became clear that the civil resistance was not going to stop the program.[33] Despite citizen efforts and stalling efforts of the Port Authority, the SSTs went into service in New York in November 1977. The Port Authority permitted this initial service as a result of both a court order and direction by the secretary of transportation. Federal courts had once again affirmed that federal law superseded the Port Authority and considered the Port Authority's ban "discriminatory, arbitrary and unreasonable." Local Concorde opponents called the Port Authority "inept" and "incompetent" for devising limits that failed to sustain legal challenges. It is difficult to imagine how the Port Authority could have actually devised a rule that would have banned the Concorde but still allowed other aircraft to continue operations, because Concorde subsonic operations nominally met existing (if lax) decibel standards when flying over neighborhoods. Concorde supporters seemed to have won the battle.[34]

Pete Hamill wrote the eulogy on the resistance to the Concorde in the *Daily News*. Concorde supporters on the inaugural day were "dressed in expensive woolen suits. . . . They had the tight, glossy, clean shaven faces that come with the franchise when you are in the business of making money for a lot of generations." He contrasted their fine tastes with "the working people on the tarmac" who "would never do anything with the Concorde except help it to park, handle its luggage." The Concorde, he concluded, "was designed as a limousine service for the corporate rich." He chatted up a deplaning investment banker who was excited that he could wedge a full day's work, including two transatlantic crossings, into one day; such speed was an obvious advantage to the global elite concentrated in New York and London in this period. The Concorde became another business service that gave New York renewed power as a financial capital.[35]

Ordinary New Yorkers also viewed the beginning of Concorde service as a clear example of "the big-money interests" buying their way to victory. One study estimated that 172,000 people would feel the impact of Concorde operations in the New York area despite the planes serving just a few people per flight.[36] And the planes, while few in number compared with aviation generally, were uniquely noisy. In spite of the relatively small number of operations in the first year (698 Concorde operations versus 167,313 subsonic operations), the number of Concorde complaints remained heavy. Between November 1977 and June 1978, there were 1,754 complaints about noise from the Concorde versus 2,583 complaints for all subsonic craft.[37] Neighborhoods such as Howard Beach, Cedarhurst, and Rosedale stood out for complaints. Over Cedarhurst, for instance, EPNdB for landings over the community averaged about 99.9 in early operations, generally higher than the subsonic craft operating at the time.[38] The Port Authority and the airlines continued to claim that they were meeting noise standards, but residents of many towns continued to complain of the deep roar and vibration caused by the planes. A resident of Atlantic Beach claimed "that thunderous roar is beyond comprehension." The PNdB rating system, once the cutting edge of noise regulation, now failed to protect communities.[39]

As the years passed, however, the Europeans appeared to have won the battle and lost the war. The Concorde was never allowed to operate freely as a result of coordinated resistance. Concordes became loud, caged birds. FAA restrictions severely limited long-term commercial possibilities for the program that ultimately doomed it.[40] The Concordes under the FAA rules could not exceed the speed of sound on American territory and were only allowed to operate between 7:00 A.M. and 10:00 P.M. Additional Concordes would have to meet higher noise standards in the future (by 1985 they had to meet the standard of the noisiest subsonic planes), and local airports could bar the airliner as long as the rules were fair to all aircraft.[41] The Port Authority thus aimed by 1985 to have in place a general and more restrictive decibel limit for all planes and pursued a broad rule that would not single out the Concorde (and thus be able to survive legal challenges). These types of restrictions, combined with the fuel costs per passenger, led to the cancellation of the next generation of Concorde that might have achieved better fuel and noise performance. In practice, these restrictions meant that the program would expire when the planes aged out of service and would never achieve greater economies of scale.

Concorde service remained a niche in the decades that followed. Most New York and European business and professional travelers could not sufficiently support the high-cost service as a legitimate personal or business expense. The costs were simply too high per seat. On average, in the first part of the twenty-first century, passengers paid $6,000 to go just one way to Europe on the Concorde; even rich people had to pause at that price, especially as the planes aged. A horrid crash in 2000 that killed all aboard scared away many customers and closed service for sixteen months. The program never recovered and was abandoned by its corporate and government sponsors.

Local residents, of course, were excited about the end of the Concorde service: "While pampering the rich and famous, the Concorde touched lives, perhaps 100,000 people living near the airport. . . . It reached into homes, teaching adults to glue their China to cabinet shelves, and into schools, teaching children the letters SST before ABC." Neighbors claimed, "It caused ceilings to crack, eardrums to ring, houses to shake, windows to rattle . . . and car alarms to blare."[42] Others admitted, on balance, "no one went deaf or insane from the noise of the jet, as some had predicted" and "no one's property values fell."[43]

The Concorde's history reflects both the strengths and weaknesses of the New York context. The New York region had the wealth to attract the most advanced aircraft of the age, but the environmental impact of that system in a crowded urban location meant tight limits on the use of this technology that, in part, proved its undoing. The Concorde system had little chance of survival in any case, but its decline does illustrate the pivotal role of environmental and noise politics at JFK and for the nation as a whole. Even in the face of modern technologies and key support by many in the city's business and political arenas, the Concorde program could not escape restrictions that limited its viability.

Air Cargo as Urban Microcosm

In 2014, JFK was still the dominant air-cargo port in the New York region, focusing on key New York consumables and exports rather than dominating the entire air-cargo industry as it once did. Serving the New York region is a solid, lucrative airport business and reveals another hidden strength of the metropolitan context, but it is a more modest role than global leader. In spite of every effort to keep JFK as the leading national air-cargo port, the deregulation of transportation and the complexity of its urban situation made New York's long-term national leadership unlikely to continue forever.

In 1981, the Air Cargo Center at JFK remained the "largest in the world" and was "served by the highest number of flight frequencies, and forwards the greatest amount of total tonnage in the country. This tonnage included almost all half of the air imports and exports for the United States." The air-cargo complex sprawled across 344 acres in 22 buildings with 2.5 million square feet of space. Both on airport grounds and on the edge of the airport, mainly in nearby Queens, hundreds of air-cargo forwarders, consolidators, customs brokers, and truckers coordinated the customs process and movement of the imports to their final destinations.[44]

The Blackball shipping lines, which in the early nineteenth century had gathered coastal exports in New York for European shipment, had been renewed for the air age. Administrators in 1979 boasted that JFK had "national supremacy." One impressive figure illustrates the importance of JFK: of the thirty-seven all-cargo 747 jumbo jets in operation worldwide on a daily basis, twenty-six were based out of JFK International. The jumbo jets had truly become the clipper ships of their day.[45] While the region's aerospace companies, such as Grumman or Sperry, had long relied on air cargo to receive and ship high-value goods, even a Midwestern company such as Honeywell, Inc., producing a range of defense and electronic products in factories across the United States, in the early 1980s sent 140 tons per month of its electronics through JFK for global shipment to Europe and other points. According to executives at the company, JFK had "the greatest number of flights to world destinations of any American airport and offers us great flexibility."[46]

JFK's freight industry updated facilities to a level that at that time were at the front of the class, in contrast to the situation in passenger terminals by the time. These advantages were so extensive that a great deal of cargo never left the airport but simply moved from one plane to another in order to take advantage of the first-class facilities available. Shippers sometimes flew freight from Europe to Africa via the New York air-cargo center to obtain faster service. Other freight came by truck from across the Northeast and Mid-Atlantic region for air shipment at JFK.[47] New York-style corruption remained, but the Port Authority had rationalized the process and reduced the human element as much as possible: "The cargo shed of yesterday has become a giant robot terminal. Automated machinery loads, unloads, and stores containerized airfreight. Computers control documentation. Handling has been speeded to the point of loading and unloading a 747 in less than two hours."[48] The emphasis on mechanization and computerization paralleled the changes at the containerized Elizabeth, New Jersey, seaport where a similar strategy rationalized and streamlined an industry once dependent on large numbers of workers and managers.

U.S. Customs in the 1980s implemented automated cargo clearance to increase efficiency. Rather than poorly screening the mass of goods, customs inspectors now highlighted shippers and their violation rates in order to discern between high- and low-risk shipments for closer examination.[49] A massive foreign trade zone created in the 1980s at JFK created a duty-free air-cargo district within the airport in order to encourage transshipment of goods. "Goods, both finished and unfinished, can be stored, repackaged, exhibited, assembled, or remanufactured in the zone, all without paying any duties until the goods leave." The very real estate of the airport was thus "globalized" legally in order to benefit from and foster the globalization of trade.[50]

Even though it was expensive to operate in New York, the tremendous profits generated by such industries as electronics and pharmaceuticals, and a weak dollar, offset the high cost of labor and real estate. The main air commodities in the mid-1990s included such high-value items as office machinery, electric machinery, precious stones, aircraft parts, works of art, and pharmaceuticals.[51] The critical role of air transportation in the fast-paced global production systems such as fashion is indicated in the fact that apparel alone accounted for about one quarter of New York's air-cargo trade in 1990.[52]

New York City's influx of immigrants boosted New York's specialty air-cargo industry. The famous Korean groceries that opened in New York sourced some of their inventory from "Korean wholesalers and importers who provide the local services sector with new links not just to their home country but to the emerging economies of Southeast Asia as well."[53] By 1995 the New York region accounted for one-fifth of the air cargo to the Far East, with a notable increase in South Korean trade.[54] Local consumption and production became important factors in the air-cargo operations. Yuppie and immigrant taste for exotic fish and sushi boosted importing at JFK, and "the surge seems primarily to be in the big-ticket fish products that are destined for the tables of affluent diners at gourmet restaurants and luxury hotels."[55] In response, the Port Authority added a large Perishable Center at JFK in 1988,[56] the "first at any U.S. airport built solely for the use of handling perishable goods." Only Narita Airport in Japan had more food traffic than JFK. Asian electronics, flooding the American market, frequently arrived on these same cargo flights.[57] Air cargo in the region in the 1980s was still a major driver of economic activity regionally. Air cargo, primarily at JFK, in 1984, for instance, alone counted for $2 billion in wages and $5.3 billion in business activity, and for 93,000 jobs, either direct or related.[58]

The airport proved its resiliency in partnership with a recovering city. Yet the airport's national supremacy in air cargo, as in passenger service, began its slow fade. In 1977 air-cargo deregulation took place under Public Law 95–163. Deregulation opened the door to the rise of competition from such *global* integrated cargo carriers as Federal Express (FedEx) and UPS that now challenged traditional cargo carriers and airlines that moved cargo in their holds, businesses that had made JFK what it was in global and domestic air cargo. Under deregulation, packages, even commercial and industrial shipments, from around the globe and across the nation no longer had to go through separate freight forwarding, frequently changing hands multiple times, but could be delivered door-to-door by integrated carriers such as FedEx (who offered their own freight-forwarding and customs services). FedEx also created aggressive public-relations campaigns that promised, and mostly delivered, extraordinarily fast service.[59]

This shift to a more competitive market hurt the traditional air-cargo carriers; by 1990 integrated carriers dominated 90 percent of the domestic market in the United States: "Federal (Express) and its imitators redefined the cargo market. . . . They cut out domestic forwarders. Today forwarders handle less than 10 percent of domestic air cargo shipments—a far cry from their hold on the business a score of years ago."[60] The New York region became the leader in 1995 for small-package air express business for FedEx and UPS only because of the concentration of business services and media services in the city. Firms such as FedEx concentrated their activities as much as possible at Newark airport because of its superior location in terms of transportation.[61] At the same time, integrated express carriers were "moving more deeply into the low-yield, low-service basic airfreight business," including international shipping. Many of the old-line air-cargo companies that had made JFK a national leader failed or were absorbed by integrated carriers, including Braniff, Western, Frontier, Seaboard, Flying Tigers, and National.[62]

Deregulation undercut New York's highly specialized aviation niche in global freight as well. The specialized skills acquired by forwarders and brokers over decades lost much of their value. Surviving forwarders often moved out of the city to save money on rent. New York experienced a 7 percent decline between 1970 and 1986 in forwarding and customhouse brokerage, whereas in the nation as a whole such business grew by 60 percent. More shocking was the New York region's, primarily JFK's, loss of preeminence in its share of total national freight, *slipping from 32 percent in 1970 to just 19 percent in 1986.* Florida and California airports, for instance, aggressively expanded their air-cargo businesses. Major terminals of the integrated carriers at more remote spots, such as Memphis (Federal Express), Louisville (UPS), and Anchorage (FedEx and UPS) leveraged a global network with low cost land and labor in far less congested and regulated regions. Cargo movement on large 747s, so important to JFK's centrality in global trade, declined as companies added a wider range of smaller aircraft that better suited the high-speed, decentralized integrated cargo system emerging with deregulation.[63]

The dramatic deindustrialization of the New York region contributed to this slippage. With the end of the Cold War in 1991, consolidation of defense-related aviation firms blew a hole in a key Long Island industry from which the region's manufacturing base never recovered. The large aerospace companies of the postwar era, such as Grumman, have been absorbed or closed by rival companies and now employ few workers in the New York region. New York City, too, was at one level a classic rust-belt city that shed approximately a million industrial jobs in the postwar period. The new model of production was in low buildings and production lines in the Sunbelt, Mexico, China, and other developing nations. Queens alone lost 27,200 manufacturing jobs between 1982 and 1994, leaving a trail of shuttered factories and unemployed workers in such fields as metalworking, which, according to one report, was "decimated" during this period.[64] Apparel production was particularly hard hit as well by low-cost manufacturing abroad. Still, in 2004, transportation and warehousing constituted an impressive 37.6 percent of the borough's industrial jobs, many of which were connected to the air-cargo industry.[65] Globalization thus cut both ways in New York: policies that encouraged immigration and global trade benefited certain interests, but the same policies (many of which were designed to improve the economies of the nation's global partners during the Cold War) consciously left most American workers vulnerable to global competition.

The major integrated air carriers, such as UPS and FedEx, had plenty of other reasons to limit their exposure to New York for practical reasons. New York City, after all, had the worst cargo transportation system imaginable. The nagging problem of mob racketeering was one issue. The Port Authority claimed long-term success in its war on crime, in partnership with law-enforcement agencies such as the Department of Justice and technological improvements such as containerization that made theft more difficult, but there were those who had their doubts. In 1988, for instance, $72 billion worth of cargo passed through JFK and just (depending on your perspective) 1.5 cents of every $1,000 was stolen. Port Authority officials were proud to say that the figure was down from 32 cents per $1,000 in 1969.[66]

With so much attention to theft, outright stealing proved less lucrative than extortion, which was far more difficult to prosecute. The Teamsters union (including Harry Davidoff) and the Lucchese crime family were finally convicted in the 1980s of a variety of crimes, including, most notably, the continuing extortion from air-freight trucking companies for the right to operate safely at the airport.[67] As one company manager who had been at JFK for twelve years explained in 1986, "This place is a microcosm of the city. For some people around here, crime is a way of life. The time is not right for me to talk to freely about what has happened here. . . . But it's still not totally clean." While Davidoff and his partners were able to get high salaries for their workers and get a piece of the action in criminal enterprises, the corruption hurt JFK's air-cargo business. An attorney pursuing corruption at the airports reported the following disturbing trend for New York: "Because of the presence of corruption and the union situation, air freight companies regard JFK as the worst place to do business" and cited dropping market share of JFK as evidence.[68] After the crackdown on the Lucchese family and Davidoff, many believed the criminal activity simply shifted to the Gambino and Colombo crime syndicates.[69]

Even if cargo successfully ran the mob gauntlet, there was the matter of the roads. Moses's outdated concept of the leisure parkway had outlived its utility for a regional road system. The continuing restrictions that kept trucks off parkways made life better for drivers and some neighborhoods, but it also concentrated trucks on the few interstates, such as the Van Wyck and Long Island Expressways rather than spreading them more evenly among the region's roadways. In a survey of businesses, "congested roadways and highways were considered the region's most important transportation problem by over 40 percent of all respondents and by nearly 50 percent of firms in New York City boroughs other than Manhattan."[70] On a daily basis in 1985, six thousand light trucks and six thousand heavy trucks fought their way to and from JFK.[71] In New York, a traditional transit-intensive city otherwise, 90 percent of goods were moved by truck (as opposed to 42 percent nationally) because of the lack of an integrated freight rail network between Long Island and the mainland. It was as expensive to move a truck from New Jersey to Long Island as it was from New Jersey to Pittsburgh because of tolls, delays, and high labor costs. The trucking fleet because of delays lost $12 billion per year; companies frequently favored night routes to avoid "further delays encountered traveling south along the Van Wyck Expressway."[72] The Clearview Expressway extension through Queens might have shifted much of this longer-distance truck traffic away from the Van Wyck, but citizens and Governor Rockefeller effectively stopped the connection in 1971 that would have blasted through many middle-class neighborhoods.[73] A planned freight railroad connection that would have integrated Long Island with the mainland, while called for at least since the 1920s, has not been completed as of 2014, thus leaving JFK and many employers with very few, and very pricey, shipping options. The lack of a centralized planning body undercut the economic competitiveness of the region.

The New York region, as a result of development and zoning restrictions on development both in the city and in Nassau County, was unable to take full advantage of the global economic connections at JFK. The city has not developed an aviation-oriented urban center—including, potentially, factories, offices, hotels, meeting spaces, and residences. Unlike the emerging "Aerotropolis" districts around many emerging airports—which included industrial, commercial, and other allied activities—the Springfield Gardens neighborhood adjacent to JFK contained only a very small and rundown industrial zone: "This Queens neighborhood was never intended to be a major commercial center and is perpetually bemoaned for its old buildings, narrow streets, poor drainage system, high crime rates and lack of parking spaces."[74] Nor did there seem to be much hope of increasing the size of the industrial district in other directions. Neighbors around the airport complained of truck traffic related to air cargo. One local activist identified the problems in Springfield Gardens: "They create traffic hazards and our children have been struck by these trucks. There are no traffic signs posted to keep them off the side streets. . . . The rumbling is hazardous to the foundations of the homes."[75]

The Port Authority and city government generally failed to use the airport to leverage competitive advantages for declining neighborhoods near the airport despite making many plans for developing such connections. Mayor Abraham Beame had said in 1977, "We want to make Jamaica the 'headquarters city for aviation,'" but this has never happened. Manhattan and the suburbs still remain dominant in business services, and Jamaica has complicated social and development issues that have stymied the creation of a business center in the area near the airport.[76] The Port Authority has created the Queens Air Service office "to generate more aviation industry business for Queens companies" and claimed $15 million in contracts for three hundred firms over a six-year period (1984–1990), but this was in no way going to change the fundamental disconnect between the airport and its surrounding, mostly residential, urban neighborhoods.[77]

At some point, in a bizarre twist, the Port Authority began to claim that the comparative lack of cargo infrastructure was forward thinking. The Port Authority confessed in 1992: "We don't add or construct new air cargo warehouse space at our airports anymore. That's because we don't warehouse air cargo anymore. Instead we build air cargo transit facilities to accommodate the speedy transit of cargo through our airports for the final leg of its journey to ultimate consignee." The new facilities accommodated just-in-time inventory, a popular and leaner way of running industrial operations. In a disturbing trend, however, some large air-cargo operators

did not abandon fixed infrastructure but simply moved their entire operations from JFK to Newark.[78] SAS claimed, for instance, that operating in
Newark was more efficient for them because not only was Newark their
passenger hub but "pickup and delivery from New York, New Jersey and
Pennsylvania is faster and easier." By 2000, "most of the major overnight
freight companies, which thrive on speed, have greatly reduced their presence at JFK."[79]

Moving to Newark was less critical to JFK's economic well-being than
the ongoing national shift of the air-cargo industry. The success of the
airport in such high-value goods as diamonds, electronics, and food supported growth in the value of cargo and even modest upticks in volume,
but not an expansion in employment. Nippon Airways, for instance, moved
its major air-cargo units to Chicago in order to lower costs, shorten the
distance, and speed the movement of its goods.[80] Other cities expanded
their cargo operations: "Officials at Miami International Airport commissioned a master plan in the mid-1990s. . . . The blueprint called for demol-
ishing archaic cargo facilities and erecting 18 state-of-the-art facilities by
mid-2001." By 2000, fourteen had already been constructed.[81]

That JFK in the mid-1990s still handled 90 percent of the New York
region's international cargo sounded impressive. The total value of air
cargo of the New York region (primarily JFK) was over $84 billion and
constituted 24 percent of the total value for the United States.[82] As strong
as that sounds for the region, it was not enough to keep JFK from slipping
out of the top ranks in the global air-cargo business by volume.[83] The early
lead finally ran out in the 1990s; ironically, the airport as a whole at that
time started to experience sustained growth again.[84] Until 1990, JFK had
handled more cargo than any airport in the world, but just a decade later
in 2000, JFK had slipped to fifth in the world and third in the United States.
The total volume of air cargo has declined at JFK by approximately one
third since 2000.

Nearby, Newark International's air cargo traffic rose a healthy 126 percent
between 1991 and 1999, whereas JFK's air cargo business grew just 37 percent.[85] Newark International's impressive growth primarily resulted from the
growing dominance of integrated carriers, FedEx and UPS primarily, that
accounted for more than half of that airport's cargo trade. The technologically
advanced system at Newark could unload a plane in just one hour, and these
goods could be on the regional highway system faster, giving the integrated
carriers major advantages.[86] Long tractor trailers (fifty-three feet) that carry

multiple containers, which have played an expanded role in domestic movement of air cargo since the September 11 terrorist attacks (reducing screening costs to shippers), are allowed at Newark but faced a ban on operations in New York City until 2014 when the city's Department of Transportation finally allowed them to travel on a limited number of (already crowded) highways to JFK. Nor has the Port Authority been an aggressive manager of the air-cargo area at JFK, by most accounts, with limited marketing and administrative oversight.[87] These shifts contributed to loss of airport employment at JFK: the total number of airport employees declined from 40,558 in 1986 to 37,396 in 1999 (air cargo accounted for just under half of all positions at JFK), whereas, at Newark, the number of employees increased from 14,438 to 24,270 in the same years.[88]

The relative decline nationally of JFK's status in air-cargo operations parallels that of the passenger business. The dismantling of a regulatory regime that favored New York and had been built on historical precedents also fostered a steady erosion of the city's leadership in air cargo. On balance, JFK maintained its core regional business and even built new business on the basis of New York's many daily foreign departures (with the aircraft holds doing double-duty for cargo), existing cargo infrastructure, and the unique character of the city in such areas as finance, diamonds, apparel, and ethnic specialties. JFK's New York character grew every year and maintained *national* leadership in key areas: 83 percent of diamonds, 55 percent of art and antiques, and 47 percent of perfume and cosmetics. Even today, 40 percent of the nation's seafood exports leaves through JFK. Fish, diamonds, clothes, antiques, art, cosmetics, and pharmaceuticals: this list of enduring trade items sums up a lot of New York's life. Political and business leaders in many cities would, of course, be delighted to have such a valuable trade.[89]

JFK International may have been unpleasant and frustrating for many travelers, and declining in national importance, but these weaknesses obscured hidden strengths. The declining terminals and airlines, flight delays, growth limits, aggressive competition, and crime undermined the airport but did not destroy its importance, in large measure because of the metropolitan context. The region's financial health, the tourism industry, and immigration provided enough financial and passenger pressure to push the airport forward as a leading, if not the leading, airport in the United States. The continuing popularity of the airport, despite so many troubles, also finally forced the Port Authority to rethink its policy of benign neglect.

Reappraisal

Sheila Bair, former Federal Deposit Insurance Corporation (FDIC) chair, recounted for *Fortune* readers in 2013 her horrible experience at JFK, including air-traffic control delays, dangerous broken floor tiles, and "the strong aroma of raw sewage" from a bathroom. JFK compared unfavorably with her recent experience in Beijing's sparkling new airport. Bair's impressions of JFK are not unique. JFK International is still rated among the country's worst airports by the traveling public.[1] Indeed, JFK compares unfavorably in many respects to new airports both in the United States and abroad. But in light of the airport's complex history and context, is it fair to say that JFK is an objectively terrible airport? The slow pace of change has made it difficult for New Yorkers or other travelers to appreciate the upgrades, but the changes are real. The environment at JFK that travelers experience today is almost entirely transformed from the unpleasant, crowded airport that existed from the 1970s to the 1990s. Airport reconstruction, incorporating billions of dollars in new construction, has wiped clean nearly every trace of the original Terminal City.

This ambitious reconstruction had its roots in the widespread unhappiness with the quality of airports in New York City. Inciting already touchy New York officials was evidence that Newark International seemed to be the Port Authority's spoiled pet, known as it was then for more modern terminals and streamlined immigration. Newark also became a hub both for People's Express, an early and flawed trial of deregulated fares in the 1980s, as well as the global hub for Continental Airlines, one of the more successful airlines in the deregulated era. Newark even had its own internal monorail system to connect the terminals; meanwhile, JFK passengers still choked on diesel fumes from crummy old shuttle buses as they lurched from one terminal to another.[2] The money generated by the airports appeared to be sloshing around the Port Authority, just not to the benefit of New York City's airports.[3] Between about 1995 and 2000, for instance, JFK and LaGuardia pumped in $664 million in net income for the Port Authority while its faltering PATH system alone lost $900 million in the same period.[4]

The Regional Plan Association, the New York region's leading voice for business-related planning, also decried the airport's unpleasant reality: "New York serves as a gateway for tourism from overseas, and the absence of first-class access from our airports, particularly Kennedy, creates a decidedly poor first impression of the region. Reaching our airports is time-consuming, unreliable, inconvenient and lacking in the amenities air passengers value and expect. The absence of quality befitting a world-class city is especially acute."[5] The Port Authority deserved blame for the declining IAB, poor roadways, and unintelligible signage at JFK, but decline of the other unit terminals had more complex roots. As described above, the deregulated airline industry bankrupted the owners of many of the terminals (such as Pan Am, TWA, and Eastern) or made the new owners, such as Delta, unable or reluctant to invest in a captive and profitable market. As one airport administrator admitted, "Airports do make money—they have extremely high credit ratings and are very good for municipal credit. Airlines have had a hard time making money, but the hope is that the industry is re-adapting itself so that it can compete." In the meantime, they were going to wring every dollar they could out of existing facilities.[6]

The Port Authority, in a bid to upgrade the airport's service quality and restore public confidence in its management skills, announced dramatic multibillion-dollar investments in 1989 as part of what was called "JFK 2000." The plans included an entirely revamped internal roadway system to allow more direct access for travelers to their particular terminals; a new air-traffic control tower; and, above all, a monumental central terminal complex from which passengers would stream out in automated vehicles on a spaghetti-like underground distribution system to their gates and terminals.[7]

Architecture critic Paul Goldberger loved the central terminal plan and praised the boldness of architect Henry Cobb of Pei, Cobb, and Freed who he believed had "effectively turned the airport inside out." In the new plan, the unit terminals "would have been rendered secondary to a vast structure of granite, glass and metal that at its center would have contained a domed, sky lighted arrival hall. . . . Perhaps the closest our age has come to the grand and uplifting public space of the great railway terminals." The terminal building was only $450 million of the $3.2 billion project,[8] but the airlines rejected the design as too expensive. There were also some serious doubts about the wisdom of putting so much of the airport's traffic into a central terminal. The rest of the JFK 2000 plan, however, did move ahead: new parking garages, more logical roadways and signage, individual terminal redevelopment, and a new control tower were all realized by 2013.

The Port Authority replaced Cobb's glamorous central terminal with an incremental but equally ambitious redevelopment of individual terminals in partnership with the airlines. This choice meant that the image and experience of JFK as a whole, Terminal City, would change only very slowly. Yet the strategy of preserving the unit terminal system made sense not only from a cost perspective, as the terminals and roadways represent billions in existing investments, but also from an operational point of view. One expert argued that the "unit terminal concept remains valid for JFK because although the proportion of passengers changing planes has risen compared to the early days of Terminal City, the growth has been in online connecting traffic."[9] The unit terminal concept has thus been modified, in partnership with airlines, to better meet the needs of deregulated global travel in 2015. Some unit terminals, including those run by JetBlue and American, still serve only one airline; British Airways upgraded Terminal Seven; and American Airlines created new terminals for Eight and Nine. Six of the nine central area terminals also have on-site immigration facilities, "providing passengers a welcome change from the rush-hour crush in the old IAB" that made arriving in New York particularly unpleasant.[10] While a unified complex like that proposed by Cobb might have been more legible and grand, the AirTrain rail connections (which opened for service in 2003) between terminals have greatly reduced the effective distance and hassle, thus removing much of the justification for an expensive redesign of the plan as a whole.

For other terminal renovations, and the site of the former IAB, the Port Authority has integrated many airlines under one roof and built in more flexibility as part of the multibillion-dollar rebuilding plan. The first of the new era terminals was Terminal One, which opened in 1998 on the former site of the Eastern Airlines terminal. It was a joint development project of

Table 1. Airport Investments: Port Authority Capital Expenditures
by Facility (current dollars, in millions)

Year	Kennedy	Newark	LaGuardia	Teterboro	Stewart	Passenger Facility Charge	All Facilities
2000	124	180	57	6	—	—	367
2001	117	452	40	14	—	—	623
2002	125	349	65	12	—	—	551
2003	116	191	59	9	—	—	375
2004	80	102	72	26	—	—	280
2005	114	50	59	47	0.2	167	437
2006	295	55	38	34	0.1	135	557
2007	378	165	93	23	1	—	660
2008	259	203	136	24	9	—	631
2009	306	156	148	28	20	—	658[a]
2010	269	107	104	25	16	—	521[b]
Totals	$2,183	$2,010	$871	$248	$46	$302	$5,660[c]

[a] $100 million from 2009 capital expenditures are from Queens swap.

[b] The 2010 amounts are budgeted dollars.

[c] Expenditures of $1.9 billion on the AirTrain increases the total investment to $7.258 billion.

Source: Port Authority. Reprinted from Jeffrey Zupan, Richard Barone, and Matthew Lee, *Upgrading to World Class: The Future of the New York Region's Airports* (New York: Regional Plan Association, January 2011).

Air France, Japan Airlines, Lufthansa, and Korean Airlines, funded through the sale of hundreds of millions of bonds in the private market. The JFK manager boasted that "for the first time in 20 years, we will have a brand-new terminal at JFK." Few regular JFK users were likely surprised that it had been that long.[11] The terminal earned immediate praise for its "swooping roof with skylights supported by an enameled white aluminum structure" and "750 foot long glass curtain wall with steel columns" that offered visitors uncluttered views of the airfield and the distant skyline. The four-lane, two-level roadway also untangled arriving and departing traffic.[12]

The rebuilding of the IAB as Terminal Four started in the mid-1990s. Terminal Four, largely financed by Lehman Brothers, was designed for the deregulated and constantly shifting nature of air travel. Unlike the old IAB, which featured permanent sections for individual foreign-flag airlines,

Table 2. Airport Investments: Private Sector Capital Expenditures by Facility (current dollars, in millions)

Year	Kennedy	Newark	LaGuardia	Teterboro	All Facilities
2000	500	234	15	11	760
2001	529	120	32	36	717
2002	253	32	56	3	344
2003	100	18	3	28	149
2004	109	17	4	5	135
2005	579	26	5	2	612
2006	134	17	17	27	195
2007	116	33	13	8	170
2008	138	69	13	3	223
2009	46	100	37	1	184
2010	67	13	43	0.1	123
Total	$2,571	$679	$238	$124	$3,612

Source: Port Authority

Terminal Four featured "common user check-in desks and lounge and office space that can easily be remodeled and re-let." In other words, when an airline failed or capacity needs changed, as happens frequently in a less regulated air system, so can the terminal.[13] The revised plan included other improvements, including "dual level roadways; consolidated ticketing and baggage; larger hold rooms; consolidated and expanded immigration and customs facilities; increases in contact gates; well-located retail; and accommodation for domestic operations."[14]

After four years of intense rebuilding, the new Terminal Four opened in 2001. The new terminal took its design cues from the global airport style dominant today, including extensive glass walls and soaring open spaces to maximize natural light. Shopping areas, using a Main Street mall model, were designed to maximize revenues. Public art projects, including one that mythologizes "New York Streets," enlivened an otherwise standardized global structure. Reflecting the industry and airport's constant flux, Terminal Four underwent a $1.4 billion renovation and expansion in 2013 as part of its repurposing as Delta's primary hub in New York (as well as its continuing role as the primary IAB). The refitting included contemporary interior design, upscale eateries, and expanded gate and terminal facilities to replace the former Pan Am Worldport adjoining Terminal Four (which has been demolished).[15] The terminal unit idea has evidently not outlived its usefulness, at least from the perspective of the airlines.

One of the most curious of the new unit terminals is Terminal Five, opened in 2008 by JetBlue. Because of New York's powerful preservation movement, any chance of destroying TWA's iconic Saarinen-designed terminal was ruled out. The New York City Landmarks Preservation Committee designated the TWA terminal a protected landmark in 1994 after it was threatened with redevelopment. JetBlue, when it came time to build its own terminal in 2008, was thus forced to wrap its new unit terminal around the TWA terminal. The historic terminal, which had suffered some physical decline, has been partially restored by the Port Authority for $20 million. Yet Saarinen's building has been reduced to serving as one of the most striking pieces of urban sculpture in the world. Its final use has yet to be determined and it has no real functionality beyond vaguely signifying the importance of art and creativity to arriving and departing JetBlue passengers. Not many places in the world would preserve such a large, nonfunctional object in the middle of its airport, but then New York in recent decades has aggressively expanded the scope of its preservation and landmark powers. The Saarinen terminal is also not just any terminal but one of the great buildings of the twentieth century. New York's current emphasis on historic preservation and artistic expression has clearly shaped this unique, if less than logical, terminal arrangement.[16]

In sum, Terminals One, Four, Five, and Eight are new, while Terminals Two, Three, Six, and Seven are in various stages of redesign or redevelopment. Another $7 billion in investments are slated over the next five years; the Port Authority is determined to remake JFK as a "twenty-first century" airport and to make up for its lack of focus on quality service at its transportation hubs. As of 2014, JFK's plan and roadways were still bewildering for first-time visitors, but nearly every terminal, including the massive IAB, has been redeveloped, or is being redeveloped today, to meet contemporary global standards of design and capacity. David Dunlap of the *New York Times* provided a perceptive contrast between the old Terminal City and the new terminals that are united by "an understated aesthetic that is gradually replacing the world's fair variety of the original Terminal City, where architects outdid one another with eye-catching three-dimensional billboards. The new style—call it airfoil modern—is characterized by the roof lines as gently bowed as the top of an aircraft's wing and silvery surfaces as smooth as a fuselage skin."[17] Today's dominant approach is closely linked to the pioneering work of architect Norman Foster and has been widely imitated globally. So even though the firm of Skidmore, Owings and Merrill designed both the IAB in the 1950s and the new Terminal Four, the two terminals reflect the different design ideals of their respective eras. The original unit terminals by and large shared in a modernist aesthetic that made the individual terminals more similar than different one from the other, despite a distinctive silhouette, materials, and so forth. The same could be said for their modern replacements, all of which reflect an edited and updated version of global modernist aesthetics.

Even more important for airport experience is that post-9/11, security is very tight at the airport. While those seeing off their families are no longer welcomed beyond control gates at the various terminals, neither are the homeless and hustlers of another era. The zero-tolerance policy at airports nationally after 9/11 has also upgraded security a great deal at JFK. There is very little public space left at JFK that is accessible for nonpassengers. A lot of "helpful" staff members have been added to keep an eye on the spaces surrounding the airport, such as Airtrain platforms. The Port Authority and various airlines hope to expunge the undesirable aspects of the New York character, replacing the grit with a smooth, tightly regulated, globalized experience. They seem to be getting closer.

The most important question today is will the reconstruction finally recast the airport's reputation? The incremental process of rebuilding so frustrated Mayor Rudy Giuliani in 1999, for instance, that he proposed privatization of the airports. His effort failed, but the criticism has continued.[18] Younger travelers, who never experienced the old JFK, are likely to be more easily influenced by the new materials and designs. When asked about JFK, my New York City college students are surprisingly upbeat about the airport. For many older travelers, however, the decades of reconstruction and other negative experiences have left such bitter feeling and memories that they can never be fully expunged. The heavy use of the terminals also takes a quick toll on the modern and less robust materials used in the airport. By the time one round of renovations is complete, early renovations have already started to decline. Major upgrades are still warranted in runways and air-traffic control. The open secret that the Port Authority continues to divert hundreds of millions of dollars in profits annually from airports to such money-losing operations as the PATH system, the Port Authority Bus Terminal, and non-revenue producing infrastructure projects designated by governors (not to mention the World Trade Center redevelopment) raises questions about the Port Authority's ability to maintain world-class aviation facilities. Many critics believe that reorganization of the Port Authority's management structure and assets is the only way to take airports like JFK to the next level.[19]

New York Governor Andrew Cuomo, in the aftermath of scandals in 2014 surrounding New Jersey Governor Chris Christie and his Port Authority appointees, vowed to take a more aggressive role in the redevelopment of New York's airports. Cuomo announced a design competition, for instance, to generate visionary rethinking of JFK and LaGuardia. The Global Gateway Alliance, a group of business executives and researchers critical of Port Authority management, co-sponsored the competition as part of its goal of raising airport quality regionally. The longstanding consensus of the political and economic elite that the Port Authority is best suited to the designing, building, and managing of world-class aviation facilities, tested many times over the decades, appears to have finally fractured. The many legal, financial, and operational advantages enjoyed by such a powerful and wealthy public corporation like the Port Authority makes it unlikely, however, that it will be replaced as manager of the region's airports. Organizational reform and more aggressive rebuilding, as a result of continued pressure from private and public leaders, is the probable future for Port Authority aviation facilities including JFK.[20]

JetBlue and the Limits of Success

There remains the crucial matter of both getting to and from the airport and leaving on one's flight on time. On both these counts, JFK still remains an underperformer. And it is hard to see how the Port Authority alone can ever resolve these issues. Billions spent on upgrades and new facilities designed to bring JFK up to a global standard can do little to address the urban and environmental context that limit the airport's operations and reputation. The New York region provides many advantages, such as the booming tourism trade and financial services, but other factors, such as noise pollution control and environmental protection, have more complex effects—many of which continue to influence the quality of air service.

Despite its continuing importance in global travel, JFK continued to sink as a domestic airport in the 1980s and 1990s as the legacy lines collapsed and domestic operations shifted to LaGuardia, Newark, and more distant hubs. Domestic passenger aircraft movements dropped from

112,761 in 1986 to 95,281 in 1999. This decline was not simply larger planes replacing smaller craft because domestic passenger numbers also decreased from 12,597,588 in 1986 to 11,639,290 in 1999. International passenger movements, on the other hand, increased from 71,224 in 1986 to 100,171 in 1999.[21] What this meant in practice is that the airport's facilities were simultaneously maxed out at times essential for international travel and underutilized. The notion of JFK as an important domestic airport seemed highly unlikely.

The founder of JetBlue, David Neeleman, made this remarkable discovery on one of his tours of JFK in the late 1990s: enough slack time and runways to launch an entirely new domestic airline in the middle of the busiest air market in the United States. "What he noticed that morning stunned him. . . . It was about 10 o'clock. And at Kennedy, the biggest airport in the nation's biggest travel market, there were, for a brief moment, no planes waiting to take off." Neeleman realized, " 'There's room for us.' " Although LaGuardia and Newark had become jam-packed with domestic flights, there were large schedule holes at JFK that could be filled with domestic flights. The so-called rush hour was shorter at JFK, and federal "controls are in place only from 3 pm to 8 pm" during the peak of international arrivals and departures. JetBlue quickly made a profit on new domestic flights, most of which flew directly from JFK to their final destinations on the most modern and comfortable aircraft available. In an era of irritating transfers through such hubs as Atlanta, the direct flights, which could be filled in a dense market such as New York, gave JetBlue a great advantage. Neeleman kept his prices low by leasing aircraft, employing nonunion staff, and sticking to lower-cost arrival and departure times around the nation. JetBlue was the ideal neoliberal airline. In fact, JetBlue's innovative methods, along with other low-cost airlines, such as Southwest Airlines and AirTran, began to undermine the desirability of flying in the "hub and spoke" system for many passengers in America's domestic system.[22] So popular was JetBlue service that by 2004 this upstart airline was already flying the most passengers out of JFK.[23]

Passengers now paid a high price for the resurgence of domestic service at JFK. JetBlue's success and the continuing growth in international flights reminded many people of the reasons that flights were curtailed in the first place. Since the 1990s there have been steep increases in total passenger numbers and aircraft operations in both domestic and international travel at JFK. Competitors looking to match JetBlue, and other airlines expanding into a very profitable market, have started to jam the airport once again. The 9/11 attacks and subsequent recession only temporarily stalled air traffic in the New York region before the power of the New York market, economic recovery, and further deregulation of New York's airspace brought back New York's air traffic to new records. In 2004, for instance, JFK handled 37.5 million passengers and had once again become one of the fastest-growing airports in the nation.[24] More traffic, alas, also meant more delays. Even JetBlue could not entirely avoid the pitfalls of operating in crowded airspace. It lost tremendous goodwill after it stranded passengers on JFK's runways during a winter storm in 2007.

The zeroing out of the FAA restrictions in 2007, much desired by airlines aiming for expanded service and profits, without any concomitant increase in the number of air controllers or the long-promised modernized air-traffic control system (NextGen), inevitably clogged the airport. This simple change in restrictions alone increased use by 23.5 percent in just one year: "Airlines quickly added flights, creating record delays not only at Kennedy, but also at airports where flights from New York were headed."[25] The situation became fairly brutal. At JFK in 2007, for instance, almost 32 percent of departures and 38 percent of arrivals were delayed. New York's other airports had similar delay issues.[26] Between 4:00 and 5:00 P.M., for instance, airline officials had scheduled 111 flights for takeoff from JFK, an impossible feat to carry out under the best of conditions. Even if a passenger was lucky enough to taxi out at JFK, on average that passenger ended up waiting thirty-six minutes on the tarmac before taking off. Nationally, the average was only sixteen minutes, and JFK was the worst of the three area airports. Another congesting factor was an old one: high-status New Yorkers zooming around regional airspace in small, private aircraft. Private aviation still accounted for about 30 percent of all operations in New York airspace. Business and political leaders were concerned enough to demand changes in operations; the FAA in 2008 reinstated caps of 81 landings or takeoffs per hour at JFK (and still allows only 83 in 2014). One study calculated that in 2008 flight delays at the three airports combined cost the region $2.6 billion. Without significant investment, the regional losses, in terms of employment and commerce, will total $79 billion by 2025.[27]

Above all, JFK has not, as a result of pressure from surrounding areas, undergone major runway expansion and reconfiguration programs as have other cities such as Atlanta and Chicago, which either already possess, or will soon possess, multiple runways in parallel configurations that allow for simultaneous multiple plane operations and thus much greater volume. JFK's runways, however, are more or less in the same configuration, if much more modern and longer, that they have had since the 1950s. At certain times of the day, as indicated above, the runways at JFK are sufficient to handle traffic. At other times, however, the system (particularly in poor weather) inevitably bogs down. Adding more runways would remedy some of these problems and help JFK catch up with global airports expanding massively, but the likelihood of physical expansion is remote.[28]

Familiar solutions to congestion have been discussed. Some called for new restrictions on private planes while other planners called for a third parallel runway to bring JFK up to the national standards of the day (when O'Hare's redevelopment is finished, there will be eight runways). The authors of one study for the Regional Plan Association in 2000 admitted, however, that such a plan would demand filling in part of Jamaica Bay, making it nearly impossible from a policy point of view: "With virtually no excess land at the airport, the only possible option is to fill in part of Jamaica Bay and build a runway there. But any plan to do this will be vigorously opposed by environmentalists and community groups." Despite the apparent collapse of the ecology of the bay, it is off limits.[29] The unrealistic idea of building an island off the coast for a new airport has once again been floated and has received publicity from the Regional Plan Association without generating much serious consideration. In light of Hurricane Sandy's damage to the airport in 2012, it is even less realistic to imagine placing billions of dollars of infrastructure in New York's waterways.

Perhaps the greatest hope still lies in the FAA's NextGen air-traffic control systems that switch out traditional radar and air traffic control with modern technology such as satellite-based global positioning systems. NextGen allows planes to fly in tighter, higher configurations near airports, increasing operations while having less noise and pollution impact on most surrounding neighborhoods. During poor weather conditions in the New York region, which often disrupt travel across the country, the system would also reduce cancellations and delays by allowing pilots and controllers to better navigate around thunderstorms and other weather obstacles. At JFK, for instance, while the full system had not yet been implemented (and will not be for at least another decade), NextGen control systems in 2014 have already reduced the amount of time and fuel that planes waste waiting in line for takeoff. Greater utilization of larger aircraft like the A380 also has potential to reduce airspace congestion.[30]

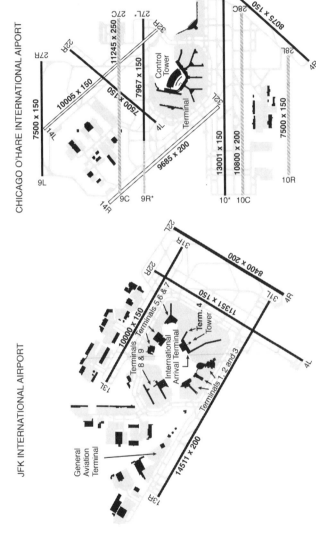

FIGURE 30. JFK's limitations in terms of operations are evident when comparing it to a competitor such as O'Hare, where an airfield reconstruction and expansion program will significantly boost capacity. Courtesy of the Regional Plan Association.

Looking back over the decades of air congestion, it is hard not to con-
clude that delays of all types are simply the cost of doing business in New
York and thus part of JFK's intrinsic identity. The airlines, or new competitors seeking to profit from the regional air market, will likely quickly fill
any increase in capacity. Are the crowded terminals of JFK, then, simply
the modern equivalent of the teeming docks and warehouses of centuries
past? Perhaps crowds are simply what a modern, successful New York
port—surrounded by an equally congested city—looks like. On the other
hand, it is also likely that other cities will continue to benefit from the
crowding and other management issues at JFK and New York's other
regional airports.

The Surprising Success of AirTrain

Ground congestion remained JFK's other curse. Cars were not much use
once passengers arrived at the airport, especially at peak times. During the
peak afternoon times of arrival in the summer months in the late 1980s, it
took an estimated ninety minutes to just go around the internal runway at
JFK International and another forty-five minutes to get to the Van Wyck
Expressway or Belt Parkway.[31] Richard Rowe, the general manager of JFK
in the 1990s, explained that "with the roadway system not being able to
absorb the traffic during peak—you have double parking, triple parking,
plus a large vehicle can't get into the curb, those kind of things—you never
know when the bus is going to arrive." Reconstruction and widening of the
airport's roads in the past decade, as part of the JFK 2000 plan, has significantly reduced internal congestion.[32]

Getting to and from the airport on roadways unfortunately remains just
as dreadful as it always was. And there is no clear solution, expensive or
otherwise, that can clearly undo this mess. Reducing automobile congestion
is complex because "most local passengers live and work in the suburbs of
Long Island, Westchester and Connecticut, which means they are more
likely to come in private cars or taxis." This is a metropolitan airport, after
all, not the city airport envisioned by Mayor La Guardia more than half a
century ago. In the 1990s, 82 percent of those surveyed arrived in low-
occupancy vehicles such as taxis, limos, and private cars,[33] while only about
one-third of daily air passengers at JFK actually traveled to Manhattan.[34]

Thousands of travelers and employees availed themselves of the vast parking lots on site (fifteen thousand total parking spaces on site in 2013). The Port Authority's goal of building an airport linked to the region by highways worked out exactly as planned.[35]

The potential for rail travel to the airport remained relatively untapped until a decade ago. A patched-together rail connection created by the MTA did operate from the late 1970s until 2003. The JFK "Train to Plane" service, integrating a long subway ride from the city on the A line and a coach connection at Howard Beach to the terminals, the so-called JFK Express, started in 1978. The system tallied impressive numbers in spite of its lackluster performance. The best a traveler to Manhattan might hope for was a sixty-seven- to seventy-six-minute ride from 57th Street to the airport. From the World Trade Center at peak times, it would take between fifty-two and sixty-one minutes. In a nonscientific test run by the *New York Times* in the early 1980s, the JFK Express took about an hour and a half from Times Square and was slower than both a taxi and hotel limousine—at least in good traffic.

By the 1980s, the JFK Express carried on an annual basis over a million riders a year, although many of these riders actually aimed for destinations en route, such as Aqueduct Raceway.[36] The lackluster service attracted few additional passengers and only modestly increased its ridership from 1,176,005 passengers in 1986 to 1.3 million passengers in 1999; these numbers are even less impressive than they seem because only about 50 percent of the ridership total actually constituted airport-related trips. But a transit planner could see from these figures that a real train-to-plane system might inherit hundreds of thousands of riders who had endured a long and more annoying system.[37] There were also thousands of Airport Coach passengers who might switch to a mass-transit option rather than enduring long bus trips on crowded highways and streets.[38] Finally, a train system that doubled as a terminal linking system would free up a lot of unlucky passengers using JFK's dismal airport internal bus system; use of that system, connected to reductions in domestic service, declined from a high of 899,147 in 1986 to 620,274 in 1999.[39]

The dream of mass transit at first remained stalled in the 1990s despite the long-term congestion. Expert studies consistently concluded that a relatively low percentage of travelers would choose mass transit. A 1989 study estimated that only 6 percent of travelers would use mass transit because the system, as planned, would not, among other things, provide a one-seat ride to Manhattan. The consultants of that study also believed that employees resist transit because of "an ingrained automobile habit, close-in residence locations where a mode shift is less welcome, dispersed job locations at JFK, and subsidized or low cost parking at the airport." On the other hand, a rail system that shifted 6 percent of the approximately 28.5 million passengers (1989 figure) using JFK would have contributed to a reduction in regional congestion because of how many passengers traveled to and from the airport in low occupancy vehicles.[40]

The experience of other American cities, such as Boston, Baltimore, and Chicago, provided cautionary tales. In Chicago, for instance, the extension of the Blue line of the city's elevated system to O'Hare in 1983 had little impact on transportation patterns to the airport.[41] By 1999, only seven thousand people per day total used the train link (40 percent of whom were airport workers); and just 1.8 percent of daily airline passengers used the rail link. There are, after all, about twenty-two thousand public parking spaces available at O'Hare for a metropolitan region with a population significantly smaller than New York's. Chicago has developed along even more decentralized, suburban lines during the postwar period than New York.[42] Based upon Chicago's experience, combined with the fact that so many suburban travelers even in New York reside in areas with limited or complicated mass transit, it was hard to make the case for mass transit at JFK.

But New York is not Chicago: New York's density, massive central business and residential districts, high cost of long-term parking, bridge and tunnel tolls, and the horror of dealing with traffic and cabs in and out of the airport make many car-loving Americans surrender to mass transit. The Port Authority had deliberately ignored the importance of mass transit (even a less than ideal system) to the region's population, particularly in the city. And while the Port Authority was claiming that an air-to-train system would never work for JFK, it actually installed what became a very popular monorail system at Newark Airport in the 1990s that featured integrated driverless, computer-controlled trains (with links to Amtrak and regional commuter trains) that could carry up to 2,600 passengers per hour. The Port Authority chairman in 1992 threw salt on the wounds of New Yorkers by bragging, "if we can build a new international terminal, the monorail, and a real connection, it will be the best airport in the Northeast." Wasn't that supposed to be JFK International?[43]

A solution to the problem of potentially low ridership, high costs, and right-of-way issues was finally found in running an elevated rail line up the center of the Van Wyck Expressway to Jamaica Station in order to capitalize on both urban and suburban riders. At Jamaica Station, a mix of city and suburban air travelers could be linked to the Long Island Rail Road and subway. From the Port Authority's point of view, of perhaps even greater importance was the role that the air link would play in finally linking together the distantly separated terminals within Terminal City. The Port Authority's willingness to invest in this system also resulted from the passage in 1990 of the federal Passenger Facility Charge legislation that allowed airports around the country to add fees to passenger tickets for airport capital improvements. This allowed the Port Authority to circumvent the limits set on its participation in mass transit. New York governor Mario Cuomo, seeing broad possibilities for the system in transforming Queens (his hometown), championed rail links in 1991, and the FAA approved the three-dollar surcharge to pay for the system in 1992. It would take many more years and continuing pressure from elected officials and the Port Authority to overcome opposition by airlines and local residents.[44]

Such a rail system was less than the "one-seat ride" to midtown or lower Manhattan that many experts concluded would be more popular, but many supporters felt that not only was a real system better than nothing, but the demonstration of the viability of the system could encourage major upgrades at a later date. The proposed system, which strongly resembled the one actually built, entailed transfers to subways or commuter rail lines for passengers traveling to Manhattan. The subway express E and F lines to which passengers would transfer after the AirTrain run quickly (thirty to forty minutes) to the East Side and Midtown from Jamaica Station. The LIRR also connects at Jamaica Station and would open up both a fast Midtown connection (fifteen to twenty minutes) and a rail commuting option for airport travelers coming from Nassau County. Even the A train subway connection in the new system was made simpler with a direct stop on the AirTrain as opposed to a bus transfer in the old system, thus maintaining connections to lower Manhattan and Brooklyn. The AirTrain system, while less than ideal, was a regional solution that the Port Authority felt it could support.

The early proposals in the 1990s included a route that would run through Jamaica Center and all the way to LaGuardia Airport. Particular emphasis was placed on using such a system as a potential north-south connector in Queens, which suffers from the fact that most transit lines run east to west.[45] Local politicians and many residents, however, continued to doubt the wisdom of a route that would have limited stops in Queens yet might be disruptive to neighborhoods; airlines as usual objected to any additional costs to them or passengers.[46] Some city officials were also concerned that a large portion of the cost for construction would be slyly transferred to the city by deductions from the "profits" of the airport, which were otherwise due to the city and not forthcoming from the Port Authority. This may, in fact, have happened. In any case, the link to LaGuardia was eventually dropped. The legal challenge to the link also failed and construction commenced in 1998.[47]

As the construction of the link for $1.9 billion link pressed ahead, the initiative was not even undermined by a spectacular and embarrassing derailment during testing. The city got a makeover of the shabby Jamaica Station into a global-style rail hub as part of the project. The AirTrain includes internal stops for all terminals, parking lots, and rental cars, as well as at Howard Beach (A train) and Jamaica Station (LIRR or express E subway). JFK still lacks a "one-seat ride" to Manhattan that would make the Airtrain that much more popular. There is also an unnecessarily confusing transfer point at Jamaica where passengers leaving the AirTrain must figure out how, often with help of staff, to pay for their AirTrain ride and buy tickets for either the LIRR or subway. The lack of administrative coordination between the Port Authority and MTA is glaringly obvious here. The difference in amenity level is also striking between the spaces run by the LIRR and that of the Port Authority: the areas within the AirTrain structure, run by the Port Authority, have shiny floors, lots of staff, an airport-style food court, and clean bathrooms while the LIRR sections are typically drab.

In spite of all the concerns about sufficient ridership raised during the development of the AirTrain, just six months after opening in December 2003, the system had already carried 1 million paying passengers (those who leave the airport); 2.6 million travelers had also used the internal circulation system. Average daily ridership was about 26,000, which was just shy of the projection of about 34,000 daily users. The AirTrain proved to be particularly useful to airport employees who had been using bus service and automobiles to get to work; it did not take that much to convince many workers in the New York region to abandon their cars or MTA buses. In 2011, 5.5 million people paid to use AirTrain, roughly double the number who paid at Newark, and millions more rode in comfort between

Table 3. How Do Passengers Get to the Airport?

Mode	Kennedy		Newark		LaGuardia	
	Manhattan	Other	Manhattan	Other	Manhattan	Other
Rail	15.4%	8.4%	24.7%	5.9%	0.0%	0.0%
Bus (private and public)	5.0%	4.1%	9.8%	2.5%	8.8%	11.7%
Van/Shuttles	12.1%	14.5%	15.9%	7.9%	7.3%	6.7%
Taxi and limousine	35.0%	20.5%	34.0%	19.1%	74.5%	45.6%
Rental car	2.7%	4.0%	1.1%	11.9%	1.3%	7.4%
Drove or dropped off	29.9%	48.5%	14.6%	52.7%	8.0%	28.6%

Source: 2008 Port Authority Survey

terminals. Paid parking has declined significantly since the AirTrain began service despite major increases in air traffic. The system is now far and away the most popular airport-city link in the country and, if current growth patterns continue, will easily exceed early ridership projections in the years to come. After all, New York traffic is not getting any better.[48]

The Port Authority's overwhelming focus on automobile connections and parking appears in retrospect as a blind spot. The simple future that leaders like Austin Tobin envisioned in the 1950s, of cars speeding across the region on expressways, had become more complex by the turn of the century. The executives at the Port Authority had overlooked the fact that millions of people within New York City maintained connections, through travel and work, with the airport. Many European and Asian travelers, in addition, were more than willing to take mass transit to an airport. The growing immigrant populations in Queens (many who worked or traveled through JFK), in particular, may have thrown off the results of earlier studies that used typical American habits to predict transit use for the projected systems. The suburbs clearly sustained JFK, but a revived city has influenced the airport in surprising ways as well.

About as Quiet as Can Be Expected

The regional pressure from environmental activists in the New York area continued, from the 1970s to the present, to define the outer limits of transportation at JFK. Despite the fact that in the 1990s there might have been 110 takeoffs and landings per hour, one every thirty seconds, the simple fact is that decades of citizen activism have significantly reduced noise. That said, the surrounding communities and the Port Authority have been forced time and again to confront the airlines and the federal officials concerned more about a mixture of safety and profits than about neighborhood tranquility. The Port Authority's pro-growth stance and lackluster sound control in its own backyard, however, have generated significant opposition from surrounding communities fearful of proposals for even more operations, albeit with today's "quieter" aircraft and NextGen control systems. The era when the Port Authority viewed itself as simply the defender of the people against the airlines has long passed.[49]

On a daily basis, according to the City's Department of Environmental Protection, regular aircraft operations frequently exceeded the 100-decibel limit.[50] In 1975 the Port Authority was thus pushing for more retrofits as only 20 percent of JFK traffic was then carried on the quieter 747s, DC-10s, and L-1011s. Boeing 707s and DC-8s, the "oldest and noisiest jets in the fleet," still accounted for 40 percent of aircraft movements at JFK.[51] The FAA allowed the airlines to keep their loud DC-8s and Boeing 707s in service as long as they were buying new planes. There were many planes still out of compliance in the early 1980s, but airlines claimed that it was essential to use these planes for basic profitability in the more competitive deregulated system. In 1984, for instance, about 5 percent of the planes measured in one day were in violation of the noise limit. This sounds small as a percentage, but on an annual basis, it meant that thousands of operations per year were out of compliance: certainly enough to infuriate long-suffering neighbors.[52]

The Port Authority in the 1980s put in place its own rules that more aggressively restricted the loudest engines. This phase-out began in 1982 and focused on cargo shippers such as FedEx and DHL that scheduled older planes in the night hours.[53] By 1989, in fact, only twenty-four planes were allowed to land between the hours of midnight and 6:00 A.M. among all three airports.[54] The Port Authority's regulations were considered at the time far in excess of anything else in the country. While they no doubt helped hundreds of thousands sleep better, they were another limiting factor on the growth of air cargo and passenger service.

The Port Authority's rules were complemented by new federal regulations coming online in the 1990s. The Airport Noise and Capacity Act of 1990, while stripping airports of a great deal of control, is considered to be the first national aviation noise-policy legislation with teeth. The legislation

aimed to eliminate 85 percent of the older and louder stage-two engines by 1999.[55] The introduction of large numbers of 757s on order in the mid-1980s gave further hope. JFK in 1991 was already a bit better off than some other airports when it came to airline utilization of quieter stage-three engines (70 percent of the airplanes into JFK were so equipped) because of the large number of modern 747s. The new 757s coming into service would further help the situation not just at JFK but more crucially at Newark and LaGuardia.[56] The FAA, in characteristic form, was slow to pressure the airlines to make updates required under the laws[57] and even threatened the Port Authority with financial penalties if it tried to put in place more stringent regulations, but in time most of the stage-two aircraft were retired from service.[58]

As usual, the Port Authority quickly trotted out the victory banner for surrounding neighborhoods. The Port Authority in the 1990s credited "quieter jet engines, new flight paths and better use of runways with reducing significant airport noise for hundreds of thousands of people" in Queens. It claimed that whereas in 1990, 862,239 people lived under areas of flights at 65 decibels or higher, by 1994 they reported that the number had dropped to just 210,995.[59] On the whole, it claimed that between 1992 and 2003, there was a 92 percent reduction in the number of people affected by noise.[60] They gave credit to the Noise and Capacity Act, stage-three engines, and new flight paths.[61] A few caveats in this success must be noted. First is the fact that over two hundred thousand residents were still living in environments that regularly experienced over 65 decibels of noise—anywhere else and that might be considered a great many aggravated souls. Second, although the fleet was much quieter, there were more flights using JFK and other regional airports as traffic picked up again. More planes, even quieter ones, were still an additional annoyance to many residents. Between 1995 and 1997 alone, twenty thousand flights were added at LaGuardia and JFK.[62] The high-density rule was thus extended until 2007 under pressure from the Queens delegation in Congress.[63]

Even with new planes and quieter engines that were the result of regional political cooperation, flight paths sometimes pitted New York neighborhoods against each other. These conflicts, according to many participants, reflected the major social divisions in the region.[64] Within the Rockaways, for instance, many residents believed they were victims of environmental racism. In the 1990s, Friends of the Rockaways "charged that flights are directly over poor and minority neighborhoods—not the richer,

whiter neighborhoods." Arverne and Edgemere, "two struggling areas with large public housing projects," constantly had flights overhead, while Belle Harbor, Breezy Point, and Neponsit, affluent neighborhoods in the Rockaways, appeared to be less affected. The Port Authority and FAA made some efforts in the early 1990s to fairly space these overflights in the Rockaways among the various communities.[65]

Everyone in the Rockaways could at least agree, however, that they were getting the short end of the stick in the big picture: "Over the past decade, the number of flights that roar over the Rockaways has doubled, while more affluent areas—such as the Five Towns area in Nassau—have been left virtually untouched." The noise maps seem to reflect this inequality between affluence and everyone else, but an aggressive fair-share program has attempted in the past decade to spread landing paths over a mix of affluent, middle-class, and poor neighborhoods in the region (including both the city and Nassau County). The neighborhoods close to the airport, however, are always going to be highly affected, and many are, for a variety of reasons having nothing to do with the airport, poorer with higher numbers of minority residents. Public housing communities in the Rockaways, for instance, are frequently directly under major landing routes for JFK because their communities are directly aligned with a major runway.[66]

The remaining impact of the airports might have been mitigated somewhat if the Port Authority had been more aggressive with soundproofing. Port Authority airports in 2000 had spent less than the fifteen other busiest American airports on noise reduction, even though they are collectively the busiest in the country. At this point, the airports were collecting three dollars per airline ticket for noise reduction but spending almost nothing: "Airports nationwide are spending millions in per ticket charges to soundproof homes, schools and build quieter runways, yet in New York and New Jersey, the Port Authority seems to be taking money for nothing." Chicago, by contrast, has earned praise for soundproofing tens of thousands of homes and many schools affected by aircraft noise. Between 1983 and 2000, in comparison, the Port Authority paid for just seventy-three schools to be soundproofed. Residents have also expressed their dismay about the comparatively small number of noise monitors in the area compared to other cities.[67] A study by the mayor's Council on the Environment found that "nearly 70% of residents who live in the paths of overhead airplanes perceive themselves to be in poorer health, describe more sleeping difficulties, and report that noise interferes with their daily activities." Many residents

in Queens and Nassau County are now (2014) fighting the implementation of new landing patterns, made possible by NextGen satellite technology, that would significantly boost operations at JFK and LaGuardia. Many residents of the region are well aware that changes in flight patterns that provide benefits to the region as a whole in reduced noise and pollution may still negatively influence their local quality of life if they are unlucky enough to be under the new routes; because New York is so densely populated, the numbers of affected families for any change is usually always counted in the thousands. That so many of the affected residents in Queens and Nassau County are middle-class or wealthier, with strong voter turnout, makes a difference in the attention they receive from elected officials.[68]

In sum, despite significant progress, there are still opportunities for mitigating noise pollution. The Port Authority, by most accounts, has been more aggressive adjusting flight patterns and pushing for new jet and air control technology (which costs the Port Authority very little of its own money) rather than more expensive mitigation including soundproofing and buying out the most affected homeowners. The long history of aircraft noise at JFK nevertheless provides reason for hope that a balance can still be struck between environmental concerns and the bottom line. Rather than destroying aviation, as many air executives once prophesied, or entirely destroying the quality of life as many activists feared, regulation has encouraged innovation in airplane design, air-traffic systems, and everyday flight operations.

A Losing Battle for the Bay

The post-1990s rebirth of JFK Airport included new terminals, roadways, a people-mover system, tighter security, and even a slow but steady diminution in aircraft noise, but the long-term crisis of Jamaica Bay, despite some upgrades here and there, continues. While the further deterioration of the bay might in some places create a call for airport expansion into a now degraded environment, New York is heroically trying to rescue this neglected space.

Critics of the Port Authority in 1992 reported, "A petroleum slick has surfaced on Jamaica Bay, traced to a vast lake of jet fuel beneath Kennedy Airport that the Port Authority was ordered to clean up more than a decade ago." Estimates put the size of the spill underground between five million and nine million gallons. It was so bad that reportedly "at low tide, fuel can be seen bubbling from Kennedy's rocky shore."[69] For a number of decades, underground lines had leaked, and the Port Authority had made matters worse by pumping a toxic blend of fuel and water out of the fuel tanks and simply dumping it on the ground or in area waterways. A JFK manager admitted, "In just one year they spilt 60,000 gallons of fuel in daily operations."[70] The Port Authority was still playing catch-up in the 1990s, building an underground wall to stop underground oil from leaking into the bay, pumping out the remaining oil, and cleaning the separated water. No doubt the damage to many areas nearby is already done.[71] The Natural Resources Defense Council also listed LaGuardia and JFK as "among the five largest sources of industrial volatile compounds and nitrous oxide in the NYC area."[72]

Airport managers have a lot to answer for in terms of pollution, but airport pollution was just one of many factors that undermined the surrounding ecology. On a daily basis, for instance, Jamaica Bay treatment plants still discharge 250 million gallons of treated wastewater. This treated water includes high levels of nitrogen (and many toxic metals, including cadmium, lead, copper, nickel, and zinc) that may be having a negative effect on marsh grass.[73] Pollution had also long ago leaked into the edges of Jamaica Bay from a municipal landfill in Brooklyn close to the Starrett City (Spring Creek) development. One estimate counted between 20 million and 30 million gallons of polychlorinated biphenyl-infused oil in the landfill that was dumped illegally between 1974 and 1978 as a result of bribes. Visitors to the city were also greeted in the 1970s and 1980s by illegally dumped vehicles rotting within sight of the Belt Parkway.[74]

Even as New York finally dragged out the cars and demanded cleanup of the most toxic sites, an even more menacing environmental threat has emerged: rising sea levels. Climate change may cancel out the decades of efforts to upgrade the marshlands. It also bears noting that the accelerated production of carbon dioxide is, in part, a product of the growing popularity of air travel. Jamaica Bay for the past decade has been losing on average 40 acres of wetlands a year. One estimate finds that the marshland may be entirely gone by about 2025.[75] The marshes have already declined from 3,300 acres in the early 1900s to 2,200 acres in 2002.[76] Efforts are under way to restore marshlands, but it is not clear if the efforts can work. Sand was dredged and sprayed into a marsh, for instance, to increase its elevation so that new marsh grass can grow. Hurricane Sandy, however, swamped most of the bay in 2013, with still unknown consequences to ecology.[77]

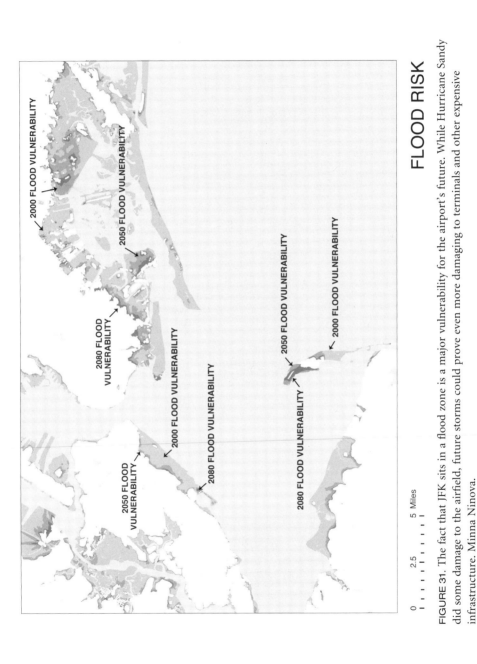

FLOOD RISK

0   2.5   5 Miles

FIGURE 31. The fact that JFK sits in a flood zone is a major vulnerability for the airport's future. While Hurricane Sandy did some damage to the airfield, future storms could prove even more damaging to terminals and other expensive infrastructure. Minna Ninova.

One of the few thriving species in the bay are the gulls. Just like New Yorkers struggle for every square inch of urban space, so too do the laughing gulls that enjoy the grassy open spaces around the airport and nesting spots in the bay. The tarmac, for instance, proved an excellent surface for breaking clamshells. Some of the gulls' food also comes from the landfills in the area, but the airport proved a rich hunting territory as well. Taxi drivers provide a good bit of food as they waited around for fares; even dumpsters at the rental-car parking lots provide good eating. In 1990, JFK may have been only twentieth in airport operations in the United States, but it was first by ten times in the total number of bird strikes per ten thousand operations. In 1998, there were 7,629 gull nests on islands adjacent to JFK. Gulls loved the bay! It is notable that the major colonies were right where the runway was extended into Jamaica Bay in 1962. The National Park Service encouraged cutting of grass, reducing puddles, and chasing off birds, but the humane path has not been entirely successful.[78]

Taking a harder line is not easy, however, in activist New York. Animal-rights activists and the federal government are understandably interested in protecting animals in the wildlife refuge: "But any attack on the laughing gull . . . will pit Kennedy officials against federal laws protecting migratory species, as well as the National Park Service, which oversees the Jamaica Bay refuge where the birds now safely nest and raise their young." The Port Authority tried cannons, for instance, to scare gulls away and even played tape recordings of seagulls in distress.[79] Tipping scales in favor of more radical and violent measures have been major collisions between gulls and airplanes. In 1989, for instance, there were 187 bird-plane collisions at JFK; two 747s had to make emergency landings in 1991 after smacking into birds. In 1991 the animal damage control unit went out and laid low almost 15,000 gulls; the strikes had declined 70 percent by that September.[80] Since 1991, Port Authority wildlife biologists have regularly killed hundreds of bird per year and used other techniques including close-cut grass, pyrotechnics, birds of prey, lasers, and close tabs on cabbie snacking. Bird strikes are still high at JFK but much reduced from the past.[81]

The airport's environmental context is still influencing operations in a dramatic fashion. With a valued wildlife refuge as its neighbor, the Port Authority has limited options for waste disposal, expansion, and airplane safety. Like noise regulation, striking a better balance between airport neighbors (in this case, animals and plants) and commerce is difficult. Larger aircraft and better air control have meant that many more passengers can come over the bay without filling in more of it; new technologies promise more humane ways of mitigating damage. In the long term, however, global competition may once again force residents and politicians of the New York region to trade natural resources such as clean air, thriving bird populations, and marshlands for economic growth. For now, however, quality of life and environmental protection remain dominant values in the region.

Gateway to the Metropolis

JFK, in partnership with LaGuardia and Newark, remains a functioning, if imperfect, gateway to a long settled, wealthy, diversified, and crowded postindustrial urban region of approximately 18 million people. In other words, they get the job done, and safely, nearly every day. In spite of its manifest flaws, JFK International in particular has helped New York achieve and sustain regional renewal in the postwar era. JFK may have fallen from the top ranks of global international airports, but there are reasons to believe that this slipping rank, while a cause of concern, is not quite as apocalyptic as many believe. First, JFK is again the number one airport in the United States for international travel. The continuing popularity of New York for tourists, the strong business community, the short distance to Europe, and the aviation demands of 18 million residents, many of whom are recent immigrants, maintain this powerful lead.

JFK has fallen behind competing global airports in the total numbers of international passengers (sixteenth globally in 2012), but lists of this type are frequently misleading. The world's busiest international airport, London's Heathrow, for instance, processed approximately 64 million international passengers in 2012 as opposed to JFK's modest 24 million. Yet European nations with leading international hubs, such as London or Paris, have a much more limited number of international airports, possess nationally dominant cities, and are part of a continent with many small countries (and growing economic and political ties) and thus many international travelers covering comparatively short distances. More than half of all international travelers out of Great Britain's airports, for instance, are moving to or from Europe. The airports in the developing world now exceeding JFK's passenger numbers often benefit from massive state investment in airlines and terminals (Singapore, Dubai, Hong Kong) and a limited number of international hubs nearby.[82] Among the important differences between JFK and its global competitors are the numerous urban

Table 4. Summary Statistics for the Three Major Regional Airports

Airport	Acres	Daily Movements	Runways	Longest Runway (ft)	Gates	Parking Spaces
Kennedy	4,390	1,260	4	14,572	141	17,150
Newark	2,207	1,150	3	11,000	104	22,000
LaGuardia	680	1,126	2	7,000	74	11,344
Total	7,277	3,536	9	14,572	319	50,494

Source: Port Authority

rivals in the United States for international travel (including Newark International), the turbulent history of airlines post-deregulation, the comparative isolation of the United States geographically from the developing world, modest national population growth, and the less regulated market context.

If lists like this do matter at some level, then the totals for the metropolitan area can soothe the most worried New Yorkers. JFK, Newark, and LaGuardia considered as a single regional system, in the manner of the Port Authority when it presents totals, moves over a hundred million passengers per year, making it second in the world in terms of total passengers. In fact, in an era of airline consolidation and perpetual boom and bust cycles, the New York region is pulling away from many cities in the nation, such as Pittsburgh (which lost its USAirways hub), in terms of air-service quality. A passenger might likely be delayed and frustrated in New York, but JFK and area airports still provide direct flights to almost anywhere around the globe every day; this simply is not the case for a smaller city like Cleveland or Pittsburgh. Airlines, in order to cover escalating fuel costs, have restructured to emphasize full flights circulating among the most populous urban centers both nationally and globally. In the process, they have cut less profitable routes to smaller cities, reducing the ability of these cities to compete with a global metropolis like New York.

Examining JFK without a global score card reveals other strengths despite widespread unhappiness. JFK alone makes a $31.5 billion contribution to the regional economy, generates 224,000 jobs, and contributes $11.3 billion in wages. Approximately 36,000 New Yorkers (from across the region) are still directly employed at the airport. The employee levels alone make JFK a leading regional central business district in its own right.[83] Air cargo is still a lucrative industry for the region, which leads the nation in total value of cargo. JFK also still bestows great advantages for firms and travelers despite its poor reputation. Fortune 500 companies based in the area, such as PepsiCo and Pfizer, and other companies and hedge funds are heavy users of both commercial and general aviation regionally.[84] Nearly all the aviation activity in New York State also still takes place at LaGuardia and JFK (84 percent of airport economic impact) despite efforts to develop smaller and more distant airports, such as Stewart and Macarthur, as major regional hubs.

The rumor of New York's demise, and that of JFK, continue to be exaggerated. The New York metropolitan area suffers from many long-term issues—high costs, taxes, climate vulnerability, traffic jams—but the combination of global connectivity, diversified economy, luxuriant suburbs, upscale urban districts, low crime, and good infrastructure (clean water, good schools, and decent roads) is frequently overlooked in one-dimensional global comparisons such as these. Despite the growing challenge from rising world cities, the New York region in 2012 still ranked number one according to an *Economist* benchmarking of global city competitiveness, receiving very high marks for economic strength, physical capital, financial maturity, institutional effectiveness, and social and cultural character.[85] Hundreds of millions of people in India and China may, for instance, enjoy brand-new airports, but getting enough power, clean air, employment, good public schools, public safety, and clean water can be a struggle on a day-to-day basis. Many mobile, educated people from these countries still come to live permanently in the New York region for these reasons. And when they need a flight home, they can easily catch one, usually that day.

The current resurgence of JFK, however, is no time for complacency. The early leadership in aviation of JFK International relied upon the vision of Mayor La Guardia, Robert Moses, and Austin Tobin, the historical wealth and density of the city, and a highly regulated transportation system. The airport's long-term growth—despite major design flaws, deregulation, uneven management, and citizen resistance—has depended upon the metropolitan area's diversified economy and wealth. Historical chance may no longer be enough. The metropolitan area's haphazard transportation planning and lackluster management at JFK by the Port Authority have not mortally harmed the airport, but they have not helped it either—

particularly as global competitors seek to divert global transportation routes away from the Western hemisphere. The quality of airport management at the Port Authority and cooperation among regional players are poised to be major challenges during these coming decades if New York is to maintain its status as an important global city.[86]

NOTES

INTRODUCTION

1. There have been some standard histories of JFK by the Port Authority, including Geoffrey Arend's *Kennedy International* (New York: Air Cargo News, 1981) and George Scullin's *International Airport: The Story of Kennedy Airport and U.S. Commercial Aviation* (New York: Little, Brown, 1968). A few architectural studies have discussed JFK, among other topics, including Mark Blacklock, *Recapturing the Dream: A Design History of JFK Airport* (London: Blacklock, 2005); Alastair Gordon, *Naked Airport: A Cultural History of the World's Most Revolutionary Structure* (Chicago: University of Chicago Press, 2008); and Hugh Pearman, *Airports: A Century of Airports* (New York: Abrams, 2004).

2. Reyner Banham, "The Obsolescent Airport," *Architectural Review* October 1962, 252; William Burrows, "Time Runs Out at JFK," *New York*, 29 July 1968, 14–21. The 80 percent estimate is from Thomas Leslie, "The Pan Am Terminal at Idlewild/Kennedy Airport and the Transition from Jet Age to Space Age," *Design Issues* 21, no. 1 (Winter 2005).

3. On urban renewal in New York, see recent books by Samuel Zipp, *Manhattan Projects: The Rise and Fall of Urban Renewal in Cold War New York* (New York: Oxford, 2010); Nicholas Bloom, *Public Housing That Worked: New York in the Twentieth Century* (Philadelphia: University of Pennsylvania Press, 2008); Suleiman Osman, *The Invention of Brownstone Brooklyn: Gentrification and the Search for Authenticity in Postwar New York* (New York: Oxford University Press, 2011); Hilary Ballon and Kenneth T. Jackson, *Robert Moses and the Modern City: The Transformation of New York* (New York: Norton, 2007); Joel Schwartz, *The New York Approach: Robert Moses, Urban Liberals, and the Redevelopment of the Inner City* (Columbus: Ohio State University Press, 1993); and Robert Caro, *The Power Broker* (New York: Knopf, 1974). Those looking for details on individual projects would do well to consult Robert Stern, *New York 1960: Architecture and Urbanism Between the Second World War and the Bicentennial* (New York: Manacelli, 1995), as well as Kenneth T. Jackson, editor, *The Encyclopedia of New York City* (New Haven, Conn.: Yale University Press, 1995).

4. My perspective on suburban and regional issues has been shaped by works such as Louise Mozingo, *Pastoral Capitalism: A History of Suburban Corporate Landscapes* (Cambridge, Mass.: MIT Press, 2011); Caro, *The Power Broker*; Kenneth T. Jackson, *Crabgrass Frontier: The Suburbanization of the United States* (New York: Oxford University Press, 1985); Joel Garreau, *Edge City: Life on the New Frontier* (New York: Anchor, 1991); Robert Fishman, *Bourgeois Utopias: The Rise and Fall of Suburbia* (New York: Basic, 1987); Roger Panetta, *Westchester: The American Suburb* (New York: Fordham University Press, 2006); and Robert Bruegmann, *Sprawl: A Compact History* (Chicago: University of Chicago Press, 2006). I also have been influenced by the planning perspective on sprawl, although not necessarily their recommendations, in works such as Andres Duany et al., *Suburban Nation: The Rise of Sprawl and the Decline of the American Dream* (New York: Macmillan, 2001), as well as standard urban planning textbooks such as J. Barry Cullingworth et al., *Planning in the USA: Policies, Issues and Processes* (New York: Routledge, 1997).

5. John D. Kasarda and Greg Lindsay, *Aerotropolis: The Way We'll Live Next* (New York: Farrar, Straus and Giroux, 2012).

6. The literature on airports, and even on JFK, is large, but the historical treatment of airports is much smaller. On national airports and the airport industry, see works such as Janet Bednarek, *America's Airports* (University Station: Texas A&M University Press, 2001); Mark Rose and Bruce Seely, *The Best Transportation System in the World* (Philadelphia: University of Pennsylvania Press, 2010); and Mark Salter, editor, *Politics at the Airport* (Minneapolis: University of Minnesota Press, 2008). See also general aviation history, such as T. A. Heppenheimer, *Turbulent Skies: The History of Commercial Aviation* (New York: Wiley, 1995).

7. Robert Moses, "The Future of Jamaica Bay and the 'Experts,'" *Park East*, 8 April 1971, AQL.

8. Robert Caro provides a colorful but short description of O'Dwyer's decision. See Caro, *Power Broker*, 776–77.

9. See Jameson Doig, *Empire on the Hudson: Entrepreneurial Vision and Political Power at the Port of New York Authority* (New York: Columbia University Press, 2001).

10. Historical accounts of New York subways include Clifton Hood, *722 Miles: The Building of the Subways and How They Transformed New York* (New York: Simon and Schuster, 1993); Julia Solis, *New York Underground: The Anatomy of a City* (New York: Routledge, 2005); and Peter Derrick, *Tunneling to the Future: The Story of the Great Subway Expansion That Saved New York* (New York: New York University Press, 2001).

11. Discussion of the challenges of regional governance and the role of the Port Authority in that scenario is provided by Michael Danielson and Jameson Doig, *New York: The Politics of Urban Regional Development* (Berkeley: University of California Press, 1983). More general books on the problems related to regional governance include Jon Teaford, *The Metropolitan Revolution: The Rise of Post-Urban America* (New York: Columbia University Press, 2006), and Myron Orfield, *Metropolitics: A*

Regional Agenda for Community and Stability (Washington, D.C.: Brookings Institution Press, 1997).

12. Researchers such as Saskia Sassen, Margaret O'Mara, John Findlay, and William Rohe have made strong cases that technology clusters, for instance, are highly influenced by their surroundings. See, for example, Margaret Pugh O'Mara, *Cities of Knowledge: Cold War Science and the Search for the Next Silicon Valley* (Princeton: Princeton University Press, 2005); John Findlay, *Magic Lands: Western Cityscape and American Culture After 1940* (Berkeley: University of California Press, 1992); William H. Rohe, *The Research Triangle: From Tobacco Road to Global Prominence* (Philadelphia: University of Pennsylvania Press, 2011); Saskia Sassen, *The Global City: New York, London, Tokyo* (Princeton: Princeton University Press, 1991), and *Deciphering the Global: Its Scales, Space and Subjects* (New York: Routledge.

13. On Jane Jacobs, see *The Death and Life of Great American Cities* (New York: Random House, 1961); Alice Alexiou, *Jane Jacobs, Urban Visionary* (New Brunswick, N.J.: Rutgers University Press, 2006); Anthony Flint, *Wrestling with Moses, How Jane Jacobs Took on New York's Master Builder and Transformed the American City* (New York: Random House, 2009); Roberta Brandes Gratz, *The Battle for Gotham: New York in the Shadow of Robert Moses and Jane Jacobs* (New York: Nation, 2010); Max Page and Tim Mennel, editors, *Reconsidering Jane Jacobs* (Chicago: American Planning Association, 2011); and Timothy Mennel, Jo Steffens, and Christopher Klemek, *Block by Block: Jane Jacobs and the Future of New York* (New York: Municipal Art Society, 2007).

14. The many annual reports of the Port Authority in this era document the scale, ambition, and technology embraced at the time. See Port Authority of New York-New Jersey (hereafter PANYNJ) Annual Reports, 1948–1970. These reports also document many of the troubles faced by the Port Authority with management, capacity, and expansion. Copies of most of these reports can found in the research collection of the New York Public Library. The September 11 attacks unfortunately destroyed the Port Authority's extensive archive; as a result I have been forced to use some remaining materials copied by Jameson Doig as well as various reports and publications created by the Port Authority and now stored in libraries across the city and country.

CHAPTER 1. FROM IDLEWILD TO NEW YORK INTERNATIONAL

Epigraph: Joseph McGoldrick, "Report of the Board of Estimate of the City of New York to Accompany the Proposed Airline Leases at the Municipal Airport at Idlewild," 23 August 1945, New York Public Library (hereafter NYPL).

1. "New York as an Air Center," *New York Times*, 23 July 1944.

2. James Kaplan, *The Airport: Terminal Nights and Runway Days at John F. Kennedy International* (New York: Morrow, 1994), xix–xx.

3. "Industries: Airplane Production in Queens," *Queensborough*, May 1918, 1.

4. Harry Berkowitz, "We've Lost an Engine," *Newsday*, 19 August 1991.

5. See T. A. Heppenheimer, *Turbulent Skies: The History of Commercial Aviation* (New York: Wiley, 1995), for an overview of this process and the national picture.

6. "Answers of the Port of New York Authority to Questionnaire of Civil Aeronautics Board, Dated May 4, 1943, Relating to Long-Range Problems in Civil Aviation," 28 May 1945, Box 96, Municipal Archive (hereafter MA).

7. Ibid.

8. See the classic by Thomas Kessner, *Fiorello H. La Guardia and the Making of Modern New York* (New York: McGraw Hill, 1989).

9. Alastair Gordon, *Naked Airport: A Cultural History of the World's Most Revolutionary Structure* (New York: Henry Holt, 2004), 112.

10. Roy Carlton, "Idlewild Was Envisioned," *Long Island Daily Press*, 29 July 1948.

11. "Idlewild Airport Wins Council Test," *New York Times*, 6 December 1941, 33.

12. Regional Plan Association, *Graphic Regional Plan*, 1929, vol. 1, p. 306. Elmer Holmes Bobst Library, New York University (hereafter NYU)

13. "Air Tour," *Long Island Journal*, 4 December 1941, Archives at Queens Library (hereafter AQL)

14. "Jamaica Bay," *Brooklyn Daily Eagle*, 24 May 1896, AQL.

15. "Miracle on the Bay," *Long Island Daily Press*, 2 December 1957, AQL.

16. City of New York, "Report on the Main Drainage and Sewage Disposal of the Area Tributary to Jamaica Bay," 1917, 14–15, AQL.

17. 14 November 1954, paper not noted, Jamaica Bay Vertical Files, AQL.

18. "Awards Approved for Airport Site," *New York Times*, 14 January 1942, 23; "Location of the Idlewild Airport Neighborhood in Relation to the 5 Boroughs of New York," Board of Education City of New York, 1945, Box 96, 1934 to 1945 subject files, MA

19. Robert Moses to Board of Estimate, Robert Moses (hereafter RM) Papers, 10 June 1948, Box 99, Folder 1948, NYPL. Any number of promotional articles are available at the AQL in clipping files related to Jamaica Bay: see, for instance, Hermann De Selding, "The Harbor of New York," *Record and Guide*, 23 March 1918.

20. Jeffrey Kroessler, "The Greatest Port That Never Was," *Seaport*, Spring 1993, AQL.

21. Robert Moses to Fiorello La Guardia, 18 July 1938, included in a report entitled the *Future of Jamaica Bay*, Department of Parks, City of New York, 18 July 1938, AQL.

22. Geoffrey Arend, *Great Airports: Kennedy International* (New York: Air Cargo News, 1981), 32.

23. "LaGuardia Field Banned," *Long Island Star*, 30 July 1948, AQL.

24. See Ted Steinberg, *Gotham Unbound* (New York: Simon and Schuster, 2014).

25. Fiorello La Guardia, "Finest Airport in the World," *New York Times*, 21 January 1945.

26. Robert Moses to Fiorello La Guardia, 4 June 1945, NYPL Special Collections.

27. Jeffrey Kroessler, "The Greatest Port That Never Was," *Seaport*, Spring 1993, AQL.

28. Robert Moses to Fiorello La Guardia, 18 July 1938, included in a report entitled "The Future of Jamaica Bay," Department of Parks, City of New York, 18 July 1938, AQL.

29. *Long Island Daily Press*, 22 September 1938, AQL.

30. Robert Moses to Vincent Impellitteri, RM Papers, 10 June 1948, Box 99, Folder 1948, NYPL.

31. Fiorello La Guardia, "Finest Airport in the World," *New York Times*, 21 January 1945.

32. Josef Israels, "21st Century Airport Now," undated and marked article, ca. 1943, AQL.

33. Leo McDermott, "Idlewild Airport," address given to the city council finance committee, 16 December 1943, Box 96, MA.

34. "Awards Approved for Airport Site," *New York Times*, 14 January 1942, 23.

35. Mayor La Guardia to Comptroller McGoldrick, 17 November 1941, Box 96, MA.

36. "Idlewild Airport Wins Council Test," *New York Times*, 6 December 1941, 33.

37. Airline Observes 50,000 Crossing," *New York Times*, 28 June 1955.

38. "New Idlewild Radar," *Long Island Press*, 6 July 1958, AQL.

39. "$48,028,800 Voted for Relief in City," *New York Times*, 4 January 1942, 1.

40. "Idlewild Airport Site Costs $6,079,731," *New York Times*, 26 February 1945; Fiorello La Guardia, "Finest Airport in the World," *New York Times*, 21 January 1945.

41. "Idlewild to Wipe Out," 27 February 1945, unknown newspaper, AQL; figure for total land costs from Joseph McGoldrick, "Report of the Board of Estimate of the City of New York to Accompany the Proposed Airline Leases at the Municipal Airport at Idlewild," 23 August 1945, p. 7, NYPL.

42. Fiorello La Guardia, "Finest Airport in the World," *New York Times*, 21 January 1945.

43. Chairman Howard Cullman to Mayor William O'Dwyer, 15 January 1947, MA; "Idlewild Plan Cut to Save 20 Million," *New York Times*, 25 August 1946.

44. "An Authority for Airports," *New York Times*, 29 January 1946. See Gail Radford, *The Rise of the Public Authority: Statebuilding and Economic Development in Twentieth Century America* (Chicago: University of Chicago Press, 2013); and Jameson Doig, *Empire on the Hudson: Entrepreneurial Vision and Political Power at the Port of New York Authority* (New York: Columbia University Press, 2001). See also Louise Nelson Dyble, *Paying the Toll: Local Power, Regional Politics, and the Golden Gate Bridge* (Philadelphia: University of Pennsylvania Press, 2009); and Janet R. Bendarek, "Layer upon Layer: Public Authorities and Airport Ownership in St. Louis, 1947–1980," *Journal of Planning History* 8, no. 1, (February 2009), 3–26.

45. Chairman Howard Cullman to Mayor William O'Dwyer, 15 January 1947, Jameson Doig Papers, New Jersey State Archive (hereafter JDP); "Idlewild Plan Cut to Save 20 Million," *New York Times*, 25 August 1946.

46. The outlines of the shift in management is tracked in such articles as "LaGuardia Is Set for Radio Finale," *New York Times*, 30 December 1945, 18; Warren Moscow, "Moses Emerges as 'Strong Man' of the O'Dwyer Administration," *New York Times*, 8 January 1946, 1; Paul Crowell, "O'Dwyer Sees City $6,000,000 'In Red,'" *New York Times*, 10 January 1946, 1; "Airport Authority Is Set Up for City in Bill Due Tonight," *New York Times*, 28 January 1946, 1; "Idlewild Cost Plan Is Cut, Says Moses," *New York Times*, 22 February 1946, 30; "Sharp Rise Asked in Idlewild Rents," *New York Times*, 10 July 1946; "Guggenheim Quits Airport Authority," *New York Times*, 19 July 1946; "Airport Authority May Be Scrapped," *New York Times*, 22 July 1946, 21; "Drastic Reduction in Idlewild Costs Sought by Mayor," *New York Times*, 23 July 1946, 1; "Idlewild Critics Scored by Moses," *New York Times*, 12 July 1946, 19; "Airport Proposal Derided by Moses," 25 July 1946, 11; "Idlewild Cost Discussed," *New York Times*, 1 August 1946, 31; "Airlines to Press Idlewild Speed-Up," *New York Times*, 17 January 1947, 25; "Airport Hearings on Wednesday," *New York Times*, 22 January 1947.

47. "Experts Submit New Airport Plan," *New York Times*, 23 December 1946.

48. "Another Idlewild Plan," *New York Times*, 24 December 1946, 16; Paul Crowell, "Experts Submit New Airport Plan," *New York Times*, 21 December 1946.

49. "Airport Authority Named by O'Dwyer," *New York Times*, 7 April 1946.

50. "O'Dwyer Fights Plan," *New York Times*, 9 February 1946.

51. See Jameson Doig's *Empire on the Hudson*, chapters 11 and 12, for a rich and full portrait of Tobin's approach to development and his successful battle to gain control of regional airports.

52. Editorial, "Idlewild Airport," *New York Times*, 11 August 1944.

53. Doig, *Empire on the Hudson*, 254.

54. "Tobin Cites Gains of Port Authority," *New York Times*, 7 August 1948, 27.

55. "Cullman Promises Speed on Airports," *New York Times*, 17 May 1947. See also Doig, *Empire on the Hudson*, for more on the history of the Port Authority up until the 1940s.

56. Robert Bellaire, "Battle of the Airports," *Colliers*, 31 March 1945, 22.

57. "City Officials Cool to Airport Offer," *New York Times*, 20 December 1946, 10.

58. "We Favor the Port Authority," *New York Times*, 16 January 1947, 24.

59. Regional Plan Association, *Thirteenth Annual Report*, December 1942, 4, NYU.

60. "Cullman Promises Speed on Airports," *New York Times*, 17 May 1947.

61. "Port Body Offers to Run Idlewild," *New York Times*, 19 December 1946, 1; "City Delays Action on Airport Plans," *New York Times*, 16 January 1947; Mark Blacklock, *Recapturing the Dream: A Design History of New York's JFK Airport* (London: Blacklock, 2005), 7.

62. "LaGuardia Scores Airport Handling," *New York Times*, 10 April 1947; "City Board Backs Airport Compact," *New York Times*, 17 April 1947, 29.

63. "Port Body Offers to Run Idlewild," *New York Times*, 19 December 1946, 1; PANYNJ, "Summary of Proposal for the Development of New York City Airports," *New York Times*, 18 December 1946, 9; William Conklin, "Port Authority Airport Offers Wins Favorable City Action," *New York Times*, 27 March 1947.

64. "Truman Will Open Idlewild," 1947, unknown publication, AQL. Note that the airport was briefly named for Major Anderson as well.

65. "Truman May Help to Open Idlewild," *New York Times*, 17 September 1947.

66. Saul Pett, "World's Biggest Airport," *Long Island Sunday Press*, 27 June 1948, 4, AQL.

67. PANYNJ, Annual Report, 1948, pp. 22, 29, NYPL.

68. "Name of Idlewild to Be City Airport," *New York Times*, 30 May 1947.

69. "Airport System Takes Shape Here," *New York Times*, 8 May 1950.

70. Saul Pett, "World's Biggest Airport," *Long Island Sunday Press*, 27 June 1948, 4, AQL.

71. George McSherry, "New York International Airport," *Rockaway Review*, June 1949, AQL; "International Airport," *Queensborough Magazine*, August 1948, 7–8, AQL; George Scullin, *International Airport: The Story of Kennedy Airport and U.S. Commercial Aviation* (New York: Little, Brown, 1968), 111–12.

72. "Idlewild Airport Nears Operation," *New York Times*, 29 April 1947.

73. For a more generous appraisal of Tobin and a more detailed account, see Doig, *Empire on the Hudson*, 248–391.

74. "Giants of Airports Costliest to Run," *New York Times*, 27 June 1949.

75. Port Authority of New York (hereafter PANYNJ), Annual Report, 1950, 53; and Annual Report, 1951, page unmarked. NYPL.

76. PANYNJ, Annual Report, 1957, 4, NYPL; "Idlewild Dispute Is Ended," *New York Times*, 6 August 1949, 1.

77. PANYNJ Annual Report, 1948, p. 26, NYPL.

78. Stuart Rochester, *Takeoff at Midcentury: Federal Civil Aviation Policy in the Eisenhower Years, 1953 to 1961* (Washington, DC: U.S. Department of Transportation, FAA, 1976).

79. Heppenheimer, *Turbulent Skies*, chap. 7, 170–95.

80. "Radar to Relieve Air Traffic Jams," *New York Times*, 14 April 1955.

81. "Aviation: Airports," *New York Times*, 11 September 1949.

82. Sidney Goldstein, General Counsel, PANYNJ, "Jet Noise at Airports," Washington, D.C., 29 October 1965, 7, (JDP). Folder and box numbers are not included with these documents as the collection was not yet processed by archive staff.

83. Scullin, *International Airport*, 105; Heppenheimer, *Turbulent Skies*, 127.

84. Mark Rose and Bruce Seely, *The Best Transportation System in the World* (Philadelphia: University of Pennsylvania Press, 2010), 76.

85. Port Authority, "History of NYIA," April 1956, AQL. See also Rose and Seely, *Best Transportation System in the World*, 78.

86. "Aviation: New Luxury," *New York Times*, 7 September 1952.

87. "Clipper London Bound," *New York Times*, 28 April 1952.

88. Blacklock, *Recapturing the Dream*, 8, 14; see also Rose and Seely, *Best Transportation System in the World*, 84. Values calculated using Measuring Worth, 2014, available at http://www.measuringworth.com/uscompare/relativevalue.php.

89. Port Authority, "Metropolitan Transportation—1980," 1963, 257. The Port Authority provides one figure for the New York region in this document, but for reference there were 60,169 overseas airline movements at JFK in 1960 and only 25 at Newark. One can assume with some assurance then that the international travel figures are those of JFK. See Port Authority, "Airport Statistics," 1987, Table I-15–17. NYPL.

90. Answers of the Port of New York Authority to Questionnaire of Civil Aeronautics Board, Dated 4 May 1943, Relating to Long-Range Problems in Civil Aviation," 28 May 1945, Box 96, MA.

91. Gene Jones, "The Forwarder and the Air Cargo Industry," *Via Port of New York New Jersey*, September 1990, 6–7, NYPL.

92. "Export Air Trade Gains Acceptance," *New York Times*, 22 August 1948; Scullin, *International Airport*, 251.

93. William F. Clarke, "Long Island's Industrial Lift," *Long Island Business*, September 1956, 9–10.

94. Richard Cook, "Flying Freight," *Wall Street Journal*, 18 December 1956, 1.

95. Brendan Jones, "Big Rise Forecast in Air Commerce," *New York Times*, 13 June 1954.

96. On highways and car culture, see Christopher Well, *Car Country: An Environmental History* (Seattle: University of Washington Press, 2012); and Owen Gutfreund, *Twentieth Century Sprawl: Highways and the Reshaping of the American Landscape* (New York: Oxford, 2004).

97. "1st Departure Late at Idlewild," *New York Times*, 11 July 1948.

98. "Air Tour," *Long Island [———?] Journal*, 4 December 1941, Clipping File, AQL

99. "Airport of Tomorrow," *New York Herald Tribune*, 1 July 1943.

100. Robert Bellaire, "Battle of the Airports," *Colliers*, 31 March 1945, 22.

101. "Boulevard Extension Approved," *New York Times*, 17 September 1942, 28; "Air Traffic Cops Are Seen by Mayor," *New York Times*, 11 December 1943, 17.

102. "Idlewild Airport Viewed by Mayors," *New York Times*, 3 July 1945.

103. "New Airport Needs a Subway," *Long Island Daily Press*, 15 January 1948, 14.

104. Robert Moses to Nat Schlausky, RM Papers, 18 October 1935, Box 97, Folder 1934–35, NYPL.

105. "Airport's Highway Lags on High-Cost," *New York Times*, 10 May 1948.

106. B. K. Thorne, "New Expressway Shortens Trip to Idlewild," *New York Times*, 22 October 1950.

107. Robert Caro, *The Power Broker* (New York: Knopf, 1974), 908–11, 954–58.

108. Robert Moses to Einar Eriksen, RM Papers, 23 September 1937, Box 97, Folder 1937, NYPL.

109. "Cullman Promises Speed on Airports," *New York Times*, 17 May 1947.

110. Robert Moses to Justice Henry Ughetta, RM Papers, 15 July 1948, Box 99, Folder 1948, NYPL.

111. "Speedier Routes to Airports Urged," *New York Times*, 5 March 1949.

112. B. K. Thorne, "New Expressway Shortens Trip to Idlewild," *New York Times*, 22 October 1950.

113. "Cullman Defends Agency's Policies," *New York Times*, 13 January 1950, 25.

114. Austin J. Tobin, "Changes in Transportation: Effect on Railroads of Growing Use of Autos and Trucks Discussed," *New York Times*, 31 May 1955, 26.

115. PANYNJ, "Summary of Proposal for the Development of New York City Airports," 18 December 1946, 26. NYPL.

116. PANYNJ Annual Report, 1948, p. 26, NYPL. See also John Jakle and Keith Sculle, *Lots of Parking: Land Use in a Car Culture* (Charlottesville: University of Virginia Press, 2004); and Eran Ben-Joseph, *ReThinking a Lot: The Design and Culture of Parking* (Cambridge, Mass.: MIT Press, 2012).

117. Alastair Gordon, *Naked Airport: A Cultural History of the World's Most Revolutionary Structure* (Chicago: University of Chicago Press, 2008).

118. "Big Crowd Attends," *New York Times*, 1 August 1948.

119. See Cradle of Aviation Museum, "Grumman Hellcat," http://www.cradleofaviation.org/history/aircraft/a_fourth_of_july_remembrance.html.

120. Adam Rome, *The Bulldozer in the Countryside: Suburban Sprawl and the Rise of American Environmentalism* (Cambridge: Cambridge University Press, 2001); Chris Sellers, *Crabgrass Crucible: Suburban Nature and Environmentalism in Post WWII America* (Chapel Hill: University of North Carolina Press, 2012). On the reshaping of the New York landscape for profit and growing environmentalism, see also Steinberg, *Gotham Unbound*. For the general patterns of sanitary reform, see Martin Melosi, *The Sanitary City* (Baltimore: Johns Hopkins University Press, 2000). For the experience of another city and the relationship of technological improvement to regulation, see Joel Tarr, editor, *Devastation and Renewal: An Environmental History of Pittsburgh and Its Region* (Pittsburgh: University of Pittsburgh Press, 2005).

121. "Foes of Plane Noise Make Idlewild Tour," *New York Times*, 10 October 1940.

122. "Big Airliners to Be Restricted," *New York Times*, 6 November 1948.

123. Sidney Goldstein, General Counsel, Port of New York Authority, "Jet Noise at Airports," Washington, D.C., 29 October 1965, 1, JDP,

124. "Big Airliners to Be Restricted," *New York Times*, 6 November 1948.

125. "CAA Fees It's Done All It Can to Ease Low-Flying Plane Nuisance," *Long Island Press*, 24 July 1949.

126. Alexis Faust and Dina Taylor, "Aircraft Noise, 1948–1972," for Jameson Doig, 28 October 1986, JDP, 2.

127. Ibid.

128. "10 Airlines Agree to Divert Traffic," *New York Times,* 16 February 1952.

129. "Airports Reroute Half of Runs Here," *New York Times*, 15 April 1954.

130. John Wiley, "What Aviation Means to Queens," Address, 22 November 1957, JDP.

131. "Long Island Groups Protest Big Airports," *New York Times*, 11 March 1952.

132. "Airport Closings Sought," *New York Times*, 22 April 1952.

133. "Jamaica Plane Hit," *New York Times*, 9 April 1952.

134. Frederick Graham, "Aviation: White Noise," *New York Times*, 15 February 1953.

135. "800 Homeowners Sue Airlines and PA," *Long Island Daily Press*, 20 December 1961. See also Sidney Goldstein, General Counsel, Port of New York Authority, "Jet Noise at Airports," Washington, D.C., 29 October 1965, 10, JDP.

136. "Cullman Predicts More Air Travel," *New York Times*, 23 April 1952.

137. Seymour Marks, "Giant Plane Repair Base," *Long Island Daily Press*, 29 January 1953.

138. Rochester, *Takeoff at Midcentury*. See also Heppenheimer, *Turbulent Skies*, for a full description of the development of jet engines during World War II and after.

139. Sidney Goldstein, General Counsel, Port of New York Authority, "Jet Noise at Airports," Washington, D.C., 29 October 1965, 1, JDP.

140. C. R. Smith to Austin Tobin, 10 October 1952, JDP.

141. John Wiley, Draft White Paper for Congressional Testimony, 6 March 1962, JDP.

142. Alexis Faust and Dina Taylor, "Aircraft Noise, 1948–1972," for Jameson Doig, 28 October 1986, 5–8, JDP.

143. Ibid., 12.

CHAPTER 2. TERMINAL CITY'S SUBURBAN FORM

1. "A Great Air Terminal," *New York Times*, 5 December 1957.

2. PANYNJ Annual Report, 1954, p. 33, NYPL.

3. "Idlewild Airport Plan," *Architectural Forum*, March 1955.

4. PANYNJ Annual Report, 1954, p. 33, NYPL; George Scullin, *International Airport: The Story of Kennedy Airport and U.S. Commercial Aviation* (New York: Little, Brown, 1968), 8.

5. PANY Annual Report, 1963, p. 19; PANY Annual Report, 1951, page unmarked. NYPL.

6. "Of Idlewild," *Today's Living*, 24 April 1960.

7. "Idlewild Feature," *Architectural Record*, September 1961.

8. Geoffrey Arend, *Great Airports: Kennedy International* (New York: Air Cargo News, 1981), 84–89.

9. Alastair Gordon, *Naked Airport: A Cultural History of the World's Most Revolutionary Structure* (New York: Henry Holt, 2004).

10. "Idlewild Airport Plan," *Architectural Forum*, March 1955.

11. Mel Elfin, "New Idlewild Layout," *Long Island Star Journal*, 3 December 1957.

12. Gilbert Millstein, "Airport of the Jet Age," *New York Times*, 8 November 1959.

13. Michael Thomas, "JFK's IAB: Back to the Future," *Via Port of New York New Jersey*, September-October 1995, 23–25, NYPL

14. John Wiley, "What Aviation Means to Queens," address, 22 November 1957, JDP.

15. James Kaplan, *The Airport: Terminal Nights and Runway Days at John F. Kennedy International* (New York: Morrow, 1994), 13.

16. Port Authority, "The History of New York International Airport," April 1956. AQL.

17. "Wonderful World That Aviation Built," *Today's Living*, 24 April 1960, 4.

18. "Synagogue Is Started at Idlewild," *New York Times*, 30 June 1959.

19. PANYNJ Annual Report, 1960, p. 5, NYPL; *Airport News*, 10 July 1959, 2. NYPL.

20. T. A. Heppenheimer, *Turbulent Skies: The History of Commercial Aviation* (New York: Wiley, 1995), 126.

21. "Transport News," *New York Times*, 9 December 1957.

22. PANYNJ Annual Report, 1954, p. 33, NYPL.

23. "Cost of Terminal at Idlewild Rises," *New York Times*, 30 July 1956; Mark Blacklock, *Recapturing the Dream: A Design History of New York's JFK Airport* (London: Blacklock, 2005), 38.

24. Paul Friedlandersy, "Idlewild Transformed," *New York Times*, 8 December 1957.

25. Jeffrey Hardwick, *Mall Maker: Victor Gruen, Architect of an American Dream* (Philadelphia: University of Pennsylvania Press, 2010). My book on James Rouse explores similar efforts: *Merchant of Illusion: James Rouse, America's Salesman of the Businessman's Utopia* (Columbus: Ohio State University Press, 2004).

26. Paul Friedlandersy, "Idlewild Transformed," *New York Times*, 8 December 1957.

27. Morris Gilbert, "Idlewild Speeds Its Passenger Processing," *New York Times*, 16 March 1958.

28. "Cost of Terminal at Idlewild Rises," *New York Times*, 30 July 1956; Blacklock, *Recapturing the Dream*, 38.

29. Scullin, *International Airport*, 153.

30. *Airport News*, 29 May 1959, p. 10, NYPL Science and Technology Library.

31. Gilbert Millstein, "Airport of the Jet Age," *New York Times*, 8 November 1959.

32. Arend, *Great Airports*, 192.

33. Carol Willis, *Form Follows Finance: Skyscraper and Skylines in New York and Chicago* (Princeton: Princeton University Press, 1995).

34. "Airline Planning Umbrella Ramp," *New York Times*, 5 April 1957. For a detailed description of the changing Pan Am Terminal, see Thomas Leslie, "The Pan

Am Terminal at Idlewild/Kennedy Airport and the Transition from Jet Age to Space Age," *Design Issues* vol. 21, no. 1 (Winter 2005), 63–80

35. Blacklock, *Recapturing the Dream*, 20, 138.

36. Scullin, *International Airport*, 154.

37. *The TWA Terminal: Photographs by Ezra Stoller*, introduction by Mark Lamster (New York: Princeton Architectural Press, 1999). See also Eeva Liisa Pelkonen and Donald Albrecht, editors, *Eero Saarinen: Shaping the Future* (New Haven: Yale University Press, 2006).

38. Serianne Worden, "Eero Saarinen's Flight Center," in *Terminal Five*, curated by Rachel Ward, October 2004–2005 (New York: Lukes and Sternberg, 2004), 42–43.

39. Blacklock, *Recapturing the Dream*, 20.

40. *Queensborough Magazine*, December 1978, AQL

41. "Terminal Hailed in Idlewild," *New York Times*, 24 November 1960.

42. Dave Rosenbluth, "Sky City in Transition," *Newsday*, 24 February 1960.

43. "Idlewild Buses to Be Linguistic," *New York Times*, 5 July 1959.

44. "Aviation: Ground Time," *New York Times*, 7 October 1951.

45. "CAB Approves a Helicopter Line," *New York Times*, 6 December 1951.

46. "Aviation: Helicopters," *New York Times*, 22 July 1956.

47. PANYNJ Annual Report, 1955, p. 21, NYPL.

48. "New Rotocraft in New York's Future," January 1960, publication unclear, JFK Documents/Aviation Vertical File, Queens Library Long Island Division, 1950–1969.

49. The Port Authority Aviation Department, "The Public Demand for Air Terminal Services," Aviation Economics Division, September 1961, Virginia Tech Library.

50. Airport Statistics, 1987, Port Authority Aviation Department, 1988, Table II-8, NYPL

51. Blacklock, *Recapturing the Dream*, 85.

52. Richard Cooke, "Jetliner Puzzle," *Wall Street Journal*, 15 October 1958, 1; Scullin, *International Airport*, 132–37. See also Heppenheimer, *Turbulent Skies*, for a full description of the race to develop superchargers and jet engines.

53. Gordon, *Naked Airport*.

54. Richard Witkin, "Idlewild Opened to Jet Airliners," *New York Times*, 4 October 1958.

55. Alexis Faust and Dina Taylor, "Aircraft Noise, 1948–1972," for Jameson Doig, 28 October 1986, p. 19, JDP. See also John Wiley, Draft White Paper for Congressional Testimony, 6 March 1962, JDP, for a detailed description of the process of developing PNdB.

56. Richard Witkin, "Idlewild Opened to Jet Airliners," *New York Times*, 4 October 1958.

57. Richard Witkin, "Sound and Fury over Jets," *New York Times*, 21 September 1958.

58. "Idlewild Check Test Stirs Mixed Noise," *New York Times*, 4 May 1957.

59. "Boeing Says Its Sound Suppressor Cuts Noise of Jet Liner Sharply," *Wall Street Journal*, 3 September 1958, 7.

60. Port Authority Internal Notes, 1 September 1956, p. 14, JDP.

61. Port Authority Internal Notes, 7 December 1957, p. 10, JDP.

62. "Measurement of Comet's Jet Noise," *Fairplay*, London, 21 November 1957.

63. "Weekly Report to the Commissioner from the Executive Director," 15 March 1958, JDP; Austin Tobin to unknown, 23 July 1958, JDP.

64. Richard Witkin, "Sound and Fury over Jets," *New York Times*, 21 September 1958.

65. Richard Cooke, "Jetliner Puzzle," *Wall Street Journal*, 15 October 1958, 1.

66. "Weekly Report to the Commissioner from the Executive Director," 22 November 1958 and 24 June 1959, JDP.

67. PANYNJ Annual Report, 1958, p. 24, NYPL.

68. Edward Hudson, "Jet Noise Rules Tightened Here," *New York Times*, 1 May 1959; Heppenheimer, *Turbulent Skies,* 185.

69. Alexis Faust and Dina Taylor, "Aircraft Noise, 1948–1972," for Jameson Doig, 28 October 1986, p. 22, JDP.

70. Kaplan, *The Airport*, 152.

71. "Hot Weather Adds to Jet Noise," *Aviation Week*, 22 June 1959.

72. Heppenheimer, *Turbulent Skies,* 190–91.

73. Michele Ingrassia, "Where Do They Get Their Rubber Decibel Stretcher?" *Newsday*, 17 November 1975.

74. Joseph Martin, "What's with the Jets?" *Daily News*, 11 November 1959.

75. "More Anti-Noise Motorcades Threatened," *Long Island Daily Press*, 3 September 1959.

76. "Capital Gets Queens Plea," *Herald Tribune*, 27 August 1959; "U.S. State Laws Urged on Jet Noise," *Long Island Daily Press*, 27 August 1959.

77. "Nassau Gets Behind PA on Jet Noise," *Long Island Daily Press*, 29 October 1960.

78. Myron Becker, "Airport Neighbors Agree There's Less Noise Now," *Long Island Daily Press*, 20 September 1959; "Idlewild Adopts New Rules to Cut Airplane Noise," *Long Island Daily Press*, 26 June 1959.

79. Weekly Report to the Commissioner from the Executive Director, 24 June 1959, JDP.

80. "Queens Building Boom Spurred by Airports," *Aviation News*, 10 July 1959, 2.

81. "Queens Industry Led by Airports," *New York Times*, 28 August 1959.

82. "The Influence of a Major Airport on the Economy of Surrounding Areas," PANY, Aviation Development Division, January 1960, University of California, Institute of Transportation Library.

83. "Do You?" National Air Transport Coordinating Committee, New York, 1960, JFK International Clipping File, AQL.

84. Advertisement, *Aviation News*, 19 August 1960, 9, NYPL

85. *Airport News*, 29 May 1959, 15; *Airport News*, 10 July 1959, 2, NYPL.

86. "Do You?" National Air Transport Coordinating Committee, New York, 1960, AQL.

87. John Wiley, "What Aviation Means to Queens," address, 22 November 1957, JDP.

88. "U.S. Fashions en Route," *Via Port of New York New Jersey*, April 1961, 9.

89. S. Sloan Colt, "The Importance of Queens' Airports," *Rockaway Review*, June–July 1961, AQL.

90. "Export NYC: A Roadmap for Creating Jobs Through Exports," report by Manhattan borough president Scott Stringer, June 2013, 17, author's collection.

91. PANY, "Airport Requirements and Sites to Serve the New Jersey–New York Metropolitan Region," December 1966. NYPL.

92. Port Authority, "A Report on Airport Requirements and Sites in the Metropolitan New Jersey-New York Region," 1961, 12. NYPL.

93. Port Authority, "Airport Requirements and Sites to Serve the New Jersey-New York Metropolitan Region," December 1966, 13. NYPL.

94. Ibid., 11.

CHAPTER 3. HOW THE OTHER HALF WAITS

1. Port Authority, "Metropolitan Transportation—1980," 1963, 255, NYPL.

2. Ibid., 245.

3. George Scullin, *International Airport: The Story of Kennedy Airport and U.S. Commercial Aviation* (New York: Little, Brown, 1968), 12–13.

4. "Kheel Says That Port Authority Hoards Profits," *New York Times*, 17 April 1970, 53.

5. Jeffrey Zupan, Richard Barone, and Matthew Lee, *Upgrading to World Class: The Future of the New York Region's Airports* (New York: Regional Plan Association, January 2011), 16.

6. Mark Blacklock, *Recapturing the Dream: A Design History of New York's JFK Airport* (London: Blacklock, 2005), 17, 30, 37.

7. PANY, "Airport Requirements and Sites to Serve the New Jersey–New York Metropolitan Region," December 1966, 39, NYPL.

8. "Idlewild Closing in on Saturation," *Long Island Daily Press*, 8 June 1963.

9. Philip Boffey, "Clogged Airports," *Wall Street Journal*, 22 August 1966, 1.

10. David Bird, "Kennedy Airport Faces Traffic of the 60s with a 40's Design," *New York Times*, 18 August 1968, 90.

11. PANYNJ Annual Report, 1961, pp. 22, 25, NYPL; PANYNJ Annual Report, 1950–60, p. 5, NYPL.

12. Leonard Victor, "Our Crowded Skies," *Long Island Press*, 18 January 1968, AQL; "Landing Fees Boosted," *Wall Street Journal*, 21 November 1967, 12.

13. PANYNJ Annual Report, 1970, p. 25, NYPL.

14. Leonard Victor, "If Not a Jetport . . . Why Not a Wetport?" *Long Island Press*, 19 January 1968, AQL.

15. Michael Unger, *Newsday*, 29 February 1972, Clipping File, AQL.

16. Bruce Lambert, "Agencies Assail LI Wetport," *Newsday*, 15 January 1972.

17. Leonard Victor, "Our Crowded Skies," *Long Island Press*, 18 January 1968, AQL; Martin Arnold, "United Weighing a Cut in Flights," *New York Times*, 23 July 1968.

18. Mohamad Bazzi, "Unlimited Flights Opposed," *Newsday*, 8 February 1999.

19. PANYNJ Annual Report, 1969, p. 25, NYPL.

20. "The Jetport Crisis," *Daily News*, 3 September 1968, 51.

21. Joseph Novitski, "Delays Persist at Airports Here," *New York Times*, 22 July 1968.

22. PANYNJ Annual Report, 1969, p. 25, NYPL.

23. "Tobin for Forcing Air Rescheduling: If Lines Don't, Government Should Step In, He Says," *New York Times*, 29 July 1968, 62.

24. Dave Behrens, "Air Traffic Is Smooth," *Newsday*, 2 June 1969.

25. PANYNJ Annual Report, 1968, p. 10, NYPL.

26. PANYNJ Annual Report, 1970, p. 25, NYPL.

27. Port Authority, "Metropolitan Transportation—1980," 1963, 257, NYPL.

28. Richard Cooke, "Airlines Unhappy with Delays in New York," *New York Times*, 27 October 1967, 34.

29. "Facilities at JFK to Be Exanded," *Wall Street Journal*, 9 September 1966, 11; "Air Transportation," *Rockaway Review*, Summer 1967, AQL.

30. Geoffrey Arend, *Great Airports: Kennedy International* (New York: Air Cargo News, 1981), 193.

31. "Radically Different Facility," *Wall Street Journal*, 14 November 1968; Richard Cooke, "Jumbo Jet Service," *Wall Street Journal*, 27 September 1968, 12.

32. Blacklock, *Recapturing the Dream*, 18, 83.

33. Thomas Leslie, "The Pan Am Terminal at Idlewild/Kennedy Airport and the Transition from Jet Age to Space Age," *Design Issues*, vol. 21, no. 1 (Winter 2005), 76.

34. PANYNJ Annual Report, 1964, pp. 33–34, NYPL.

35. PANYNJ Annual Report, 1973, pp. 27–28, NYPL.

36. PANYNJ Annual Report, 1969, p. 26, NYPL.

37. Betty Beale, "Idlewild Run 'by Ugliest Americans," *Long Island Daily Press*, 3 August 1961.

38. Mrs. Darrell Burkhardt, Letter to the Editor, *New York Times*, ca. 1964.

39. "The Jetport Crisis," *Daily News*, 3 September 1968, 51.

40. "Planners Study Kennedy Road Jams," *New York Times*, 2 January 1969.

41. Port Authority, "Metropolitan Transportation—1980," 1963, 260, NYPL.

42. "Kheel Says That Port Authority Hoards Profits," *New York Times*, 17 April 1970, 53.

43. Port Authority Aviation Department, "The Public Demand for Air Terminal Services," Aviation Economics Division, September 1961, NYPL.

44. PANY, "Airport Requirements and Sites to Serve the New Jersey–New York Metropolitan Region," December 1966, 35, 39, NYPL.

45. "Kheel Says That Port Authority Hoards Profits," *New York Times*, 17 April 1970, 53.

46. "PA to Spend $425 Million on 3 Metropolitan Airports," *Long Island Press*, 1 September 1967, AQL; "Snow Thwarts Bus," *Wall Street Journal*, 4 December 1967, 14.

47. "New York to Spend $1.6 Billion," *Wall Street Journal*, 29 February 1968, 18; PANYNJ Annual Report, 1969, p. 27, NYPL.

48. Frank Prial, "Port Authority to Spur Mass Transit," *New York Times*, 22 June 1972.

49. "Queens Bloc Stalls Rail Link to Kennedy," *Long Island Press*, 20 March 1973.

50. The case and background is described in detail in *United States Trust Co. vs. New Jersey*, 431 U.S. 1 (1977), Justia U.S. Supreme Court, available at http://supreme .justia.com/cases/federal/us/431/1/case.html. It is also discussed in Michael Danielson and Jameson Doig, *New York: The Politics of Urban Regional Development* (Berkeley: University of California Press, 1983).

51. Dennis E. Gale also documents the spread of gangsters to New Jersey in this period: see Gale, *Greater New Jersey: Living in the Shadow of Gotham* (Philadelphia: University of Pennsylvania Press, 2006)

52. See, for instance, Colin Davis, *Waterfront Revolts: New York and London Dock-workers, 1946–1961* (Urbana: University of Illinois Press, 2003); Henry Hill, *Gangsters and Goodfellas* (New York: M. Evans, 2004).

53. "$35,000 Pearls Stolen," *New York Times*, 26 January 1952.

54. See James Kaplan, *The Airport: Terminal Nights and Runway Days at John F. Kennedy International* (New York: Morrow, 1994).

55. Charles Grutzner, "Airlines Unable to Halt Crime Flourishing at Kennedy Airport," *New York Times*, 12 May 1968, 1.

56. "Five Arrested," *Wall Street Journal*, 15 April 1970, 3.

57. Charles Grutzner, "Airlines Unable to Halt Crime Flourishing at Kennedy Airport," *New York Times*, 12 May 1968, 1.

58. Fred Cook, "The Jackals at JFK," *New York Times*, 12 April 1970.

59. Ibid.

60. Arend, *Great Airports*, 142–50.

61. Scullin, *International Airport*, 269–77.

62. Joseph Martin, "JFK: How Mob Still Rules Airport," *Daily News*, 1 June 1971.

63. Dick Meyer, "Panel Finds . . ." *Long Island Press*, 5 December 1973.

CHAPTER 4. NEIGHBORHOOD BATTLES

1. Ken Johnston, "Jamaica Bay Area . . .," publication unknown, 7 November 1954, AQL.

2. "New Little Jones Beach Urged," *Long Island Star Journal*, 27 August 1957.

3. Robert Moses to Harry Levy, 28 December 1956, RM Papers, Box 100, Folder 1956, NYPL.

4. Robert Moses, "The Future Development of Jamaica Bay," *Rockaway Review*, April 1945.

5. Edward Brady, "Jamaica Bay Wildlife Refuge," ca. 1950s, AQL.

6. U.S. Department of the Interior, Jamaica Bay Waterfowl Use Survey, 1967–1968, AQL. The National Audubon Society and Sierra Club were listed as anti-expansion groups.

7. Harry Levy to NYC Transit Authority, 13 December 1956, RM Papers, Box 100, Folder 1956, NYPL.

8. Seymour Marks, "Jamaica Bay," *Long Island Daily Press*, 16 December 1968.

9. "Jamaica Bay and the Rockaways, a Report by the Park Association of New York City on the Interagency Conference," 28 May 1968, AQL.

10. PANYNJ Annual Reports, 1948–1970, NYPL.

11. Interview with Jerry Biscardi, JFK's general supervisor for aviation fueling, in James Kaplan, *The Airport: Terminal Nights and Runway Days at John F. Kennedy International* (New York: Morrow, 1994), 134.

12. U.S. Department of the Interior, Jamaica Bay Waterfowl Use Survey, 1967–1968, 5, AQL.

13. U.S. Department of the Interior Fish and Wildlife Service, "Jamaica Bay Waterfowl Use Survey, 1967 to 1968," AQL.

14. Save the Bay Committee, Brooklyn, Carol Crawford and others, 23 May 1970, AQL.

15. "Wydler Opposes Longer JFK Runways," *Daily News*, 15 August 1970.

16. "Charge PA Pollutes," *Long Island Press*, 31 July 1970. See Ted Steinberg, *Gotham Unbound* (New York: Simon and Schuster, 2014), for a detailed examination of recent environmental destruction.

17. U.S. Department of the Interior Fish and Wildlife Service, "Jamaica Bay Waterfowl Use Survey, 1967 to 1968," AQL.

18. Jameson Doig, "The Best as Enemy of the Good: The Port Authority's 4th Jetport, Lindenthal's Massive Span over the Hudson, and the George Washington Bridge," *Journal of Urban History*, vol. 10, no. 10, November, 2014, 1–15.

19. Richard Witkin, "Airlines Seek to Expand Kennedy Airport," *New York Times*, 13 May 1969. See also Port Authority, "Airport Requirements and Sites to Serve the New Jersey-New York Metropolitan Region," December 1966, 24, NYPL.

20. Bernard Rabin, "Armada Cruises," 12 October 1970, AQL.

21. "Heckscher Assails Runway Extension into Jamaica Bay," *Long Island Press*, 5 January 1970.

22. "Map Battle over at JFK Expansion," *Long Island Press*, 17 September 1970.

23. "Heckscher Rips Airport Expansion," *Long Island Press*, 27 August 1970. See also Steinberg, *Gotham Unbound*, and Adam Rome, *The Bulldozer in the Countryside:*

Suburban Sprawl and the Rise of American Environmentalism (Cambridge: Cambridge University Press, 2001).

24. "FAA Report Called Airline Whitewash," *Long Island Press*, 11 September 1970.

25. National Academy of Sciences, *Jamaica Bay and Kennedy Airport: A Multidisciplinary Environmental Study; a Report* (Washington, D.C.: National Academy of Sciences, 1971), 7.

26. Ibid., 11.

27. Ibid., 25.

28. Robert Moses, "The Future of Jamaica Bay and the 'Experts,' " *Park East*, 8 April 1971.

29. Paul Friedlander, "Air Traffic Control," *New York Times*, 18 December,1960.

30. Charles Hall, "Moses Given Green Light on Bay Park," *New York Times*, 11 October 1945.

31. "Jet Noise: The Dilemma of Long Island Airports," *New York Herald Tribune*, 11 November 1962.

32. "Jamaica Bay and the Rockaways, a Report by the Park Association of New York City on the Interagency Conference," held 28 May 1968, AQL.

33. "Land Bank Urged," *New York Times*, 6 March 1961.

34. Ronald Maiorana, "U.S. Aide Suggests L.I. Air Corridors," *New York Times*, undated.

35. National Academy of Sciences, *Jamaica Bay and Kennedy Airport*, 15.

36. "Desolate Marshlands Give Way to Burgeoning New Communities in Queens," *New York Times*, 12 July 1959.

37. Gene Gleason, "The Towns Organizing for Growth," *New York Herald Tribune*, 22 November 1964.

38. Leonard Victor, "All About Jet Noise," *Long Island Star*, 27 May 1963.

39. Alexis Faust and Dina Taylor, Unpublished chronology, "Aircraft Noise, 1948–1972," for Jameson Doig, 28 October 1986, 29–30, JDP.

40. Ibid.

41. Ibid., 41; Sidney Goldstein, Port Authority, "Jet Noise at Airports," 29 October 1965, 20–33, JDP.

42. Alexis Faust and Dina Taylor, "Aircraft Noise, 1948–1972," for Jameson Doig, 28 October 1986, 37, 38, JDP.

43. Albert Odell, "Jet Noise at John F. Kennedy Airport," June 1966, 21–22, JDP.

44. John Wiley, Draft White Paper for Congressional Testimony, 6 March 1962, 22–23, JDP.

45. Alexis Faust and Dina Taylor, "Aircraft Noise, 1948–1972," for Jameson Doig, 28 October 1986, 37, JDP.

46. Edward Hudson, "New Flightpath Upsets Brooklyn," *New York Times*, 22 August 1962.

47. "Idlewild Praised by FAA on Noise," *New York Times*, 26 July 1961.

48. "Jet Noise—Whose Fault?" *Rockaway Review*, August 1961.

49. Jane Gerard, "New FAA Plan," *Newsday*, 19 July 1961.

50. "New Airport Noise Abatement System," *Long Island Press*, 16 October 1964.

51. Albert Odell, "Jet Noise at John F. Kennedy Airport," June 1966, 23, JDP.

52. Alexis Faust and Dina Taylor, "Aircraft Noise, 1948–1972," for Jameson Doig, 28 October 1986, 49–50, JDP.

53. Edward Hudson, "Increased 'Stacking' Disquiets Air Passengers," *New York Times*, 24 July 1968.

54. "FAA Chief," *Long Island Star Journal*, 22 September 1964.

55. "LI Jet Noise Foes," *Long Island Daily Press*, 21 September 1961.

56. Leonard Victor, "Jet Hush at Limit," *Long Island Star Journal*, 23 May 1963.

57. Albert Odell, "Aircraft Noise: The Sounds and the Fury," *Port Authority Review*, Spring 1971, 11.

58. "Idlewild Experiment May Ease Jet Noise," *Long Island Star Journal*, 6 September 1961.

59. Austin Tobin, "A Letter of Protest," *Long Island Star Journal*, 6 October 1962.

60. Leonard Victor, "The Case of People vs. Jet Noise," *Long Island Daily Press*, 5 June 1963.

61. David Anderson, "L.I. Plane Noises Heard in Court," *New York Times*, 25 September 1964; David Hoffman, "New Attack on Jet Noise," *New York Herald Tribune*, 17 November 1963.

62. "Hempstead Loses Jet Noise Battle," *Long Island Press*, 18 July 1968.

63. Town-Village Aircraft Safety and Noise Abatement Committee, Memo, "Jet Aircraft Noise Pollution," ca. 1971, AQL.

64. Alexis Faust and Dina Taylor, "Aircraft Noise, 1948–1972," for Jameson Doig, 28 October 1986, 46, JDP.

65. "Demand Action on Jet Noise," *Leader-Observer*, 23 November 1967.

66. "Cariello's Aviation Committee," *Rockaway Review*, Summer 1968.

67. See Mansel Blackford, *Making Seafood Sustainable: American Experiences in Global Perspective* (Philadelphia: University of Pennsylvania Press, 2011), for parallel trends in federal environmental regulation.

68. TVASNAC Memo, "TVASNAC," ca. 1971, AQL.

69. Metro Suburban Aircraft Noise Association, "Lower the Boom," undated, AQL.

70. PANYNJ Annual Report, 1969, p. 25, NYPL.

71. TVASNAC Memo, "Public Law 90–411," ca. 1971, AQL.

72. Alexis Faust and Dina Taylor, "Aircraft Noise, 1948–1972," for Jameson Doig, 28 October 1986, 49–50, JDP.

73. National Academy of Sciences, *Jamaica Bay and Kennedy Airport*. 13,

74. "Noise Puts 3 LI Areas in Holding Pattern," *Long Island Press*, 27 July 1974.

CHAPTER 5. DECLINE AND DISORDER

Note to epigraph: Paul Goldberger, "Blueprint for an Airport that Might've Been," *New York Times*, 17 June 1990.

1. PANYNJ Annual Report, 1971, p. 33, NYPL.

2. James Kaplan, *The Airport: Terminal Nights and Runway Days at John F. Kennedy International* (New York: Morrow and Sons, 1994), 120.

3. Mark Blacklock, *Recapturing the Dream: A Design History of New York's JFK Airport* (London: Blacklock, 2005), 18.

4. Austin Perlow, "More Airline Job Losses," *Long Island Press*, 27 January 1974.

5. Kaplan, *The Airport*, 187.

6. T. A. Heppenheimer, *Turbulent Skies: The History of Commercial Aviation* (New York: Wiley, 1995), 315.

7. Henry Lefer, "A Facelift at 50," *Air Transport World*, September 1998, 66.

8. Thomas Lueck, "Revving up the 'Economic Engine,'" *New York Times*, 2 August 1987, F1.

9. Harry Berkowitz, "We've Lost an Engine," *Newsday*, 19 August 1991.

10. Alastair Gordon, *Naked Airport: A Cultural History of the World's Most Revolutionary Structure* (New York: Henry Holt, 2004). See also Betsy Braden and Paul Hagan, *A Dream Takes Flight: Hartsfield Atlanta International and Aviation in Atlanta* (Athens: University of Georgia Press, 1989).

11. N. R. Kleinfeld, "The Hot Seat," *Wall Street Journal*, 16 July 1976, 1.

12. Susan Kellum, "Air Control: Full Skies, Help Wanted," *New York Times*, 25 September 1980.

13. "The World's Airports," *Via Port of New York New Jersey*, September 1988, 7–9, NYPL.

14. Harry Berkowitz, "We've Lost an Engine," *Newsday*, 19 August 1991.

15. Airport Statistics, 1987, Port Authority Aviation Department, 1988, Table II-5; Table I-16, NYPL.

16. "Study Finds Kennedy Airport May Be Losing Gateway Status," *Newsday*, 21 November 1991.

17. Airport Statistics, 1987, Port Authority Aviation Department, 1988, Table I-4; Table II-2, Table II-5; Table I-16, NYPL.

18. Agis Salpukas, "Newark's Rise as a Global Airport," *New York Times*, 9 October 1990.

19. Mark Rose and Bruce Seely, *The Best Transportation System in the World* (Philadelphia: University of Pennsylvania Press, 2010), 87.

20. Harry Berkowitz, "We've Lost an Engine," *Newsday*, 19 August 1991; Jack Otter, "Crew Gardens," *Newsday,* 11 January 1998.

21. PANYNJ, "Demographic Trends in the NY/NJ Metropolitan Area," June 1994, NYPL.

22. James Dao, "Pan Am Sends Queens Econ into Tailspin," *Daily News*, 15 December 1991.

23. Liz Goff, "Former Pan Am Workers . . . ," *Queens Tribune,* 7 August 1992.

24. "On a Wing and a Prayer," Center for an Urban Future, October 2000. Accessed at https://nycfuture.org/research/publications/on-a-wing-and-a-prayer.

25. "Outreach Taking Off," *Daily News,* 1 October 1998.

26. Michael Kaufman, "New Arrivals: Hustlers Vying with the Skycaps at Kennedy," *New York Times,* 13 January 1989.

27. John Hughes, "JFK Airport Is Working on Beefs by Travelers," *Daily News,* 15 March 1970.

28. Alfred Miele, "Suspend the Licenses," *Daily News,* 1 November 1979.

29. Don Flynn, "Link 11 to JFK Taxi Kickbacks," *Daily News,* 29 June 1983.

30. Katherine Foran, "Trying to Make Airport Car Hustlers Play Fare," *Newsday,* 25 October 1989.

31. Patricia Hurtado, "A Drive to Halt JFK Car Thieves," *Newsday,* 10 December 1985.

32. Edmund Newton, "Shedding Light on Airport Nights," *Newsday,* 24 March 1981.

33. Ibid.

34. Katherine Foran, "Trying to Make Airport Car Hustlers Play Fare," *Newsday,* 25 October 1989.

35. Barbara Ross, "Zooming in on JFK," *Daily News,* 6 August 1986; Scott Ladd, "Heroin Halters," *Newsday,* 26 May 1992.

36. Juleyka Lantigua, "New Film Shows Colombian Mules Risking Death for Better Life," *The Progressive,* 21 July 2004.

37. N. R. Kleinfield, "Patrolling the Border at JFK," *New York Times,* 28 June 1987.

CHAPTER 6. RESILIENCE OF A GLOBAL HUB

1. John Mollenkopf and Manuel Castells, editors, *Dual City: Restructuring New York* (New York: Russell Sage, 1991); John Mollenkopf, *New York City in the 1980s: A Social, Economic and Political Atlas* (New York: Simon and Schuster, 1993); Jonathan Soffer, *Ed Koch and the Rebuilding of New York City* (New York: Columbia University Press, 2010); Nancy Foner, editor, *New Immigrants in New York* (New York: Columbia University Press, 1987).

2. Robert Aaronson, "The World's Aviation Capital," *Via Port of New York-New Jersey,* 1985, 10–11.

3. Saskia Sassen, *The Global City: New York, London, Tokyo* (Princeton: Princeton University Press, 1991), 59.

4. Stanley Brezenoff, "New Challenges, Executive Director," Port Authority, *RE:Port,* vol. 7, no. 2, May 1991.

5. Aviation Department, PANYNJ, "Economic Impact Study of Aviation," 1985, 16–18, NYPL.

6. Ibid.

7. Robert Aaronson, "The World's Aviation Capital," *Via Port of New York-New Jersey*, April 1985, 10.

8. Hugh O'Neill and Mitchell Moss, "Reinventing New York: Competing in the Next Century's Global Economy," Urban Research Center, New York University, November 1991, NYU.

9. Port Authority, "Airport Traffic Report," 1999, 21, NYPL

10. Geoffrey Arend, *Great Airports: Kennedy International* (New York: Air Cargo News, 1981), 193.

11. PANYNJ Annual Report, 1978, NYPL.

12. Aviation Department, PANYNJ, "Economic Impact Study of Aviation," 1985, 16–18, NYPL.

13. PANYNJ, "Airport Traffic Report," 1999, 49. NYPL.

14. PANYNJ, "Airport Traffic Report," 1999, 27, NYPL.

15. "274 Immigrants Arrive as Airlift Sets a Record," *New York Times*, 14 June 1956, 66.

16. Samuel Freedman, "The New New Yorkers," *New York Times*, 3 November 1985, 24.

17. Fiscal Policy Institute, *Working for Better Life: A Profile of Immigrants in the New York State Economy*, November 2007 (Education statistics from p. 41). Other summary information from the report as a whole provides background for this paragraph. Accessed at http://www.fiscalpolicy.org/publications2007/FPI_ImmReport_WorkingforaBetterLife.pdf. See also Nancy Foner, *New Immigrants in New York* (New York: Columbia University Press, 1987), and Hector R. Cordero-Guzman et al., *Migration, Transnationalism and Race in a Changing New York* (Philadelphia: Temple University Press, 2001.)

18. "Export NYC: A Roadmap for Creating Jobs Through Exports," report by Manhattan borough president Scott Stringer, June 2013, 15, no longer available online, author's collection.

19. "A 200 Bed Center to Open Near Kennedy Airport," *New York Times*, 21 January 1997, B5.

20. Fran Reiter and Joseph Rose (New York City Department of City Planning), *Newest New Yorkers, 1990–1994*, December 1996, Fashion Institute of Technology Library

21. Port Authority, "Airport Traffic Report," 1999, p. 2.7.2, NYPL

22. "Schumer: Put INS at Airports," *New York Times*, 18 February 1992.

23. Donatella Lorch, "A Flood of Illegal Aliens Enters U.S. via Kennedy," *New York Times*, 18 March 1992, B2.

24. Donatella Lorch, "Immigrants from China," *New York Times*, 3 January 1991, B1.

25. Ashley Dunn, "Greeted at Nation's Front Door," *New York Times*, 3 January 1995, A1.

26. Gus Dallas, " Stupendous Change," *Daily News*, 23 November 1977.

27. James Kaplan, *The Airport: Terminal Nights and Runway Days at John F. Kennedy International* (New York: Morrow, 1994), 193.

28. Michael Unger, "Both Sides Vow Hard SST Fight," *Newsday*, 17 June 1977.

29. Harry Pearson, "Kennedy SST Landings," *Newsday*, 1975, Clipping File, AQL.

30. U.S. Department of Transportation Federal Aviation Administration, "Concorde Supersonic Transport Aircraft," Final Environmental Impact Statement, vol. 1, September 1975, Library of Congress.

31. Harry Pearson, "EPA Head," *Newsday*, 10 December 1975.

32. Untitled, *Queens County Times*, 17 April 1975, AQL.

33. Aileen Jacobson, "A Small Turnout for SST," *Newsday*, 21 November 1977.

34. PANYNJ Annual Report, 1977, NYPL, 15; Michael Unger, "SST Closer to Kennedy Landing," *Newsday*, 18 August 1977.

35. Pete Hamill, "Fly Now—Pay Later for 'Progress,'" *Daily News*, 23 November 1977.

36. Public hearing before Senate transportation and communications committee, Senate Chamber, Trenton, New Jersey, 15 March 1976, JDP.

37. Dennis Hevesi, "It Isn't Over Yet," *Newsday*, circa 1978, AQL.

38. FAA, "Concorde Monitoring," March 1978, 37–38, Library of Congress.

39. Marjorie Kaplan, "Concorde's Roar Leaves Aftershock," *Newsday*, 19 June 1978.

40. Michael Unger, "Both Sides Vow Hard SST Fight," *Newsday*, 17 June 1977.

41. Richard Witkin, "Port Body Votes," *New York Times*, 15 December 1977.

42. Corey Kilgannon, "Covering Their Ears One Last Time for Concorde," *New York Times*, 24 October 2003.

43. Maureen Dowd, "Shangri-La by the Bay," *New York Times*, 10 February 1986.

44. Arend, *Great Airports*, 142

45. PANYNJ, "Regional Recovery, the Business of the 80s," 1979, 29. For the number of 747s, see "Internline Pipeline," *Via Port of New York-New Jersey*, February 1977, 2., NYPL.

46. "With Help from the Firefly," *Via Port of New York-New Jersey*, September 1982, 10, NYPL.

47. PANYNJ, "Regional Recovery, the Business of the 80s," 1979, 29, NYPL.

48. Ibid.

49. "JFK Accept Goes Online," *Via Port of New York-New Jersey*, September 1985, pp. 6–11., NYPL.

50. "AirPort Update," *Via Port of New York-New Jersey*, September 1984, pp. 6–7, NYPL.

51. PANYNJ, "Regional Economy: Review and Outlook," April 1996, 29, NYPL.

52. "A Look at the Bistate Ports . . . ," *Via Port of New York-New Jersey*, September 1990, 19, NYPL.

53. Hugh O'Neill and Mitchell Moss, "Reinventing New York: Competing in the Next Century's Global Economy," Urban Research Center, New York University, November 1991, 45, NYU.

54. "A Solid Showing at the Port of New York/New Jersey," *Via Port of New York-New Jersey*, July/August 1995, 26, NYPL.

55. George Anders, "At Kennedy Airport, Imports Rain Down from All Directions," *Wall Street Journal*, 18 November 1987, 1.

56. Laura Castro, "Planned Project at Kennedy to Handle Perishable Goods," *Newsday*, 18 January 1988.

57. "JFK Breaks Ground for New Building," *Crain's*, 23 September 1991.

58. "Aviation an 18 Billion Dollar Business in New York Area," 1 December 1985, NYT, 51.

59. Buz Whalen, "Trends in International Air Cargo," *Via Port of New York-New Jersey*, September 1991, 40.

60. William Boesch, "Cargo Redux," *Via Port of New York-New Jersey*, September 1990, 12–13.

61. "The World's Leading Air Cargo Center," *Via Port of New York-New Jersey*, September/October 1995, 15.

62. William Boesch, "Cargo Redux," *Via Port of New York-New Jersey*, September 1990, 12–13.

63. Cathy Lanier, Office of Business Development, "The Nature of Trade-Related Services in the New York-New Jersey Region and the Influences on their Location," PANYNJ, October 1990, WorldCat; "The Narrowbody," *Via Port of New York-New Jersey*, August 1982, 13.

64. New York State Department of Labor, "1994 Labor Conditions," December 1995, p. 3, NYPL.

65. Michael Bloomberg, City of New York, Office of the Mayor, "Protecting and Growing New York City's Industrial Job Base," January 2005, 14., NYPL.

66. Bill Sternberg, "Kennedy Pilfering Surges," *Crain's New York*, 1 August 1988.

67. Joseph Queen, "Mob Hide," *New York Newsday*, 6 February 1992.

68. Patricia Hurtado, "Airport Worker," *Newsday*, 9 November 1986.

69. Richard Esposito, "Law Man: Mob Still Strong at Kennedy," *Newsday*, 13 October 1987.

70. PANYNJ, Freight Planning Division, "Transportation's Role in Manufacturing Location Decisions," May 1985, 9, Northwestern University Transportation Library.

71. "The Time Mechanics," *Via Port of New York-New Jersey*, September 1983, 14.

72. Regional Plan Association, Working Paper No. 6, "Goods Movement in the New York Region," prepared by John Dean, March 1992, 34, University of California Berkeley Libraries.

73. "Upgrading to World Class: The Future of the New York Region's Airports," 133–34. Accessed at http://www.rpa.org/pdf/RPA-Upgrading-to-World-Class.pdf.

74. "On a Wing and a Prayer," October 2000, accessed at https://nycfuture.org/research/publications/on-a-wing-and-a-prayer, page 12. See John Kasarda and Greg Lindsay, *Aerotropolis: The Way We'll Live Next* (New York: Farrar, 2011).

75. Thomas Pugh, "They Want No Truck with JFK Cargo," *Daily News*, 28 May 1980.

76. "Beame: Jamaica . . . ," *Long Island Press*, 17 June 1977.

77. "Queens Air Services Development," *Queens Chronicle*, 5 February 1990; "Aviation Biz Campaign," *Queens Borough*, November 1984, 11.

78. James Larsen, "How to Win the Airport Game," *Via International*, May 1992, 8–10.

79. Advertisement in *Via International*, September 1992; "On a Wing and a Prayer," October 2000; "On a Wing and a Prayer," Center for an Urban Future, October 2000. Accessed at https://nycfuture.org/research/publications/on-a-wing-and-a-prayer, page 3.

80. Lydia Polgreen, "When It Positively Has to Be There Fast, J.F.K Loses Ground," *New York Times*, 10 July 2004, B1.

81. "On a Wing and a Prayer," Center for an Urban Future, October 2000. Accessed at https://nycfuture.org/research/publications/on-a-wing-and-a-prayer, page 13.

82. PANYNJ, "World Trade Boom Fuels Air Cargo Growth," September/October 1995, 16–17.

83. Aviation Department, PANYNJ, "Airport Statistics," 1987, 1988, Table I-4; Table II-2, Table II-5; Table III-4, NYPL.

84. PANYNJ, "Airport Traffic Report," 1999, 53, NYPL.

85. "On a Wing and a Prayer," Center for an Urban Future, October 2000. Accessed at https://nycfuture.org/research/publications/on-a-wing-and-a-prayer, page 2.

86. Kate Ascher, *The Works* (New York: Penguin, 2007), 85. See also Jeffrey Zupan, Richard Barone, and Matthew Lee, *Upgrading to World Class: The Future of the New York Region's Airports*, Regional Plan Association, January 2011 Accessed at http://www.rpa.org/pdf/RPA-Upgrading-to-World-Class.pdf.

87. New York City Economic Development Corporation and Port Authority, "JFK Air Cargo Study," January 2013, available at http://www.nycedc.com/sites/default/files/filemanager/Projects/Air_Cargo_Study/Exec_Sum-Sec_FINAL_MN.pdf.

88. PANYNJ, "Airport Traffic Report," 1999, 66, NYPL. Percentage of air cargo employees from "On a Wing and a Prayer," Center for an Urban Future, October 2000. Accessed at https://nycfuture.org/research/publications/on-a-wing-and-a-prayer, page 3.

89. Ascher, *The Works*, 82.

CHAPTER 7. REAPPRAISAL

1. Sheila Bair, "A Bold Plan for Rebuilding Our Roads and Bridges," *Fortune*, 22 July 2013, 41.

2. Neil MacFarquhar, "Newark Airport Is Pressing to Surpass Kennedy," *New York Times*, 24 January 1996, A1.

3. Arthur Wang, "No Way to Run Kennedy Airport," *New York Times*, 24 November 1984.

4. "On a Wing and a Prayer," October 2000. Accessed at https://nycfuture.org/research/publications/on-a-wing-and-a-prayer.

5. Regional Plan Association, Working Paper Number 13, "The Region's Airports: Two Issues," prepared by Jeffrey Zupan, March 1992, 15, University of California Berkeley Libraries.

6. Bill Decota, "Managing Growth at New York's Airports," in Pravin Raj, Syed Hoda, Howard Lock, ed., *Connected Transportation* (Walmer, Kent, UK: Torworth, 2006), 66.

7. "Slattery Awarded $55M Contract," *Ledger/Register/Journal News*, 23 November 1989, 5; Michael Moss, "$21M Tunnel . . ." *Newsday*, 16 April 1992; "PA Abandons $100M of Plans," *Newsday*, 17 April 1992.

8. Paul Goldberger, "Blueprint for an Airport That Might've Been," *New York Times*, 17 June 1990.

9. Mark Blacklock, *Recapturing the Dream: A Design History of New York's JFK Airport* (London: Blacklock, 2005), 20, 21.

10. Henry Lefer, "A Facelift at 50," *Air Transport World*, September 1998.

11. "Gearing Up for a New Era of Air Passenger Service," *Via Port of New York New Jersey*, May/June 1995, 23.

12. "$450 Million Terminal Rising at JFK," *New York Times*, 16 June 1996.

13. Blacklock, *Recapturing the Dream*, 20, 21.

14. Michael Thomas, "JFK's IAB: Back to the Future," *Via Port of New York New Jersey*, September/October 1995, 23–25.

15. Blacklock, *Recapturing the Dream*, 155.

16. David Dunlap, "TWA's Hub Is Declared a Landmark," *New York Times*, 20 July 1994.

17. David Dunlap, "A 'New' Kennedy Airport Takes Wing," *New York Times*, 26 October 1997.

18. James Rutenberg, "Rudy Acts to Wrest LaG, JFK from PA," *Daily News*, 10 February 1999; Mohamad Bazzi, "Closer Look at Deal," *Newsday*, 18 April 2001; Mohamad Bazzi, "Big Shot Backing," *Newsday*, 17 March 2001; Mohamad Bazzi, "Air Agency Grounded," *Newsday*, 10 April 2001.

19. David Dunlap, "A 'New' Kennedy Airport Takes Wing," *New York Times*, 26 October 1997. See Mitchell Moss and Hugh O'Neill, "A Port Authority That Works," Rudin Center for Transportation and Public Policy at New York University, March 2014, for a breakdown on the financial and managerial issues facing the Port Authority. Accessed at http://wagner.nyu.edu/rudincenter/wp-content/uploads/2014/04/Port AuthorityFINAL_Web.pdf.

20. This information is based upon discussions with staff of the Global Gateway Alliance and various sources on their website: http://www.globalgatewayalliance.org.

21. PANYNJ, "Airport Traffic Report," 1999, 5, 27, NYPL.

22. Randy Kennedy, "Welcome to JFK: Now with Service to Rochester," *New York Times*, 9 February 2001.

23. Micheline Maynard, "JetBlue Airways Wants to Serve La Guardia," *New York Times*, 22 January 2004.

24. Warren Woodberry, "Local Airports See Record Traffic in 2004," *Daily News*, 3 March 2005.

25. Ken Belson, "Port Authority and Airlines Offer Plans to Ease Delays," *New York Times*, 7 December 2007.

26. John Valenti, "NYC Airports at Tail End of On-Time List," *Newsday*, 4 December 2007.

27. William Thompson, comptroller, "Grounded: The Impact of Mounting Flight Delays," December 2007, New York City Comptroller's Office, Columbia University Libraries. See also Partnership for New York City, *Grounded: The High Cost of Air Traffic Congestion*, February 2009, p. 4, available at http://www.pfnyc.org/reports/2009_0225_airport_congestion.pdf.

28. "O'Hare History," Chicago Department of Aviation website, http://www.flychicago.com/OHare/EN/AboutUs/Pages/History.aspx.

29. "On a Wing and a Prayer," October 2000, Accessed at https://nycfuture.org/research/publications/on-a-wing-and-a-prayer.

30. Jeffrey Zupan, Richard Barone, and Matthew Lee, *Upgrading to World Class: The Future of the New York Region's Airports*, Regional Plan Association, January 2011, available at http://www.rpa.org/pdf/RPA-Upgrading-to-World-Class.pdf. See also the Global Gateway Alliance's post here: http://www.capitalnewyork.com/article/null/2014/04/8544197/fixing-new-york%E2%80%99s-airports-what-nextgen-can-do.

31. Kirk Johnson, "Kennedy Gridlock: Problems Seen in Costly Solution," *New York Times*, 8 July 1988.

32. James Kaplan, *The Airport: Terminal Nights and Runway Days at John F. Kennedy International* (New York: Morrow, 1994), 17.

33. Kirk Johnson, "Kennedy Gridlock: Problems Seen in Costly Solution," *New York Times*, 8 July 1988.

34. Regional Plan Association, Working Paper No. 13, "The Region's Airports: Two Issues," prepared by Jeffrey Zupan, March 1992, UC Berkeley Libraries, 27.

35. PANYNJ, "Airport Traffic Report," 1999, 65, NYPL.

36. "JFK Express Subway," *The Wave*, 9 August 1978; "Director Getting Airport Projects Off the Ground," *Craine's*, 30 September 1991.

37. PANYNJ, "Airport Traffic Report," 1999, pp. 63–65, NYPL.

38. PANYNJ, "Airport Statistics," 1987, Table IV-4; 1988, Table IV-1, NYPL.

39. PANYNJ, "Airport Traffic Report," 1999, 63–65, NYPL.

40. "A Jamaica to JFK Airport Connector," N.J. Fenwick, consultant for the Greater Jamaica Development Corporation, July 1990, p. 13, AQL.

41. Regional Plan Association, "The Region's Agenda," December 1988, NYPL.

42. "Train to the Plane or Money Down the Drain," Council of the City of New York Finance and Economic Development Committee Report, 20 April 1999, p. 16, AQL. The Chicago parking statistics are from Jon Hilkevitch, "At O'Hare, Gridlock Begins in Parking Lots," *Chicago Tribune*, 6 March 2006.

43. "Introducing the New Airport," *Via International*, May 1992, 4.

44. Regional Plan Association, Working Paper No. 13, "The Region's Airports: Two Issues," prepared by Jeffrey Zupan, March 1992, UC Berkeley Libraries, 27.

45. "Monorail System . . . ," *Queens Gazette*, 23 October 1991.

46. Joseph Queen, "Fee to Pay . . . ," *Newsday*, 24 July 1992; Michael Moss, "$3 Tax Asked on NY Air Travelers," *Newsday*, 14 November 1991.

47. "Train to the Plane or Money Down the Drain," Council of the City of New York Finance and Economic Development Committee Report, 20 April 1999, Appendix A, Library of Congress.

48. Donald Bertrand, "AirTrain Flying High as Numbers of Riders Climbs," *Daily News*, 10 June 2004; "Port Authority Announces Record Year at Region's Airports," 12 February 2012, Press Release Number 28, http://www.panynj.gov/press-room/press-item.cfm?headLine_id = 1539.

49. Kaplan, *The Airport*, 182.

50. "Airliners Often Break City Noise Rules," *Daily News*, 31 May 1977.

51. "PA Urges Congressional Action," 14 October 1975, Jameson Doig Papers.

52. Randy Banner, "Two Views of Airport Noise Issue," *Newsday*, 20 September 1984; Sharon Monahan, "Rules Eased for Noisy Planes," *New York Times*, 20 January 1985.

53. David Pitt, "3 Metropolitan Airports to Bar Noisy Night Flights," *New York Times*, 11 August 1989.

54. Katherine Foran, "Port Authority Casts Hush over Airports," *Newsday*, 11 August 1989.

55. *Newsday*, 21 November 1991, Clipping File, AQL.

56. "Draconian Battle Looming over Jet Noise," *New York Times*, 23 June 1991.

57. Sarah Lyall, "Noise Plan Delay Irks Airport Neighbors," *New York Times*, 26 September 1991.

58. "FAA Warns Port Authority . . . ," *New York Times*, 19 March 1992.

59. Pete Donohue, "Good Vibrations on Airport Noise," *Daily News*, 29 October 1995.

60. PANYNJ, "The Economic Impact of the Aviation Industry on the New York-New Jersey Metropolitan Region," October 2005, NYPL.

61. Pete Donohue, "Good Vibrations on Airport Noise," *Daily News*, 29 October 1995.

62. "Planning for Quieter Queens Skies," *Queens Tribune*, 23 September 1999.

63. Brian Lockhart, "LaGuardia, JFK to Keep Limits on Airplane Flights," *Newsday*, 17 June 1999.

64. Pete Donohue, "Plan to Dilute Jet Noise," *Daily News*, 9 June 1994.

65. Pete Donohue, "Good Vibrations on Airport Noise," *Daily News*, 29 October 1995.

66. Donald Bertrand, "Sky Wars . . . ," *Daily News*, 11 January 1999. See also the following study for more information on noise: http://www.panynj.gov/about/pdf/JFK-Runway-4L-22R-EA-FONSI.pdf. In recent years, residents of Northeast Queens (heavily impacted by operations at LaGuardia) have organized under the Queens Quiet Skies umbrella group to register their unhappiness with the Port Authority and politicians over increased noise from sources such as airspace redesign and NextGen (satelleite) implementation. See, for instance, http://www.timesledger.com/stories/2014/45/noisetask_bt_2014_11_07_q.html and http://queensquietskies.org.

67. Anthony Wiener, "PA Is Deaf," *Daily News*, 15 February 2000; Warren Woodberry, "Schools Helped on Jet Din," *Daily News*, 6 March 2000.

68. Donald Bertrand, "Sky Wars . . . ," *Daily News*, 11 January 1999.

69. Michael Moss, "What a Mess!" *Newsday*, 23 October 1992.

70. Kaplan, *The Airport*, 134, 138.

71. Interview with Jerry Biscardi, JFK's general supervisor for aviation fueling, in Kaplan, *The Airport*, 134.

72. Donald Bertrand, "Sky Wars . . . ," *Daily News*, 11 January 1999.

73. John Lauinger, "Marshland Disappearing,"*Daily News*, 9 October 2007.

74. Brooklyn College Public Relations, "Study Traces Source of Jamaica Bay Pollution," 14 February 1991, AQL.

75. Warren Woodberry, "Saving Jamaica Bay," *Daily News*, 31 March 2005.

76. Warren Woodberry, "Solving the Mystery," *Daily News*, 7 November 2002.

77. John Lauinger, "Marshland Disappearing," *Daily News*, 9 October 2007.

78. Curtice Griffin, "Birds and the Potential for Bird Strikes near John F. Kennedy International," National Park Service, July 1992, F. Franklin Moon Library, SUNY College of Environmental Science and Forestry.

79. Katherine Foran, "The Flap at Kennedy," *Newsday*, 11 October 1988.

80. James Dao, "15,000 Sea Gulls Are Shot Down," *New York Daily News*, 27 December 1991.

81. Michael Wilson, "Working to Separate Big and Small Fliers," *New York Times*, 31 December 2009.

82. Civil Aviation Authority, "Passenger Numbers at UK Airports up 1.4 Million but Still Below 2007 Peak," 18 March 2013, available at http://www.caa.co.uk/application.aspx?appid = 7&mode = detail&nid = 2217.

83. Economic Impact of Aviation, 2010 Summary Report, New York State DOT. Accessed at https://www.dot.ny.gov/divisions/operating/opdm/aviation/repository/NYS%20Economic%20Study%202010%20Exec%20Summary%20Report-Final.pdf.

84. Ibid.

85. Economist Intelligence Unit, "Hot Spots: Benchmarking Global City Competitiveness," 2012, pp. 20, 25, available at http://www.citigroup.com/citi/citiforcities/pdfs/eiu_hotspots_2012.pdf.

86. "Export NYC: A Roadmap for Creating Jobs Through Exports," report by Manhattan borough president Scott Stringer, June 2013, 7, No Longer Available Online, Author's Personal Collection. For estimates on the losses to the region in terms of employment and trade, see such documents as Partnership for New York City, *Grounded: The High Cost of Airport Congestion*, February 2009, available at http://www.pfnyc.org/reports/2009_0225_airport_congestion.pdf.

INDEX

ACKNOWLEDGMENTS

I should like to thank Professor Jameson Doig of Princeton University and Jeffrey Zupan of the Regional Plan Association for their comments. Librarians at many institutions including the New York Public Library, the New Jersey State Archives, the Archives at Queens Library, and the New York Institute of Technology (NYIT) have been patient and helpful with my requests. Series editor Professor Mark Rose has provided detailed comments on multiple occasions that have improved the manuscript. I am indebted to a report from an anonymous reader that inspired important final revisions. Senior editor Robert Lockhart at the University of Pennsylvania Press has again offered excellent direction over many years. Thanks as well to project editor Noreen O'Connor-Abel and copyeditor Pat Wieland. The opportunity to present the work to members of the Urban History Association and the Society for American City and Regional Planning History has sharpened the book's focus. The New York Institute of Technology has provided steady financial support and consistent grants to support this work. Thanks in particular to my chair, Dr. Ellen Katz; Dean Roger Yu of the College of Arts and Sciences; Provost Rahmat Shoureshi; and NYIT's President Edward Guiliano. Leanne and Roxie Bloom are, as always, encouraging and helpful partners in these research projects.